St Albans

St Albans
Life on the Home Front, 1914–1918

Edited by JONATHAN MEIN, ANNE WARES and SUE MANN

for the St Albans Home Front Project Group
St Albans & Hertfordshire Architectural & Archaeological Society

Hertfordshire Publications
an imprint of
UNIVERSITY OF HERTFORDSHIRE PRESS

First published in Great Britain in 2016 by
Hertfordshire Publications
an imprint of
University of Hertfordshire Press
College Lane
Hatfield
Hertfordshire
AL10 9AB
UK

British Library Cataloguing in Publication Data
A catalogue record for this book is available from the British Library

ISBN 978-1-909291-74-4

Design by Arthouse Publishing Solutions Ltd
Printed in Great Britain by Henry Ling Ltd, Dorchester

Contents

Figures

Tables

Foreword

St Albans & Hertfordshire Architectural & Archaeological Society is an exceptionally active and constructive local history society, so it is no surprise that they have worked so effectively on their Home Front project. Their meticulous research has borne fruit in the form of this publication.

When the Lieutenancy embarked on its project to make a film[1] commemorating life on the home front during the First World War it could not have proceeded without the help of the society's project group. A dozen topics were suggested and these formed the structure on which the filmmaking could build. I am so grateful to the group for its guidance.

I very much look forward to reading this book, not least because the Grimston family make an appearance, including my husband's beautiful Irish grandmother, who was a member of the local Voluntary Aid Detachment. She surely must have gladdened the spirits of wounded soldiers.

The Countess of Verulam
Her Majesty's Lord-Lieutenant of Hertfordshire
Patron of SAHAAS

---

1. The film referred to is *A County At War. Life on the Home Front in Hertfordshire*, commissioned by the Lord-Lieutenant of Hertfordshire and produced by the University of Hertfordshire.

Preface

This book was inspired by the discovery of quite rare records relating to military service tribunals held in St Albans between 1916 and 1918. Although the government had ordered the destruction of such material after the war, those in St Albans were among the few that survived. The minutes of the St Albans City Military Service Tribunal, together with often-lengthy news reports of hearings in the *Herts Advertiser*, St Albans city archives and other local records, enabled us to piece together essential details about how businesses and individuals coped with life on the home front.

The team of 21 indefatigable researchers who made this book possible are all members of the St Albans & Hertfordshire Architectural & Archaeological Society. Our project group includes three professional historians: Alan Wakefield of the Imperial War Museums, Julie Moore of the University of Hertfordshire and Mark Freeman of University College London. They brought academic rigour to the project, contributed an enormous amount of knowledge and helped the group to navigate their way around national and local archive collections.

This book shines a unique light on the activities of the people of St Albans throughout the war as they dealt with the sorrows, stringencies and new and constantly changing demands made upon them. At the same time it reveals how in many respects their lives continued to follow the patterns and routines of pre-war days to an impressive degree.

Jonathan Mein, Anne Wares and Sue Mann

St Albans & Hertfordshire Architectural & Archaeological Society (SAHAAS)

Founded in 1845, SAHAAS is one of the oldest historical societies in the country. It continues to thrive, with a membership of over 500 engaging in a varied series of 27 lectures a year, excursions to sites of interest and research groups. The society is joint publisher of the journal *Hertfordshire Archaeology and History*. For further details see www.stalbanshistory.org.

St Albans Home Front Project Group

Research team
Val Argue
Barry Bateman
Susan Bellamy
Helen Bishop
Patricia Broad
Romaine Byers*
Linda Clarke
Ann Dean*
Maggy Douglas*
Mark Freeman
Sheila Green*
Gareth Hughes
Philippa Hurst
Sue Mann
Jonathan Mein*
Julie Moore*
Mike North*
Anne Petrie
Elizabeth Rolfe
Alan Wakefield
Anne Wares

1911 census transcribers
Barbara Croom
Dave Girdziusz
Gill Girdziusz
Rosemary Knight
Richard Mein
Gill Tarrant

* Members involved in both parts of the project.

Mike North devised the occupational classification on which his subsequent statistical analysis of the census was based.

Chapter writers
1 Mark Freeman
2 Jonathan Mein
3 Alan Wakefield
4 Sue Mann
5 Jonathan Mein
6 Julie Moore
7 Philippa Hurst
8 Anne Wares

Acknowledgements

This project would not have been possible without the support of the St Albans & Hertfordshire Architectural & Archaeological Society, which provided not only funding but also the expertise and encouragement of the members.

In the course of our research the project team consulted many libraries, organisations and suppliers. We are grateful to the following for information, assistance and support: Kevin Bond, BDA Design and Print; British Library; Janet High, British Red Cross Museum and Archive; staff at Hertfordshire Archives and Local Studies, particularly Chris Bennett and Maggie Ramsden; Chris Reynolds, Hertfordshire Genealogy website; Frank Brittain, archivist, Hertfordshire Scouts; Matt Adams, editor, *Herts Advertiser*; Helen Little, Marshalswick Baptist Free Church; Catherine Newley at the Museum of St Albans; Gordon Leith, curator of the Archive and Library, RAF Museums, Hendon; the staff of Rothamsted Library; Michael Clayton and Bob Richardson, St Bride's Foundation Library; the vicar and parochial church council of St Saviour's, St Albans; Clare Coombe, St Albans Cathedral Library; David Kelsall, St Albans Cathedral Muniment Room; St Albans Central Library, especially Beryl Housley, Scott Chalmers and Margaret Payne; Ann Collings, cemeteries manager, St Albans City and District Council; Daniel Flitton and Lyn Henny, council officers, St Albans City and District Council; St Albans High School for Girls; Mike Neighbour of the 'St Albans' Own East End' blog; Nigel Wood-Smith and Michael Hollins, St Albans School; the Library of the Society of Friends; Sandy Norman, Sopwell Memories; James Brant, Thomas Galliford and Glenn Rawlings, history students from the University of Hertfordshire; the management board of Verulam Golf Club; and The National Archives, in particular Chris Barnes and David Langrish.

Extracts from and references to H.C. Cossins's papers and *A War Record of the 21st London Regiment (First Surrey Rifles) 1914–1919* are made courtesy of Imperial War Museums.

The project has benefited from the contribution made by many individuals who generously shared their family photos, archives, knowledge, research and skills, including: Diana Bennett, Michael Bickerton, Timothy Cornfield, Elanor Cowland, John Cox, the Debenham family, David Dorling, Phil Dutton, Peter Glossop, Chris Green, Frank Iddiols, Andy Lawrence, Tony Lord, Clive Mead, Stephen and Nick Mellersh, David Moore, Pat Moore, Kate Morris, Donald Munro, Phyllis Nicholls, Steve Peters, J.T. Smith, Jean Taylor, Ian Tonkin, Lord and Lady Verulam, Julie Wakefield and Lance Watson.

We wish to express our thanks to Thomas and Adrian Bending for the legacy from their late father, Brian Bending, which contributed to the funding of this book. Brian was a longstanding member of the St Albans & Hertfordshire Architectural & Archaeological Society.

The support of the Heritage Hub at the University of Hertfordshire has been invaluable and in particular we thank Sarah Lloyd, who reviewed earlier drafts of the book.

Without the continuing support of our families and friends throughout the project this book could not have been written.

Abbreviations

ASC	Army Service Corps
AVC	Army Veterinary Corps
CAT	County Appeal Tribunal
CMB	City Council Minute Book
CWGC	Commonwealth (formerly Imperial) War Graves Commission
DORA	Defence of the Realm Act
GRO	General Register Office
HA	*Herts Advertiser*
HALS	Hertfordshire Archives and Local Studies
HCC	Hertfordshire County Council
HD	Home Defence
HTF	Hertfordshire Territorial Force
HWAC	Hertfordshire War Agricultural Committee
HWACEC	Hertfordshire War Agricultural Committee, Executive Committee Minute Book (1917–1918)
HWACM	Hertfordshire War Agricultural Committee Minutes, 1916–1919
IWM	Imperial War Museums
LADA	London Air Defence Area
LFCC	St Albans Local Food Control Committee
LGB	Local Government Board
MCMB	City Council Miscellaneous Committees Minute Books
MOHR	Medical Officer of Health Report
n.d.	No date of publication recorded
n.p.	No place of publication recorded
NCO	Non-Commissioned Officer
NUWW	National Union of Women Workers
POW	Prisoner of War
RAMC	Royal Army Medical Corps
RFA	Royal Fleet Auxiliary
RGA	Royal Garrison Artillery
RMS	Royal Merchant Ship

SAHAAS	St Albans & Hertfordshire Architectural & Archaeological Society
SSFA	Soldiers' and Sailors' Families' Association
TCOL	Town Clerk Out Letters Book
TF	Territorial Force
TLC	Trades and Labour Council
TS	St Albans Typographical Society
UAGPC	Urban Authority & General Purposes Committee
VAD	Voluntary Aid Detachment
VD	Venereal disease
VTC	Volunteer Training Corps
WCM	Watch Committee Minute Book
WRAF	Women's Royal Air Force
YMCA	Young Men's Christian Association
YWCA	Young Women's Christian Association

Military fitness gradings in the First World War

From January 1916 to November 1917 men being enlisted into the army were given the following fitness gradings at their medical examinations:

A: General Service
B1: Garrison Service Abroad
B2: Labour Service Abroad
B3: Sedentary Work Abroad
C1: Garrison Service at Home Camps
C2: Labour Service at Home Camps
C3: Sedentary Service at Home Camps

From November 1917 the structure changed to:
Grade I: old category A
Grade II: B1 & C1
Grade III: B2 & B3; C2 & C3
Grade IV: fail

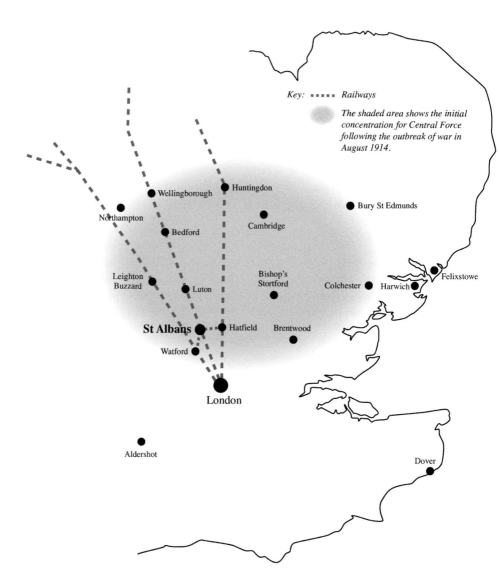

Huntingdon

Wellingborough

Bury St Edmunds

Northampton

Cambridge

Bedford

Leighton Buzzard

Bishop's Stortford

Luton

Colchester

Harwich

Felixstowe

St Albans

Hatfield

Brentwood

Watford

London

Aldershot

Dover

St Albans was designated as a Permanent War Station in plans drawn up before the First World War as part of an overall strategy to defend the country against enemy attack along the east coast. The city was chosen because it was on the main Midland railway route, with branch line connections to the Great Northern and London & North Western rail lines.

CHAPTER 1

St Albans in 1914

This chapter describes the main characteristics of St Albans at the outbreak of war in 1914. It considers the growing population and changing employment structure of the city, the ways in which it was governed, the amenities to which its people had access and the cultural and religious life that they enjoyed. The people of St Albans made their living in diverse ways, and the standard of life to which they could aspire varied considerably. However, by 1914, after a century of growth and change, the city was flourishing economically and had a lively political and associational life. The range of local services and institutions that existed at the outbreak of war would have been unimaginable to the inhabitants of St Albans 100, or even 50, years earlier.

This book examines the local impact of a war fought between great powers on the world stage. Sometimes described as the first 'total war', involving whole populations and not just the fighting forces, the First World War brought the term 'home front' into popular parlance in Britain. Almost every area of life was affected in some way in communities up and down the country: the war created new challenges for individuals, families, businesses, churches, schools and institutions of local government ranging from the police and fire brigade to refuse collection and sewage disposal. Industry, agriculture and services were affected in numerous ways, from the loss of employees to the armed forces, to restrictions on the use of premises and materials, to the increased costs of employing their staff. People's physical and mental health, religious convictions and patriotism were all tested, and the war had an impact on their diets, sleep patterns, personal finances, social activities and sex lives. At the end of the war a weakened population faced the influenza epidemic of 1918–20 as well as the tasks of reintegrating demobilised servicemen, restoring 'normalcy' in economic and social life, and finding suitable ways to commemorate the sacrifices made during the war itself.[1] This book explores how one comparatively small community – the city of St Albans in Hertfordshire, 20 miles north of London – met the challenges of the war and its aftermath. It is a local study, but one that has potentially wider relevance. As another historian of the home front has noted, 'there are no perfect microcosms' when it comes to a local study,[2] and St Albans can make no particular claim to being typical. However, the city had a diverse economic structure: it was a market town with an agricultural hinterland, a large and growing manufacturing sector and a middle-class commuter population. It became the temporary home of a large number of billeted soldiers; it was the seat of a military service tribunal whose proceedings offer intriguing insights into the economy and governance of the city; and its rich civil society left many records on which the historian can draw. It offers, therefore, an opportunity to examine in a local context the wide-ranging impact that the First World War had on a small area of England.

Population, industry and employment

By 1914 the population of St Albans had been expanding consistently for more than a century. There were just over 3,000 people in the city in 1801, exactly 7,000 in 1851 and 18,133 in 1911.[3] St Albans was growing beyond its historic core and a series of boundary extensions, in 1835, 1879 and 1913, reflected this sprawl, each bringing new areas within the government of the city. The last was the most important, incorporating large areas of housing and industry into the city. In the early years of the

Figure 1.1 Nicholson's Raincoat Co. Ltd works, Sutton Road, c.1910. © Andy Lawrence

twentieth century two significant areas of working-class housing had been constructed outside the city boundaries. These were Sandridge New Town, to the north of St Albans, adjacent to Bernards Heath,[4] and Fleetville and the Camp to the east, where new industrial enterprises, including the Salvation Army Printing Works on Campfield Road, Smith's Printing Co. Ltd's works on Hatfield Road and Nicholson's Raincoat Co. Ltd on Sutton Road, offered employment opportunities (Figure 1.1). The result of the boundary extension was that the population of St Albans increased by more than a third so that there were an estimated 24,000 people living in the city in 1914.[5] Urban growth, although it took many different forms, was a key aspect of the economic and social changes of the nineteenth and early twentieth centuries, and St Albans was not unusual among ancient towns and cities in this respect.

In one respect, though, St Albans and its surrounding areas were unusual: there was a preponderance of women in the population. This was a long-standing imbalance: at the time of the first census, in 1801, there had been just 74 males in the population per 100 females; in 1851 the figure was 84; and, by 1911, the last census before the war, it had fallen again to 81. Historically, this reflected the importance of straw plaiting and straw hat manufacture to the economy of the city and surrounding region; although straw plaiting had almost disappeared by the twentieth century, hat factories remained a feature of the urban landscape. By 1911 domestic service was the largest employer of women and girls, with around 1,300 employed, but the hat makers employed around 650, about 100 of whom worked from home.[6]

Although no longer using local straw and plait, as they had done for much of the nineteenth century, the straw hat manufacturers constituted the largest group of employers in St Albans, with just over 900 employees in total. These factories produced thousands of hats a year, men's boaters in particular, with many going to export markets. This focus encouraged two manufacturers from nearby Luton to invest in the city in the immediate pre-war years, thereby significantly extending the capacity of the local trade. One of these was Vyse, Sons and Co. Ltd, who opened a three-storey factory in Ridgmont Road late in 1909. Steam-powered radiators and external fire escapes were sufficiently novel to merit attention in reports of the building's opening.[7] They employed 100 workers and expected to recruit more. The other Luton business was Dillingham & Sons, who redeveloped an existing factory in Beaconsfield Road, investing around

Figure 1.2 Bringing in the harvest in sight of the abbey, *c*.1905. © SAHAAS

£2,000 in the process.[8] However, the most significant work was carried out by a St Albans firm, E. Day & Co. Over a period of 11 years they extended their premises off Marlborough Road on three occasions, culminating in 1913 with a new four-storey building complete with a gas compressor for lighting, a modern suite of offices and a 15-extension internal telephone system.[9] Day's, the largest hat manufacturer in the city, employed over 300 workers in 1914.[10] In addition, there were eight other locally based hat companies in St Albans, of which Horace Slade & Co. Ltd and Henry Partridge Smith were the next largest. Slade was a member of St Albans City Council and mayor at the outbreak of war in August 1914.

Although the economy of St Albans was going through a period of rapid diversification in the early twentieth century it was dependent at least in part on industries that reflected its long history as a centre for agricultural trade. Even within the city itself about 5 per cent of the workforce still derived a living from working on the land. There was a large nursery garden on Hatfield Road and two farms in the shadow of the abbey (Figure 1.2). Nine men worked the watercress beds on the chalk-based River Ver. Most of the land around St Albans was owned by the Earl of Verulam and the Spencer family, and most local farmers were tenants before the First World War. Other long-established industries also provided employment. On the outskirts of the city the flour mill at New Barnes had experienced recent substantial investment to bring it up to modern standards of production.[11] Although it is not clear if they were using locally grown barley, the two St Albans breweries sold their beer through more than 60 'tied' public houses and off-licences in St Albans and surrounding towns and villages.[12] The Abbey silk mills, established in 1802, employed around 250 people and was one of several businesses, such as Wiles & Lewis, the tallow chandlers and suet makers on Bernards Heath, which could trace its origins in the city back over 100 years.[13]

In the previous 25 years newly established industries had brought much-needed diversification to the economy of St Albans. Printing companies were fast becoming one of the city's staple trades, employing more than 600 workers, including 134 women. Firms such as F. Dangerfield Ltd and R. Taylor Ltd supplied their own niche markets. The former, having built extensive premises from scratch off Alma Road in the mid-1890s, used expensive presses to print large posters for the underground and bus companies that later became part of London Transport. Other printers, such as Smith's Printing and the Salvation Army, had arrived in Fleetville. The local newspaper, the eight-page *Herts Advertiser*, established in 1855 and owned by local firm Gibbs & Bamforth, was flourishing: its print-run in 1916 was around 9,000 copies a week.[14] It provided extensive coverage of day-to-day life in the city and the surrounding district and recorded the activities of the city council and other institutions of local government. Other industries prospered in St Albans too. For example, the large boot and shoe manufacturers John Freshwater & Co. Ltd and Edwin Lee & Sons employed around 400 workers between them. This figure included some 160 women. Brushes Ltd, based in Grosvenor Road, had more than 200 employees, and produced brushes such as the 'Kra Yard Broom', the 'Gripwell Carpet Brush' and the 'King of Scrubs'.[15] Ryder & Son Ltd, where around 70 'Ryder's girls' sorted seeds into packets in the Holywell Hill warehouse, was another prominent St Albans business and, along with Sander's orchids, Mercer's chronometers, Nicholson's raincoats and Peake's coats, it would be associated with the city for the next 30 years and more.

Lobbying groups such as the St Albans and District Chamber of Commerce were becoming a feature of local trade, although the Chamber consisted mostly of retailers, with few if any industrial members.[16] Instead each trade had its own alliance, such as the St Albans Hat Manufacturers' Association, the Home Counties branch of the Federation of Master Printers and the Hertfordshire Brewers Association, of which the firm of Adey & White was a member. Arrayed against them was the growing challenge of local trade unions. Nationally, a total of 41 million days was lost to strike action in 1912, more than in any year before the war. According to the Board of Trade there were 1,459 strikes in 1913 alone.[17] In St Albans, however, while there was involvement in national actions such as railway strikes, there are few examples of local unrest at the time.

Analysis of the 1911 census shows that around one in eight men living in St Albans worked in construction, with the firm of Miskin's probably the city's largest employer, both in this sector and in general, with a workforce of around 350.[18] With the significant growth in the local population in the Edwardian period there was plenty of business in the area for Miskin's and its competitors, as well as men working in professions such as architecture. There were at least five firms of solicitors in the city, no doubt handling conveyancing business derived from the pre-war building boom, but also benefiting from the presence of both quarter and petty session courts in the city. In all, about 15 per cent of the male population of the city was employed in professional and public service occupations; many of them commuted to work in London. In 1914 they were outnumbered by workers in the manufacturing sector – around a quarter of the working male population and a similar proportion of working women – and by female domestic servants. Among men in employment, nearly half worked in manufacturing, construction, transport or agriculture. St Albans was, in many respects, still a working-class city.

The standard of living enjoyed by the residents varied considerably. Not only were there wide variations in the pay and regularity of employment – even within individual occupations – but individual and family circumstances also differed considerably. Families with young children often experienced poverty, as did older people in the population: old-age pensions were available only from age 70, and were not universal. Workers in some trades were eligible for unemployment and health benefits following the introduction of national insurance in 1911, but these contributory schemes by no means covered the whole population, with women particularly vulnerable in cases of ill-health or loss of employment. Table 1.1 shows what some of those in work were earning in St Albans in 1914, and Table 1.2 summarises the cost of some typical items of expenditure. Although those in salaried employment, particularly men with small families or none, could enjoy a comfortable standard of living, others found themselves in precarious, poorly paid or seasonal employment, which made reliance on poor relief and charity a reality for many in St Albans. When the war started some food prices increased almost immediately, and in many cases on subsequent occasions as well.[19]

Government and politics

St Albans City Council governed the city. Its powers and responsibilities had been set out in the Municipal Corporations Act of 1835 and increased on various subsequent occasions. Some powers, notably over education, were reserved to Hertfordshire County Council, which, along with other county councils, had been established in 1889. Poor relief was organised and distributed by the Poor Law Union, whose elections were held separately from those of the other local authorities. The city council, however, was responsible for roads, sewage and refuse disposal, the market, public health and some hospitals, various public buildings and amenities, street lighting, policing and the fire brigade (Figure 1.3). The business of the council was administered by a small body of paid officials, most notably Edward Percy (known as E.P.) Debenham, who had held the office of town clerk since 1909 and was responsible for most of the council's correspondence. The council was answerable both to its local electors – who voted annually – and to the Local Government Board, which was required to authorise any borrowing that was undertaken. Both the Board and the county council had had to approve the boundary change of 1913. The incorporation of the new areas precipitated some changes to the way in which the city was governed: because of the size of the population St Albans was required to form a local pension committee under the terms of the Old Age Pensions Act of 1908; this committee would consider all claims for pensions. Under the term of the legislation most people aged 70

Table 1.1 Earnings in St Albans, 1914.

A) Waged work

Occupation	Hourly rate	Typical hours p/w	Typical earnings p/w	Weekly wage
Agricultural labourer (ordinary)	--	--	--	15s
Bricklayer	8½d	56½ (summer)	40s ¼d (summer)	--
Bricklayer's labourer	5½d	56½ (summer)	25s 10¾d (summer)	--
Compositors (machine composing, linotype)	--	48	--	35s
Horse driver	--	--	23s 6d	--
Painter	7½d	56½ (summer)	35s 3¾d (summer)	--
Police constable	--	--	--	23s 4d (min.) 31s 4d (max.)
Shop lad (aged 16 or 17)	--	--	--	10s

B) Salaried work

Occupation	Annual salary	Notes
Assistant surveyor, city of St Albans	£130	Increased to £160 in November 1914, as office-holder took on additional duties.
Cook	£22 to £28	Living in employer's house.
Headmaster	£150	
General servant	£14 to £16	Living in employer's house.
Medical officer of health for city of St Albans	£100	Had to meet own transport and secretarial costs. Was also paid for additional duties, e.g. in rural district.
Supply teacher	£83	
Teacher (certificated assistant)	£100	
Workhouse nurse	£26 (one year's experience) £27 (two years' experience)	Also received board and lodging.

Notes: agricultural labourers who worked with animals were paid a small additional sum. The wage shown was the weekly cash wage, not taking into account additional payments in kind, overtime, harvest earnings, etc. Typical earnings per week are calculated from the hours worked and hourly rate in the case of bricklayers, bricklayers' labourers and painters; given in source for the horse driver.

Sources: Herts County Council Education Committee minutes; St Albans City Council, Urban Authority General Purposes Committee minutes; *Herts Advertiser*; Board of Trade Department of Labour Statistics, Report on Changes in Rates of Wages and Hours of Labour in the United Kingdom in 1913, with Comparative Statistics (1914–16, Cd 7635); Board of Trade, Department of Labour Statistics, Standard Time Rates of Wages in the United Kingdom at 1 October 1913 (1914, Cd 7194).

Table 1.2 The cost of living, St Albans, 1914.

A) Housing

House type	Sale price	Rent
Detached, Spencer Park	£670	
Six-bedroom cottage with three sitting rooms	£800	£50 per annum
Worley Road, five-bed semi-detached		£30 per annum
Cambridge Road, three-bed house		9s per week

B) Other expenditure

Motor cycle	£17 to £35
Vauxhall car (35hp 6-cylinder)	£770
Sugar (lump, lb)	2d
Sugar (granulated, lb)	1¾d
Cheese (lb)	8d
Milk (gallon)	1s 1d
Bread (4-lb loaf)	6d
Herts Advertiser	1d
Bicycle (man's)	£3 to £4
Cinema admission	3d to 1s
St Albans Grammar School annual fee	£10 10s (aged under 12)
	£12 (aged 12 and over)
Verulam Golf Club (annual membership)	£4 4s (men)
	£2 2s (women)

Notes: St Albans Grammar School fee figures are for 1915.
Source: *Herts Advertiser*; *Kelly's Directory*; St Albans Food Control Committee minutes.

and over were entitled to receive a pension, although in 1911 only around 300 people in St Albans were described in the census as being retired.[20] The structure of the council was also changed. St Albans was now divided into three wards for city council elections – east, north and south – each of which elected six councillors. The rural areas that remained outside the city boundaries were governed by St Albans Rural District Council, established in 1894, which had responsibilities corresponding to those of the city council.

Local government spending was increasing in the years before the First World War. In 1912–13 the city council spent £20,773 and in the following year £22,815, of which just over a quarter was met by income from rents, fines, cemetery fees, government grants and miscellaneous sources, and the rest from the rates. The politics of rating were fiercely contested in this period, and across the country ratepayers' associations

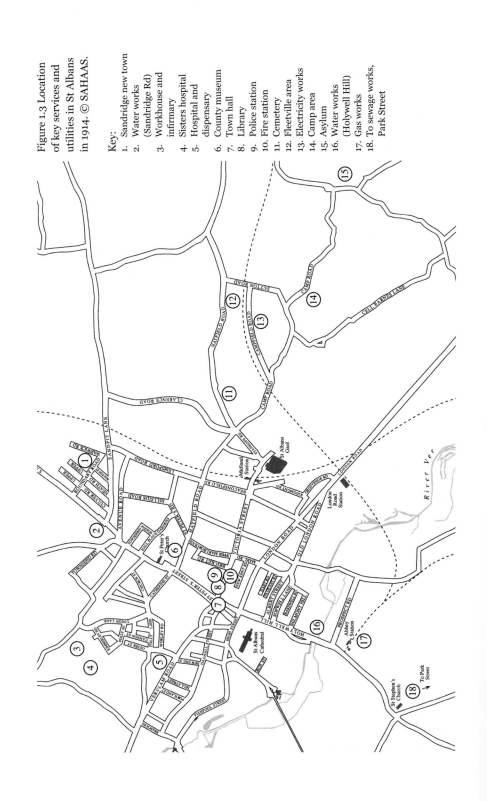

Figure 1.3 Location of key services and utilities in St Albans in 1914. © SAHAAS.

Key:
1. Sandridge new town
2. Water works (Sandridge Rd)
3. Workhouse and infirmary
4. Sisters hospital
5. Hospital and dispensary
6. County museum
7. Town hall
8. Library
9. Police station
10. Fire station
11. Cemetery
12. Fleetville area
13. Electricity works
14. Camp area
15. Asylum
16. Water works (Holywell Hill)
17. Gas works
18. To sewage works, Park Street

organised resistance to increases in local government taxation.[21] In St Albans in 1913 the Camp Ward Ratepayers' Association was prominent in the opposition to the boundary extension. Others also voiced their strong opposition, including Alfred Nicholson, managing director of the coat manufacturers, who explained that the low rates in St Albans Rural District were one of the reasons why his company chose to move there.[22] Rates were paid on the rental value of property, and the total rateable value of the city of St Albans before the extension was £106,596. The new areas were worth a total of £39,908 in rateable value, but, as housing and industry were expected to expand still further in these areas, this would increase over time, yielding a larger income for the council. Before the boundary extension the city was charging its inhabitants a rate of 4s in the pound, but because the county council and the poor law authorities also charged rates, of 3s 4½d and 1s 1½d respectively, the total rate burden within the municipal area was 8s 6d in the pound. In the neighbouring wards of St Albans Rural District the burden was significantly lower – 6s 1d in the Camp Ward and lower still in the rural areas of St Michael's, St Stephen's and Sandridge – and the services provided to inhabitants were correspondingly inferior. The extension of the boundary enabled the new housing areas to be connected to the mains sewage system of the city, although most of this work was delayed until after the war. To avoid an immediate increase in the rates, the Act of Parliament that extended the boundaries established a ten-year programme of rate assimilation, so that the new areas had a discount until 1924.[23]

St Albans had a lively political life, with contested parliamentary and municipal elections involving a number of well-known characters, many of whom had come to prominence through business and other local activities. The period from 1910 to 1914 is often characterised as one of strife and upheaval, with trade unions and women's suffrage campaigners bringing radical politics to streets and workplaces. The Labour party had been formed (as the Labour Representation Committee) in 1900, and had begun to play a role in both municipal and parliamentary politics. It stood two candidates in the local election of 1913 in St Albans, but did not meet with any success. The city council did, however, resolve in 1914 that all contracts for goods or services should require contractors to pay trade union rates and adhere to conditions agreed with unions.[24] This resolution was moved by councillor Frederick George Warwick, one of ten 'Progressive' councillors elected in the first election under the new boundaries in 1913.[25] Local government in this period was dominated by battles between 'Progressives' on the one hand – mostly Liberals – and 'Moderates', who were mostly Conservative. In St Albans the Progressives were strong in the north and east wards, whereas Moderates dominated in the south. The best-known Progressive, elected in the north ward, was the former mayor Samuel Ryder, the seed merchant and later founder of golf's Ryder Cup.[26] In terms of parliamentary politics, St Albans almost always voted Conservative: at the outbreak of war the MP was Sir Hildred Carlile, a textile manufacturer and philanthropist who defeated three different Liberal opponents in the elections of 1906, January 1910 and December 1910, with an increased majority in both 1910 polls.

Infrastructure and amenities

By far the largest item of city council expenditure, amounting to almost a quarter of the total, was the maintenance of roads. Spending under this heading was £5,390 in 1913–14, with a further £1,981 being spent on lighting. In the pre-war years a large proportion of the minuted council business related to road repairs, which were mostly routine but occasionally – such as the widening of Hatfield Road in front of the Marlborough almshouses at the northern end of the city centre – more significant.[27] Road repairs were required in the areas taken into the city after the boundary extension: in early 1914, for example, repairs were needed in Cambridge Road, Royston Road and College Road in the Camp.[28] Spending on roads increased with the growth of private motor transport and the increasing number of buses that travelled to and in St Albans. The town clerk regularly wrote to bus companies demanding payment for damage done by buses to street lamps and other council property.[29] Buses ran between the city centre and Fleetville from 1909, and the London General Omnibus Company Ltd operated a service to Golders Green from 1912.[30]

St Albans's large commuter population was served by frequent services to London on the Midland Railway, whose services had first run in 1868. The main entrance to the station was on Ridgmont Road. More than 200,000 journeys were made on this line from St Albans in 1913, a figure that had almost doubled in 20 years.[31] The railway made possible the growth of the commuter population and the development of middle-class housing. A guide to the city published in 1903 boasted: 'as a residential suburb for London, [St Albans] has claims which cannot be conceded to

Figure 1.4 Midland railway station, Ridgmont Road, c.1910. © Andy Lawrence

ordinary suburban London ... its rural surroundings and splendid train service make it an ideal place of residence for the city man'.[32] The railway created employment not only for train drivers and station staff but also for a range of others, many of whom themselves travelled to work by train: there were 446 railway workers living in St Albans in 1911. Two other railway lines carried both passengers and freight: the London and North Western line, running from the Abbey station to Watford, and the Great Northern line, which also ran from the Abbey station, in this case to Hatfield via the London Road station, which was near the place where the Midland Railway bridge crosses London Road. Railways in this period were privately owned and operated, but they created work for the council because the stations themselves generated more traffic within St Albans. In 1911 the Midland Railway Company agreed to pay a regular sum to the council for repairs to the station forecourt, but by 1915 it was clear that the council was spending more than it was receiving from the company (Figure 1.4).[33]

Residents and visitors to the city on Saturdays could take advantage of a variety of stalls on offer in the general market (Figure 1.5).[34] Exactly half the stalls carried perishable food items. Greengrocers, butchers and fishmongers made up the majority of these, but two stalls in August 1914 sold ice cream. Equally perishable were the flowers and plants for sale on three stalls: it made commercial sense for Watson's Nursery of Hatfield Road to take a stall and bring their goods direct to market, but clearly

Figure 1.5 St Albans market, c.1905. © St Albans Museums (T849)

there was a demand within the city, as one stall was taken by a Dunstable
company, William Seamons & Sons. Others who valued the opportunities
on offer in St Albans included butchers from Watford, greengrocers from
Ampthill and fishmongers from Luton. There were three drapers, as well
as dealers in books, clothes, crockery, furniture and ironmongery. Those
wishing to repair their bikes could purchase cycle fittings from Mrs Wilks
of Watford's stall and a day at the market could be rounded off with a
photograph taken by a Mr Howe, probably an itinerant traveller who took
a stall when he was in the area. It cost 1s to reserve a space at the market,
and the weekly rental of stalls cost anything from 1s 6d to 10s. In August
1914 there were 56 stallholders, 35 of whom were residents of St Albans
and thus entitled to a 25 per cent discount.

A 20-strong brigade of firemen protected the city against fire.[35] A
new fire station had been established on Victoria Street in 1899, with
stabling for three horses – there was no motor engine in the city until
1919, although the council had considered buying one before the war. The
council had a separate fire brigade committee, and the service occasioned
high expenditure in some years: £322 was spent in 1912–13, for example.
The brigade dealt with a number of major fires in the years before the

war, including one at Wiles & Lewis on Bernards Heath in 1911. There was some dissatisfaction in 1914 following delays in attending fires, a situation that was worsened by the depletion of the brigade during the war, as firemen rushed to enlist. Before the war there was particular unhappiness in Fleetville and the Camp, which were difficult for the St Albans engine to reach. There was a volunteer brigade in Fleetville, certainly in existence from 1912 and perhaps earlier, as well as a separate volunteer brigade serving the Salvation Army Printing Works on Campfield Road. Spokesmen for Fleetville at the time of the municipal boundary extension in 1913 had expressed concern about the possible amalgamation of the local brigade with the one in St Albans. Ernest Townson, a director of Smith's Printing (and later a councillor), was asked at the inquiry, 'Have you found the [St Albans] fire engine of any advantage to your ward?' He replied acidly: 'There is a legend that it came down here once.'[36] In 1914 the Fleetville brigade was incorporated into the city brigade, although the Salvation Army works brigade remained separate.

Policing was overseen by the council's Watch Committee and took the form of a separate police force that operated within the municipal boundaries, outside which the county police force was responsible. There were 35 policemen in St Albans, operating from a police station on Victoria Street, which had been built in 1893–4 at a cost of £2,100; these premises included a head constable's office, charge room and four cells.[37] The force received some central government funding, although this was not enough to cover the high cost of the service, which included uniforms and pensions in addition to salaries.[38] Crime rates were not high. In 1914 the head constable's reports show that 71 indictable offences (including burglary and larceny) were reported to police, and 252 people were proceeded against for non-indictable offences, of which 56 were cases of drunkenness.[39]

During the nineteenth century St Albans, like many other towns and cities, acquired a range of civic amenities, including water and gas supplies and sewage facilities. The water works on Sandridge Road were opened in 1865 and there were public baths at Cottonmill Lane from 1887. The water was supplied by St Albans Water Company. Sewage pipes were laid in Victoria Street in 1882 and the Park Street sewage works opened in the following year. The issue of sewage presented significant challenges for the city council and was one of the most pressing matters during the negotiations over the extension of the boundaries in 1913. Although the areas within the pre-1913 boundary benefited from mains sewage, the new houses in Sandridge New Town and Fleetville were less well provided for. The council was worried that the poor sewage arrangements, especially in Sandridge New Town, might result in the contamination of the St Albans water supply.[40] The council had agreed to fund sewage improvements in these new urban areas in return for bringing them within the city boundary and subjecting them to the higher rates charged there. For example, early in 1914 Albion Road and Cavendish Road, close to the Midland Railway station, were connected to mains sewage for the first time.[41] The war delayed the extension of the sewage system,[42] but council spending on sewage increased significantly during the war. The accounts separate the sums spent on flushing and maintaining sewers and on the 'sewage farm' itself, but the total amount increased from £1,495 in 1912–13 to £1,702 in 1913–14, and then to £2,825 in 1918–19. Significant borrowing had been undertaken to pay for sewage improvements, and by 1913–14 the council was spending £3,662 on servicing its debt. Before the war, and in the first two years of the war itself, domestic refuse collection was outsourced to John Cable Ltd.[43] According to figures in the council minute books, the total cost of this was £959 in 1912–13 and £1,042 in 1913–14. From 1908 the refuse itself was taken to the waste destructor at the electricity works on Campfield Road.[44]

These works were owned by the North Metropolitan Electric Power Supply Co., which had taken on the statutory undertaking to provide electricity to the city in 1907. Power generation had commenced in 1908 with the destructor at the heart of the process, burning the city's refuse to produce steam to supply the electricity.[45] Two diesel engines had been installed by 1914 to supplement the destructor's limited capacity.[46] By 1909 the company had 135 local consumers on the books, and this number was to increase to 619 by 1919.[47] By 1914 supply contracts had been signed with various businesses in the Fleetville and Camp areas, the most recent being with the St Albans Rubber Co. in June 1913.[48] The firm of Giffen Bros had their electrical showrooms in Chequer Street, displaying 'electric candlesticks' and an 'electric laundry iron', among many new devices. Giffen Bros were the contractors for installing supplies to various businesses, including the Rubber Co., and to residential premises such as Batchwood Hall and the White House in St Peter's Street.[49] Another new utility was also developing in the area: nearly all the businesses advertising in the 1915 *Pictorial Record* had telephone numbers.[50] There were signs of investment in the more mature utilities, too. The St Albans Water Co. had recently improved capacity with investments in a new reservoir and pumping main, probably to cater for expected growth in consumption as the city grew.[51] So too at the St Albans Gas Co., although there the most recent development was the rebuilding of worn gas mains.[52]

A number of other amenities, some provided and maintained by the council and some by private initiative, were available to the residents of St Albans. The council maintained the cemetery on Hatfield Road, opened in 1882, which was a source of income as well as an expense for the council, as were the public baths. The council was responsible for the upkeep of Clarence Park, which had been gifted to the city in 1894 by Sir John Blundell Maple.[53] Public buildings included the Corn Exchange, built in 1857, and the medieval clock tower, which had been extensively restored in 1865. A public library was first established in the 1880s, paid for by a penny rate, and this was replaced in 1911 by a new library, paid for by the philanthropist Andrew Carnegie. Close to the Midland Railway station a prison was built in 1867, in which both men and women were accommodated and executions sometimes carried out. More happily, the city's museum – known as the county museum at this time – was opened in 1898, and was one of a number of tourist attractions that brought thousands of visitors to St Albans every year.[54]

Health and education

Public health was overseen by Dr Henry E. May, the medical officer of health for both St Albans (from 1912) and the surrounding rural district (from 1911). May was responsible for the production of annual reports detailing vital statistics – birth, death and infant mortality rates – and information about infectious diseases and other public health matters, including inspections of houses, factories and workshops. May advised the council and schools about infection control, ensured that individuals with infectious diseases were isolated either in hospitals or at home, investigated the source of diseases, prosecuted parents for failing to notify the authorities of an infectious disease and closed schools when there was a serious outbreak of infection.

For the historian, May's annual reports provide an overview of conditions in St Albans at this period and of the impact of the war. In the years 1910–13 the number of births in the city annually ranged from

336 to 352, increasing to 521 in 1914 when the population was increased
by the boundary extension. The birth rate in 1914 was 20.8 per 1,000
people, somewhat lower than the national rate (England and Wales) of
23.8. The death rate was also lower: 277 people died in 1914, or 11.1 per
1,000, compared with 14.0 for England and Wales as a whole.[55] Birth and
death rates largely reflected the age structure of the population, and infant
mortality rates – deaths under one year of age per 1,000 live births – were
considered a better measure of public health. St Albans fared well in this
respect, with a consistently lower rate before the war than the country as
a whole, although one still startlingly high from a modern perspective.
In 1914 the rate was 52, compared with 105 for the whole of England and
Wales. In most years between 100 and 200 cases of infectious diseases
were notified to the medical officer: in 1914, for example, there were 179,
including 88 cases of scarlet fever. Also in 1914 there was a diphtheria
outbreak which led May to inspect the houses in St Michael's: he announced
himself 'perfectly satisfied that these cases did not arise through any
insanitary conditions either with regard to the outside premises or the
drains or sewers'.[56]

Health care was provided by three main hospitals. The St Albans Union
Infirmary was part of the workhouse on Union Lane (now Normandy
Road), and was administered by the poor law authorities. The Sisters
Hospital was close to this and specialised in treating infectious diseases:
it had been given to the city by Blundell Maple in 1893, the year before his
gift of Clarence Park, and a diphtheria block was added in 1911. The Sisters
Hospital was managed by a joint committee appointed by the city council,
the rural district council and Harpenden urban district council, and patients
from these areas were admitted free of charge. The third main hospital
was the St Albans and Mid Herts Hospital and Dispensary on the corner
of Verulam Road and Church Crescent, built in 1888 at a cost of £4,000
and enlarged in 1899 and 1912. By this time it accommodated 40 beds
and the average number of in-patients was 300 a year, with outpatients
numbering 1,100. This hospital relied heavily on annual subscriptions and
one-off donations from the public, with more than £1,000 being received
in 1914.[57] The war would put significant strain on these sources of funds.
On top of his role as medical officer of health, May was honorary medical
officer at this hospital and medical superintendent at the Sisters Hospital.
Fourteen other physicians and surgeons were listed in the city in *Kelly's
Directory* for 1914–15. Close to St Albans was the Hertfordshire County

Asylum at Hill End, which was established in 1899 and extended in 1908; by 1913 it could accommodate 820 patients.[58]

Like health care, education was a mixture of rate-financed, voluntary-aided and private provision. Elementary education was compulsory, with a school-leaving age of 13, but very few children received any secondary education, with even fewer attending a university.[59] Since 1902 the local education authority had been the county council, although in St Albans the responsibility for county council schools had been devolved to a local sub-committee, of which the town clerk was the secretary. There were ten county council schools in the city, including Alma Road, for girls and infants, built in 1882 and enlarged in 1890, and Hatfield Road, for boys, built in 1881 and enlarged twice before the war. New schools served the population of Sandridge New Town, Fleetville and the Camp. The local authority also oversaw the secular curriculum of the existing voluntary-aided church schools, and provided some funding. Including both council and voluntary-aided schools, there were over 3,900 children on elementary school rolls in St Albans in 1914.[60] Opportunities to obtain a secondary education were far more limited, being available only at the two leading fee-paying schools in the city at that time. For girls, there was St Albans High School for Girls, which had moved to Townsend Avenue in 1908 and had 157 girls in attendance in 1914.[61] Boys could attend St Albans Grammar School,[62] a medieval foundation which had been moved from the abbey itself to the old gatehouse in 1870, and which had also undergone significant expansion in the late Victorian and Edwardian period. A new building adjoining the gatehouse was constructed in 1907 at a cost of £10,000, and in 1912 a new 'head master's boarding house' was built, costing £5,000. The headmaster Edgar Montague Jones, appointed in 1902, oversaw this expansion, which enabled the school to accommodate 245 pupils in 1914.[63] The school's cadet force, which was attached to the junior division of the Officer Training Corps, numbered 102. In addition to these establishments there was also a School of Art & Craft on Victoria Street, a technical school which taught carpentry, joinery and other manual skills, as well as commercial subjects, mostly to elementary school-leavers attending day and evening classes.

Religion and culture

The religious life of St Albans – and in particular Protestant nonconformity – was strong, although church and chapel attendance had declined since the mid-nineteenth century. The expansion of the city and the construction of new housing estates resulted in new parish boundaries and new churches in addition to the long-established places of worship such as St Peter's and St Michael's and, of course, the abbey church, which had become a cathedral when the diocese of St Albans was created in 1877. By 1914 there was, in addition to the cathedral, space for around 3,000 worshippers in Anglican churches in St Albans, although no figures on actual attendance are available.[64] The newest churches were St Paul's in Hatfield Road, built in 1910 with 750 'sittings', and St Saviour's on Sandpit Lane, built in 1902 with 800. The foundation for St Saviour's parish hall was laid before the First World War and the building was opened on 5 November 1914.[65] Nonconformist churches were thriving. Marlborough Road Methodist church, built in 1898 at a cost of £7,000, had space for 950 worshippers: there had been a significant Methodist revival in St Albans in the late nineteenth century. The Methodist Sunday School continued to flourish, with over 1,000 members in the St Albans Methodist Circuit in 1908.[66] The Salvation Army Citadel and Young People's Hall on Victoria Street had around 20 meetings of various kinds each week.[67] Meanwhile, there was space for 450 at the Baptist church on Dagnall Street.[68] The Tabernacle, another Baptist church on Victoria Street, had 400 'sittings', two Sunday services and some midweek activity, and the Baptists also had a church on Verulam Road, with space for 200 but membership of just 44.[69] Baptist activities included missionary work in Sopwell Lane and the villages around the city.[70] Other religious groups included the Society of Friends (Quakers), whose meeting house was on Lattimore Road, and the Brethren in the gospel hall on the same street; both these denominations would come to prominence through their opposition to the war and support for conscientious objectors.[71] The Quakers led the St Albans adult school on Stanhope Road, which was one of 14 institutions connected to churches that operated in the city, including the Citadel. There was also a strong Congregationalist presence at Spicer Street Independent Chapel and Trinity Church on Victoria Street, with which Samuel Ryder was associated. The Roman Catholic population was served by the church in Beaconsfield Road, with an average attendance at mass of 275 in 1908; SS Alban and Stephen School was opened in 1911.[72]

Popular recreation for men, particularly working-class men, still centred on the pub, although less so than in the Victorian period. In 1871 there was one pub for every 35 or so men in the city.[73] Later in the 1870s consumption hit its peak, with per capita beer sales reaching 40 gallons a year.[74] By 1914 this had dropped to just 29 gallons as social changes such as improvements in education and mass consumerism changed attitudes to public drinking. Proceedings for drunkenness in St Albans in 1914 resulted in 44 convictions, which represented a significant decrease since the turn of the century.[75] Some drinkers changed venue: during the late Edwardian period off-licences saw a rise in business and there were around 1,400 members of clubs with their own bars, such as the city's Liberal Club and the St Albans Tennis & Croquet Club.[76] Even with the growth of the city beyond its medieval heart, the small but noisy local temperance lobby prevented the licensing of any pubs in the new working-class areas in Fleetville and around what is now Normandy Road. With these pressures bearing down on them even the publicans realised there were too many pubs in the city centre. The 1904 Licensing Act concentrated minds by introducing the so-called 'redundancy programme' to reduce the number of pubs throughout England and Wales. The act allowed payments in compensation to owners and tenants when a pub's licence was extinguished for reasons other than misconduct. Somewhat ironically, bearing in mind the 7,000 or so soldiers billeted in St Albans at the time, matters came to a head on 31 December 1914 when 11 pubs, including four in Fishpool Street, were shut under the programme either owing to insanitary conditions or because they were simply adjudged 'unnecessary', or both.[77] A notice the following day in the window of one of these redundant pubs noted: 'No more beer to be sold here for ever and ever, Amen.'[78]

Alternative sources of recreation included the theatre and, increasingly, the cinema. The County Hall Theatre in St Peter's Street had a regular programme featuring touring companies from other theatres, and was also hired out for amateur productions. The first cinema in St Albans was the Poly Picture Palace, at 166 London Road, which was opened in 1908 (as the Alpha) by the pioneering film producer Arthur Melbourne-Cooper. This was followed in 1912 by the opening of the St Albans Cinema on Chequer Street. Both showed a wide range of films and were popular with the public, being open six days a week and changing the programme every three days.[79] Before the outbreak of war St Albans Cinema showed *The Three Musketeers*, *The Man of Destiny* and a military drama called *The Boomerang*, among many other features.[80] Cinemas would become an increasingly important part of popular recreation during the interwar period, but they were emerging before the war, and in St Albans a little earlier than in most other places. Local cinemas charged between 3d and 1s for admission in January 1914, while in the same month seats for the pantomime at the County Hall Theatre ranged from 6d to 2s 6d, with children half price.[81] There were also various new opportunities for outdoor recreation. Clarence Park became the new home of St Albans Cricket Club after it was given to the city in 1894, and the club was re-formed in 1898. Large crowds watched matches in the Edwardian period. St Albans City Football Club was founded in 1908, and also made its home in Clarence Park.[82] Verulam Golf Club was established in 1905, the first scout troop in St Albans dates from 1908 and the first girl guide company from 1916.[83] Both scouts and guides would play a role in wartime St Albans.

By 1914 St Albans was a small but flourishing city with a growing industrial base and a lively political and associational life. In the latter respect, in particular, it typified the culture of voluntarism and middle-class social leadership that characterised urban communities in the early twentieth century; one historian has seen the Edwardian years as 'the apogee of British small-town life'.[84] The intertwining of politics, religion and voluntary service is seen in the varied careers of many of the leading citizens of St Albans. Samuel Ryder, with his involvement in business, the city council and Trinity Church, is one example. *Kelly's Directory*, on the eve of the war, contained a long list of associations, including choral societies, the Church of England Temperance Society, the chamber of agriculture, the Hertfordshire Natural History Society, 'lodges' of the Oddfellows friendly society, the Primrose League (a social and political organisation supporting the Conservative party) and a range of sporting, political and cultural organisations.[85] Some found an outlet for their energies in the St Albans Literary Institute or the St Albans & Hertfordshire Architectural & Archaeological Society, and both residents and tourists visited the County Museum on Hatfield Road.[86] A burgeoning civic conservation movement involved a number of prominent figures in the city and there was a strong sense of local identity and civic pride. This had been demonstrated to spectacular effect in the historical pageant of 1907, which had involved a cast of 3,000 citizens in re-enacting eight episodes from the history of St Albans, watched over several performances by many thousands of spectators, some of whom had travelled on special trains from London and elsewhere.[87] This event, and others, showcased the public face of the city and the culture of public and voluntary service that underpinned its governance. As the rest of this book will show, the war would test this culture to its limits.

Notes

1. The term 'normalcy' was used by Warren Harding in his US presidential election campaign of 1920.
2. S. Hallifax, 'Citizens at war: the experience of the Great War in Essex, 1914–1918', DPhil thesis (University of Oxford, 2010), p. 30.
3. M. Freeman, *St Albans: a history* (Lancaster, 2008), p. 210. St Albans became a city in 1877.
4. Sandridge New Town comprised the streets east of Sandridge Road and north of Sandpit Lane, including Culver Road, Heath Road and Boundary Road.
5. Freeman, *St Albans*, p. 210; Hertfordshire Archives and Local Studies (HALS), SBR/Interim Catalogue, Medical Officer of Health Report (MOHR), 1914.
6. These and other employment figures are taken from the 1911 census enumerators' books, but cover the area of the extended city of 1913.
7. 'New factory at St Albans', *Herts Advertiser* (*HA*), 25 December 1909.
8. 'Factory extension', *HA*, 10 January 1914.
9. 'Business development', *HA*, 18 January 1913.
10. St Albans Central Library, *Pictorial Record: St Albans* (London, 1915), p. 21.
11. 'Earl of Verulam's mill, St Albans', *Milling Journal*, 2 January 1915, pp. 38–40.
12. Figures based on A. Whitaker, *Brewers in Hertfordshire: a historical gazetteer* (Hatfield, 2006), pp. 197, 199. The two breweries were Adey & White in Chequer Street and T.W. Kent & Son on Holywell Hill.
13. *Pictorial Record: St Albans*, p. 17.
14. 'Adieu', *HA*, 24 January 1947.
15. *Pictorial Record: St Albans*, pp. 1, 16; analysis of the number of employees in the 1911 census indicates a workforce of closer to 100.
16. HALS, Acc 3727, St Albans & District Chamber of Commerce Executive Committee Minute Book, 1908–17, 14 September 1914.
17. BBC Radio 4, *1913: The Year Before* (2013), episode 6: 'Labour relations and the Triple Alliance'.
18. *Pictorial Record: St Albans*, p. 13.
19. 'The price of food', *HA*, 8 August 1914.
20. HALS, SBR/894A, City Council Minute Book (CMB), 27 January 1914.
21. P.J. Waller, 'Altercation over civil society: the bitter cry of the Edwardian middle classes', in J. Harris (ed.), *Civil society in British history* (Oxford, 2003), pp. 115–34.
22. City of St Alban [*sic*], *City Extension 1913, Proceedings*: bound volume in St Albans Central Library, p. 312.
23. Local Government Board's Provisional Order Confirmation (No. 12) Act, 3 & 4 Geo. V, 15 August 1913.
24. HALS, SBR/894A, CMB, 18 March 1914.
25. 'Death of Mr F.G. Warwick', *HA*, 30 July 1937.

26. P. Fry, *Samuel Ryder: the man behind the Ryder Cup* (Weymouth, 2000).

27. See, for example, HALS, SBR/894A, CMB, 9 November 1912: report of city surveyor.

28. HALS, SBR/894A, CMB, 27 January 1914.

29. See, for example, HALS, SBR/1901, Town Clerk Out Letters Book (TCOL), E.P. Debenham to secretary of Herts Motors Ltd, 5 August 1914, E.P. Debenham to secretary, London General Omnibus Company Ltd, 14 September 1914.

30. Freeman, *St Albans*, p. 272; E. Toms, *The story of St Albans* (St Albans, 1962), p. 180; T. Billings, *84 bus to St Albans: an illustrated local history* (St Albans, 2003), p. 2.

31. G. Goslin, *St Albans to Bedford, including the Hemel Hempstead branch* (Midhurst, 2003), p. ix.

32. Quoted in Freeman, *St Albans*, p. 231.

33. HALS, SBR/1901, TCOL, E.P. Debenham to general manager, Midland Railway Company, 24 March 1915.

34. All references to the market are from HALS, SBR/1666, Market Toll Account Book, 1912–22.

35. Much of the information in the paragraph below comes from A. McWhirr, *St Albans city fire brigade* (Leicester, 2007), pp. 21–32.

36. City of St Alban, *City Extension 1913*, p. 303.

37. T. Cox, 'Herts police in the Great War', Herts at War project lecture, 9 April 2015, Letchworth Garden City Heritage Foundation; *Kelly's Directory of St Albans, Harpenden and Hatfield for 1914–15* (London, 1914), p. 15.

38. The city council financial records contain detailed information on income and costs related to policing.

39. HALS, SBR/894A, CMB, Head Constable's reports.

40. City of St Alban, *City Extension 1913*.

41. HALS, SBR/894A, CMB, 27 January 1914.

42. M. Neighbour, *St Albans' own East End, volume I: outsiders* (Hoddesdon, 2012), pp. 259–60.

43. Cable had originally held the contract for those parts of St Albans Rural District that were brought into the city in 1913. In 1911 Harry Finch Reynolds had signed a five-year contract to collect the city's refuse, but was not doing so by 1914.

44. N.C. Friswell, *Northmet: a history of the North Metropolitan Electric Power Supply Company* (Horsham, 2000), pp. 42, 119.

45. Ibid., p. 43. The author conjectures that this was the earliest use of such a destructor in the country.

46. Ibid., p. 42.

47. Ibid., p. 121.

48. HALS, PUE 3/3, North Metropolitan Co. Board Minutes, 1910–17, 27 June 1913.

49. *Pictorial Record: St Albans*, p. 19.

50. Ibid., *passim*. Based on documents in the St Albans City Archive (e.g. HALS, SBR/2867) it appears that the National Telephone Co. had been developing telephone services in the city from the early 1890s onwards.

51. 'St Albans water supply', *HA*, 27 March 1915.

52. HALS, PUG 13/1/5, St Albans Gas Co. Minute Book, 1907–14, report for half-year ending 30 June 1913.

53. See Freeman, *St Albans*, pp. 239, 244.

54. B. Moody, 'The museum of St Albans, a history', copy of lecture given to SAHAAS in 1999 (available in SAHAAS library).

55. HALS, SBR/Interim, MOHR, 1914.

56. Ibid.

57. HALS, SBR/3572, St Albans and Mid Herts Hospital and Dispensary: Management Committee annual statements, 1914–19, 1914; *Kelly's Directory of St Albans, Harpenden and Hatfield for 1913–14* (London, 1913), 1913, p. 17.

58. *Kelly's Directory … 1913–14*, p. 17.

59. Unless otherwise stated, the data in this paragraph comes from *Kelly's Directory … 1914–15*, pp. 49–52.

60. HALS, HCC 21/9, Hertfordshire County Council Education Committee Minute Book, 1914–15, 22 June 1914, p. 155.

61. 'St Albans High School', *HA*, 21 November 1914.

62. The name of the school was a bone of contention between the headmaster and the governors at this time. During and after the war the headmaster discouraged the use of the word 'grammar', preferring the modern name of St Albans School: N. Watson, *Born not for ourselves: the story of St Albans School* (St Albans, 2014), p. 100.

63. St Albans School archive, E. Montague Jones to chairman of governors, 25 July 1914.

64. Calculated from *Kelly's Directory … 1914–15*, pp. 11–14.

65. W.H. Morley, *More such days, 1910–1952, being a continuation of the story of the church and parish of St Saviour, St Albans* (n.p., 1952), p. 15.

66. E.J. Gardner, *Marlborough Road, 1898–1998* (St Albans, 1998), p. 37.

67. *Kelly's Directory … 1914–15*, pp. 48–9.

68. Ibid., p. 14; *Baptists Handbook* 1915: Dr Williams's Library, London.

69. *Kelly's Directory … 1914–15*, pp. 14, 47; *Baptists Handbook* 1915.

70. D. Turner, *With cheerful zeal: a history of the Dagnall Street baptist church* (London, 1999), p. 100.

71. On the Society of Friends see C. Crellin, *Where God had a people: Quakers in St Albans over three hundred years* (St Albans, 1999), pp. 53–4.

72. J. Corbett, *Celebration: the story of a parish: SS Alban and Stephen, 1840–1990* (St Albans, 1990), p. 28.

73. The figure is based on the 1871 census return for the borough and the 86 public houses recorded in the head constable's annual licensing report: see 'Borough petty sessions', *HA*, 26 August 1871.

74. R.G. Wilson, 'The changing taste for beer in Victorian Britain', in R.G. Wilson and T.R. Gourvish (eds), *The dynamics of international brewing since 1800* (London, 1998), p. 94.

75. 'Licensing session', *HA*, 6 February 1915.

76. Figures extrapolated from HALS, PS21/4/1, St Albans City Petty Sessions, Register of Clubs.

77. For a detailed discussion of the redundancy programme in St Albans see J. Mein, *The rise and fall of the pub in Victorian St Albans* (St Albans, 2011) (available in SAHAAS library).

78. 'Eleven licensed houses closed', *HA*, 9 January 1915.

79. A. Eyles with K. Stone, *Cinemas of Hertfordshire* (Hatfield, 2002 [1st edn 1985]), pp. ix, 91–4.

80. Advertisements, *HA*, 20 June 1914, 4 July 1914.

81. Advertisements, *HA*, 12 January 1914. The cinema prices were for the Poly Picture Palace in St Albans.

82. Freeman, *St Albans*, pp. 248–9; R.G. Simons, *Cricket in Hertfordshire* (n.p., 1996), pp. 56–7.

83. F. Brittain, *Milestones of 100 years of Hertfordshire scouting* (n.p., 2008), p. 12. HALS, DP93C/29/2, St Paul's parish magazine, October 1917, celebrating the first anniversary of formation.

84. Quoted in Freeman, *St Albans*, p. 245.

85. *Kelly's Directory ... 1914–15*, pp. 53–7.

86. B. Moody, *The light of other days: a short history of the St Albans & Hertfordshire Architectural & Archaeological Society, 1845 to 1995* (St Albans, 1995), p. 2; Freeman, *St Albans*, pp. 245, 252.

87. M. Freeman, '"Splendid display, pompous spectacle": historical pageants in twentieth-century Britain', *Social History*, 38 (2013), pp. 423–55.

CHAPTER 2

Volunteering and conscription

On Tuesday 4 August 1914 Britain declared war on Germany. Almost overnight St Albans changed, as over 7,000 soldiers came to the city for training and home defence purposes. They were part of a small army that grew into millions over the next four years as the country's military situation worsened. Many volunteered to serve king and country. Others did not, and had to be compelled to join up. This chapter considers the contribution made by the people of St Albans to this colossal national effort.

N ews about the growing threat of war was slow to appear in the *Herts Advertiser*. It was not until the edition published on Saturday 1 August 1914 that readers reliant on this paper for their news would have been aware that something was afoot. Matters were serious: Austria had declared war on Serbia the previous Tuesday, prices in food markets throughout Europe were rocketing, and capital markets were shut. Tension in Britain was evident too. Army units and ships of the Royal Navy were being moved to their appointed positions, but only, as the newspaper was keen to underscore, for precautionary reasons.

By the next edition, published on 8 August, the situation had changed. Britain had declared war on Germany. The immediate response in St Albans seems to have been a degree of panic. As in Europe, cash was scarce as the banks, closed for Bank Holiday Monday,[1] remained shut for the rest of the week. Food prices rocketed here too, particularly the cost of flour and sugar. The town's grocers and provision merchants noted wealthier inhabitants buying in bulk, leaving their poorer compatriots to queue up for what was left or go without. Reports of a food riot in Hitchin cannot have helped; there was another just up the road in Dunstable.[2] Stocks could not quickly be replenished as the military, in particular the local Herts Yeomanry, seized lorries, wagons and horses in the streets, disrupting food supplies.[3] Writing 45 years later, author Ursula Bloom recalled the loss of the milkman's horse as the moment when the country's predicament was brought home to her family in Hatfield Road:

> By lunch came the point which brought the war really home
> to us, for the ancient milkman arrived nearly in tears. Usually
> his cart clopped down the road where Dollie, the pony, ate our
> hedge whilst he delivered the milk. He said: 'They stopped me
> at the corner of the road. They took my Dollie out of the shafts!
> It's downright wicked! She's old, and she won't know what's
> happening to her.' Poor Dollie had been commandeered![4]

Dollie probably joined another 250 or so horses already corralled
on Jacob Reynolds's farm on Bernards Heath, in the north of the city.[5]
Larger businesses faced supply problems as well. Reports from the straw
hat manufacturers confirmed that imports of straw plait, the key raw
material, were at a standstill as the government took control of shipping
and the railways. Rumours abounded about the likely comings and goings
of troops – mostly comings. A resident of Verulam Road, Harold Cossins,
had heard what must have been startling news that 40,000 soldiers were
likely to be billeted on the 25,000 inhabitants of St Albans.[6]

According to the Saturday 15 August edition of the *Herts Advertiser*
matters had changed again. Whatever panic there had been was now
subsiding. Food prices steadied, but there were still shortages. Having
just enlisted in the 1st Hertfordshire Battery of the Royal Field Artillery,
Ursula Bloom's brother needed socks, and she set herself to knit all night
to make him a pair before he left.

> All the young gents in St Albans were bothered about their socks,
> and a glorious army of their mothers and their sisters and their
> cousins and their aunts, were going from shop to shop to buy
> khaki wool. It was short. It had gone up in the process, which was
> a calamity to me.[7]

Panic may have dissipated but rumour remained. The Bloom family's
charwoman passed on the false rumour that two spies had been caught in
the city and shot behind the artillery riding school on Bernards Heath.[8]
More than anything else, though, there was upheaval as, almost overnight,
St Albans became a garrison town for the first time in its modern history.
Writing 50 years later, local boy Thomas Bickerton recalled his memories
as a 15 year old of the noise and colour of the arrival of the 2nd London
Division that week:

> I well remember seeing them march up Holywell Hill with their
> packs and rifles and equipment ... The field kitchens were horse
> drawn and steaming and all their equipment followed in horse-
> drawn vehicles. This was a grand sight and we had not seen
> anything like it before. Most of the battalions had their own
> regimental bands and we thought they looked fine marching up
> the hill with bands playing.[9]

Just two weeks after the declaration of war the 'town and fields swarm[ed] with soldiers'.[10] H.R. Wilton Hall, a retired schoolmaster, noted that there was to be the more acceptable number of 8,000 soldiers based in St Albans. He had two from London billeted on him in Walton Street; Bickerton's parents' house on Holywell Hill had four.[11] The *Herts Advertiser* reported that the army had already filled all spare accommodation. Space was at a premium on Bernards Heath as well, where the number of horses trebled over the week to around 800.[12]

By the end of that hectic August life on the home front in St Albans was starting to take on a shape that would remain largely constant for the next four years and more. On the one hand the city was welcoming perhaps over 7,000 territorial soldiers of the 2nd London Division and becoming accustomed to their presence (see Chapter 3).[13] By way of contrast, this chapter considers the thousands of goodbyes that were directed at local men who either volunteered to join the armed services or who, from early 1916 onwards, were compelled to do so. Put in these simple terms, the story of the successful creation of the largest army in British history, initially comprising around 2.5 million enthusiastic volunteers and then doubling in size through conscription, appears black and white.[14] What will become apparent here, through the study of the recruitment process at the local level, is a more complex picture.

The territorials go to war

The departure of the local soldiers belonging to the Hertfordshire Territorial Force (HTF) was the first of the war's many goodbyes. These volunteers belonged to a part-time army raised across the country at county level, in each case by a territorial force association,[15] in 1908 aimed at establishing a force of 300,000 men for home defence, organised and equipped along similar lines to the professional 'regular' army. Volunteers signed up to serve for between one and four years, with provision to extend service for another four. Once enrolled, a territorial soldier had to attend regular evening drill and at least eight days of a 15-day annual summer camp. In addition, men could sign the Imperial Service Obligation, indicating a willingness to serve overseas in times of emergency. St Albans had become a base in the western half of the county for 'C' Squadron, Hertfordshire Yeomanry; 'B' Company, 1st Battalion, Hertfordshire Regiment; 1st Hertfordshire Battery (Royal Field Artillery); and one section of the ammunition column.[16] The drill hall on Hatfield Road and the artillery riding school on Bernards Heath were the physical embodiment of the HTF in St Albans.[17]

In line with established mobilisation timetables the HTF was allotted to Eastern Command, charged with defending against a possible German landing on the east coast. Men of 'C' Squadron of the Herts Yeomanry were ordered to report to their HQ in St Albans no later than 1pm on 5 August, just 14 hours after Britain had declared war. This led to 80 men of the squadron being billeted in hotels and public houses around the city for three nights. The presence of men in uniform was to become commonplace in the years to come. Unlike the yeomanry, infantrymen of 1st Hertfordshire Regiment were on annual camp at Ashridge Park, near Berkhamsted, when mobilisation orders reached them on 4 August. Having the majority of men already in uniform greatly helped the regiment get onto a war footing. 'B' Company returned to St Albans, paraded at the drill hall and then visited the rifle range at Sandridge. Following this, the men marched to the London Road railway station to entrain for Hertford, their march through the city being accompanied by cheering crowds.[18]

While the yeomanry and infantry proceeded quickly overseas, the local artillery battery was destined to remain in England for another year. The day before war broke out the battery was on its way by rail to annual camp at Redesdale in Northumberland. At 6pm that day a telegram arrived recalling all units to Home Stations immediately. Once back in St Albans, 1st Battery was quickly brought up to war establishment by former members rejoining and new recruits, such as Ursula Bloom's brother, signing up. As described, sufficient horses were quickly secured and on 8 August the unit began moving to its War Station at Brentwood, later joining up with all batteries of 4th East Anglian Brigade near Thetford.[19]

Voluntary recruitment

Owing to well-laid plans, the mobilisation of the territorial force and reservists in the first few days and weeks of the war was a straightforward task for the War Office.[20] Less easy and of a greater magnitude altogether was the challenge of raising a new army. In 1914 the small regular army was little more than a well-trained colonial police force. Lord Kitchener, recently appointed secretary of state for war, expressed forcefully to his new cabinet colleagues and then to parliament just how many men would be required and for how long. In simple terms he forecast that, as this would be a war of attrition lasting years, not months, and as sea power would not by itself bring victory, an army of millions had to be established and maintained.[21]

The government had two options. It could stay with the traditional voluntary system or choose compulsion, more commonly known as conscription. Mindful of widespread riots at the introduction of a limited form of conscription in around 1800, the government did not risk testing public opinion during this August emergency.[22] Building a volunteer army was the hand the politicians dealt Kitchener and he moved quickly to start the process. On 6 August parliament agreed to increase the army by 500,000 volunteers. The next day national newspapers published his call for the first 100,000 men to step forward.

It is tempting to think there was an immediate and enthusiastic rush to the Colours. Photographs of masses of men waiting in London to enlist suggest that there was, but they reflect a process and resources suited to peacetime recruitment and unfit for the current emergency.[23] A thorough study of the *Herts Advertiser* fails to evince any August fervour in St Albans.[24] The absence of a recruiting office in the city for the first week might explain this – a district office was not opened until 11 August, at 26 St Peter's Street. However, even though the district encompassed the city and neighbouring villages and roughly 4,000 men of military age, barely 100 men enlisted there by the end of the month.[25] It should be noted that these returns for the office in the local newspaper do not provide a full view of local recruiting activity. Men could have enlisted elsewhere in St Albans, such as the HQs of recently arrived regiments, or taken the train to London or to Hertford, the home of the county force. Nevertheless, those low August figures for the district office do reflect the national situation.[26]

Was this evidence of indifference to the plight of the country? Those who did enlist that August did so for a variety of reasons, patriotism and unemployment caused by an immediate downturn in the economy being two of them.[27] For the large majority who did not, indifference was not the explanation. Rather, they had to consider whether their jobs would be

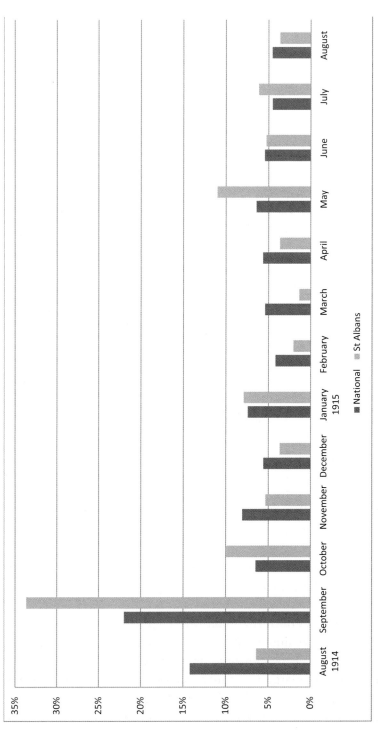

Figure 2.1 Chart showing St Albans district recruitment compared to national recruitment returns, August 1914–August 1915, expressed as monthly percentages.

open when they returned and how their dependants would be supported in the meantime. Recognising this, some employers, the St Albans City Council and the St Albans Gas Co. among them, were generous in making open-ended commitments about jobs.[28] The city's police constabulary was not alone in paying allowances to employees' families while the men were away.[29] The Grimston Tyre Co., for instance, paid 10s a week to families where official separation allowances proved insufficient.[30] The gas company regularly contributed over £400 a year in allowances to wives and dependants of employees then in the Forces.[31] Encouragement also took more passive forms. The St Albans Board of Guardians, an elected body responsible for poor law administration, issued tenders for the construction of a new boardroom with the condition that no work was to be done by single men under the age of 42.[32] The Board did not want to give any reason for them to stay at home.

It took 17 days for Kitchener to secure those first 100,000 volunteers. Yet, in the 13 days from 31 August to 12 September just over 300,000 men enlisted.[33] The returns for the St Albans office (Figure 2.1) reflect this, with 30 per cent of all recruitment at the office taking place in the month of September. What accounts for the surge? The answer lies partly in the battering the army received at the Battle of Mons, towards the end of August. Reports published in *The Times* described in surprising detail just how dominant the German army was and how beleaguered the British seemed in retreat.[34] The nation was shocked. Wilton Hall noted in his diary: 'Very disquieting news came in the Saturday evening papers, and apparently the Sunday morning papers were more alarmist still, indicating the cutting off of the British forces.'[35] These reports were a major catalyst for the upsurge. Local recruiting trends certainly underline the new-found energy. While no more than 100 men had enlisted at the district office in the last three weeks of August, in the first week of September alone 214 joined up. A further 224 followed suit the week after, making around 540 in total since the office opened.[36]

However, it would be wrong to identify the *Times* reports as the sole cause of the rush to enlist. No doubt Kitchener's decision on 27 August to raise the upper age limit to 35 for new recruits and 45 for ex-soldiers helped.[37] Moreover, with preparations starting before the news from Mons, the first of four large recruitment rallies was held on the evening of Friday 4 September, giving public form to this new spirit of enthusiasm. The *Herts Advertiser* described it as a 'memorable meeting' under the commanding headline 'Your Country Calls You'.[38] What emerges from the lengthy report is that it was a well-planned event in terms of both its staging and the arrangement of the various speeches. The town hall, with its imposing Georgian façade, was chosen as the backdrop. The atmosphere and staging of the meeting was redolent of the fervour of temperance meetings in Victorian St Albans:

> The speeches were delivered from a platform erected near the Council Chamber, and seated in the Mayor's Parlour within were several leading townsmen and military representatives who dealt with the recruits as they came forward in response to the appeals from the platform. Loud applause greeted each young fellow as he made his way across the open space kept by several companies of soldiers.

Like those going forward to sign the pledge, these new recruits crossed the 'open space' to the approbation of the audience. This interpretation chimes with the views of John Coulson Kernahan, a successful army recruiter and the son of a minister at Spicer Street Independent church in the city in the 1870s.[39] A key ingredient for successful recruitment rallies, he believed, was rhetoric that stoked up contagious enthusiasm in the crowd, something reminiscent of those earlier Victorian gatherings. He wrote that 'the assembling together of men and women with one object in view, and all with one thought in the mind, is like the laying of coal by coal when making a fire'. His approach was to focus on the moral imperative for Britain to rescue its ally, Belgium, from the inhumanity of the German invaders, and on the fear that St Albans itself might come under threat from similar atrocities if no action was taken.[40]

As the abstracts printed in the newspaper show, the speeches that September evening followed his strictures. The moral imperative was certainly present in mayor Horace Slade's speech as Belgium's fate loomed large:

> His reference to 'poor little Belgium' elicited general cheers, and he said that surely they would have been curs and churls if they had not helped them. Let them think of the men who had gone forth from St Albans ... and England, lying in the trenches against overwhelming forces only taking their part, but waiting, waiting for those at home to come.[41]

The next speaker employed Kernahan's other key tactic, namely to spread fear and uncertainty among the listeners. Representing the War Office at the rally, Sir Francis Vane said he had heard from 'good authorities' that many rumours doing the rounds about German atrocities committed on Belgian civilians were true. He also highlighted the burning of the city of Louvain and its medieval library in particular.[42] Comparing Louvain's history with that of St Albans, Vane brought the war closer to home both figuratively and geographically. He said 'A hundred miles away as the crow flies, shells were going about, and women and children were being killed by those shells.' Another speaker, the local MP Sir Hildred Carlile, echoing Kitchener's pronouncement in parliament in early August, emphasised that 'this was going to be a long war: they must not think it would come to an end shortly'. The soldiers would not be home in time for Christmas.[43]

What was the effect of the rally? As the organisers hoped, volunteers continued to flow into 26 St Peter's Street. Over the weekend there were 39 of them, a reasonable return. On Monday 7 September the organisers would have been delighted when 74 joined up. However, the success was short-lived. That Monday proved to be the high water mark, as the figures started to slide. On Thursday, four days later, just three men enlisted at the St Peter's Street office and, as Figure 2.1 shows, local recruiting returns failed to regain strength.[44] It is not altogether clear why this was. In the short term the War Office was to blame, at least in part. Again, long queues of volunteers overwhelmed recruiting offices and, this time, the regimental depots to which the men were then sent. There simply was not enough accommodation, clothing or weapons available for them. To stem the flow, officials made two surprising decisions. Already in the first week of September they had introduced 'deferred enlistment', whereby men joined up but were then sent home to await call-up. There were problems with this. For example, the scheme had not been publicly announced; it also affected many who had given up jobs to enlist and now were in receipt of just 6d a day subsistence pay.[45] The second of those two decisions, taken on Friday 11 September, was to increase the minimum height requirement for infantrymen to five feet six inches in height and the minimum chest measurement to 35 and a half inches.[46] In the longer term, the decline can also be attributed to the large munitions contracts that were issued by the War Office. Reversing August's short industrial downturn, the awards sparked a demand for labour and a consequent rise in wages. In the face

of these improving prospects, recruiting officers found even Kernahan's
emotional rhetoric failing to motivate men to enlist.

In light of these changes, Wilton Hall's diary entry at the end of
October comes as little surprise. He noted: 'I do not fancy that recruiting
is going on very briskly in St Albans and I can quite realise that it may
be necessary to push the loafers.'[47] Whether he expected the imminent
introduction of conscription is not clear. Others took matters into their
own hands. Recording examples of men being handed white feathers in
the city's streets, the editor of the *Herts Advertiser* strongly cautioned
against these practices of the 'White Feather Brigade'. He noted that,
while there were no doubt 'slackers' in St Albans, there were many reasons
why men had not enlisted, the state of their health being just one.[48] Even
an increasingly sophisticated propaganda drive failed to reverse the trend,
although successful poster campaigns publicising the bombardment of

Figure 2.2 Recruitment posters displayed on the town hall, around January 1915.
© Andy Lawrence

Figure 2.3 Herts Yeomanry recruitment poster, *c.*1915 © Hertfordshire Archives and Local Studies (DE/Yo/5/1)

Scarborough and other north coast towns by the German navy in December 1914 produced short-term improvements both locally and nationally.[49] The sinking of the *RMS Lusitania* the following May 1915 had a similar effect (Figure 2.2).

Except for these occasional spikes, recruitment in St Albans slowed to little more than a trickle in spring 1915, as Figure 2.1 shows. Various promotional schemes were tried during the voluntary phase. Nationally the most noteworthy example was perhaps the formation of 'pals' battalions', units raised by local businessmen or councils where the recruits shared attributes such as occupation and locality. There is no evidence that this was attempted in St Albans, although the endeavours of the Hertfordshire Territorial Force Association to find recruits in the county can perhaps be viewed in light of this.[50] The association met in May 1915 to discuss how to raise a further 1,576 men. Posters, as ever, would be important and the draft shown in Figure 2.3, with its explicit reference to the use of gas by the Germans, probably dates to this period. More active measures were needed, and the association discussed four possible campaigns:

1. A recruiting march through the county;
2. Recruiting meetings to be arranged by the deputy lieutenants, mayors and chairmen of district councils;
3. All employers to be approached to encourage their workers to enlist;
4. A 'census' of eligible men to be collated and sent to the secretary of the association at Hertford on receipt of which arrangements could be made for recruiters to canvass them.

The association's chairman, Viscount Hampden, thought that recruiting meetings in particular were 'absolutely useless', and that they had already tried the third option. Charles T. Part, from St Albans, agreed and called for option four. Instead, the meeting chose to organise a march through the county led by some of its soldiers and its band. Somewhat bizarrely, in light of the chairman's adverse comment, it was decided to combine the march with large set-piece rallies in towns where the march stopped.[51] At the resulting rally in St Albans, again outside the town hall, the *Herts Advertiser* recorded that 1,500 people attended but that 'a considerable majority of those present were ladies, men in khaki, men of non-military age and school children'. Perhaps the absence of eligible men was due to the rally being held at noon on a Monday. Whatever the reason, the reporter noted that, while the number of enlistments had not been large, the rally had still been 'successful'.[52]

This description was probably deliberately ironic. Frederick Usher, the paper's editor, had consistently opposed the idea of conscription both before and during the first months of the war. In a general editorial about national recruiting policy, he complained about a controversial decision taken by the HTF Association to call for the introduction of conscription. Usher expressed concern, noting that not all options for voluntary recruitment had been explored.[53]

However, by the early summer months defenders of the voluntary principle such as the prime minister, Herbert Asquith, were being assailed on all sides. There was a growing acceptance both in the national press and in parliament that, if Britain were to outlast Germany in a war of attrition, the nation's resources, including manpower, had to be managed more effectively. Proponents of conscription maintained that the indiscriminate nature of the voluntary recruitment system had impaired the nation's manufacturing capacity. Local companies had indeed been affected: Smith's Printing Co. in Hatfield Road had lost 32 men, around

25 per cent of its male workforce, in the first two months of the war alone, and the St Albans Gas Co. struggled to replace the 15 skilled men who had volunteered in 1914.[54] On a smaller scale, a motor engineer in St Peter's Street, John Davis, proudly announced in a newspaper advertisement that all seven of his workers had enlisted. Unable to find replacements, he was bankrupted in 1916.[55]

Early in June 1915 Asquith was outflanked by David Lloyd George, his Liberal party colleague in the coalition government. In his first speech as the newly appointed minister of munitions Lloyd George argued that conscription was now a matter of necessity.[56] Asquith grudgingly gave ground in this battle by permitting the introduction of the National Registration Bill into parliament late in June 1915. For conscription supporters this was the necessary first step towards calculating how many men were available for military and industrial mobilisation. The Bill was passed in the middle of July, with Registration Day set for 15 August. Every eligible person between the ages of 15 and 65 was to be issued with a certificate of registration and all were required to notify the authorities of any change of address. It was the first time that such an exercise had been carried out in Britain.

National registration

The General Register Office (GRO) was responsible for supervising the National Register, with the Registrar General acting as the Central Registration Authority. The GRO produced all the forms and instructions and compiled the final manpower statistics. Local authorities acted as the local registration authority, and were responsible for conducting registration in their area and maintaining the local register thereafter. Each authority had to enumerate all men and women resident in their area who were within the specified age range.[57] The work of data collection and collation was largely to be done by volunteers. Once complete, the register had to be kept up to date, noting changes of address and removing and adding new names over the course of the war. This was a complex set of operations for volunteer staff with little experience of this type of work, although the GRO provided the local officials in charge of the registration with training in the coding and compilation of the register.

In St Albans the town clerk, Edward Percy Debenham, briefed the city council on 19 July 1915 on the registration process. He estimated that registration would have to cover 5,750 houses in the city and that between 18,000 and 19,000 people would be eligible. The district would be divided into 54 enumeration districts, each containing about 100 houses. One enumerator would be allocated to each district.[58] An appeal for volunteers appears to have achieved a good response for, on 14 August, the *Herts Advertiser* published the full list of those who had been appointed and the districts they were to cover.[59] They included councillors William Fisk, Edwin Lee and Frederick Warwick and solicitor Thomas Ottaway.

The exercise proceeded at a swift pace. On 6 August all the enumerators met in the town hall, where they were briefed by Debenham and given their memorandum books and supplies of forms. The enumerators delivered these forms between 9 and 13 August in advance of Registration Day on Sunday 15 August. They collected the forms between 16 and 18 August and then had to complete their memorandum books and other tasks by 21 August. Processing the forms and compiling the statistics was done in the town hall. The *Herts Advertiser* noted that this work 'was in

Figure 2.4 'Bantams' advert from the *Herts Advertiser*, 31 July 1915. © Hertfordshire Archives and Local Studies

full swing', but also hinted at the growing size of the task, saying that the process was 'even more extensive than was at the outset anticipated but thanks to the willing offers of help, splendid progress is being made'.[60] While, unsurprisingly, there were issues of quality, the primary objective of producing manpower statistics was met.[61] The GRO estimated that 1,413,900 men in England and Wales were still available for military service, but cautioned that the figure should be treated as an upper limit, given the impossibility of knowing exactly how many men were fit to serve or could be spared 'without inflicting grave injury to national interest'.[62]

The voluntary recruitment phase ends

While registration ran its course, recruitment at the St Peter's Street office dropped to just 76 over the four weeks to 27 August 1915.[63] Recruiters in the Bedfordshire and Hertfordshire army district resorted to desperate measures to increase their numbers. Some of these measures were official: rules about stature were tweaked, as the advertisement for 'bantams' shows[64] (Figure 2.4). Others were not in the rule book: age limits, as in the case of 17-year-old Thomas Bickerton of Holywell Hill, were sometimes disregarded. Two years below military age when he tried to enlist in the Hertfordshire Regiment in August 1915, he was given advice by a recruiting sergeant he encountered in Chequer Street about how to pass the interview:

> He enquired my age and I said '17, but can be 19', so he replied 'Well now, look, if you go over to Hertford, what year were you born in?' 'Ah!' I said, 'Well, 1896!' 'That's the right answer' he said. 'All right, here's your railway voucher – go over there and I hope you're lucky'. So off I went on my own and called in at the Headquarters of the Third Battalion in Hertford. I saw the Doctor ... he enquired my age and I said 'Nineteen', and he said 'Alright young man, I think you'll do.'[65]

This tinkering did little to help. With the trend over the summer months flat, the country faced a perfect storm. No way to rekindle the recruiting fervour of early September 1914 had been found, casualties were mounting and War Office planning demanded that the British put a new army in the field to support the weakening French and meet commitments in other theatres. Calls for the introduction of conscription increased in volume and frequency.

In line with government wishes, the city fathers and military authorities gave the voluntary principle one last push by organising another rally in St Albans on Saturday 2 October 1915. What stands out is the element of pageantry involved. The main event was to be another set-piece rally outside the town hall, but this time four processions were organised, each starting from different points in the city and stopping at pre-arranged points on their routes to address expected crowds. In an extensive report the *Herts Advertiser* recorded that the South Ward procession assembled:

> In Longmire Road ... proceeded, headed by the bands of the 2nd North Midland Field Ambulance and the Salvation Army along Old London Road, Sopwell Lane, to Holywell Hill, down Albert Street, up Watsons Walk, down London Road, Alma Road, Alexandra Road, Lattimore Road, and up to Hatfield Road ... but owing to the absence of eligible men at any point along the route, no speeches were made, although two prospective recruits joined the ranks as the procession passed on its way.[66]

The procession in the North Ward, around the Sandpit Lane and Catherine Street areas, encountered similar problems; the other two were busier. Where had all the men gone? Were they hiding? Was this simply apathy? It is difficult to know at this distance, particularly as the *Herts Advertiser* did not comment, but Harold Cossins, who paraded as a member of the Volunteer Training Corps,[67] noted in his diary: 'I should think there were very few recruits obtained and everyone I spoke to thought the whole proceedings rather a farce. Conscription must come and it will not be unwelcome, as far as I can judge.'[68] As he predicted, there was no boom in recruitment, not even the spike seen 13 months earlier around the time of the first rally. This was the national picture too.

Cossins was also right about conscription, though it was not introduced until March 1916, still five months away. In the interim, Asquith's coalition government created the 'Group Scheme', a national recruitment campaign launched in October 1915. Better known as the 'Derby Scheme', its success depended on canvassing eligible men aged 18 to 41 on their own doorsteps asking them either to join up then and there or to attest their willingness to serve when called.[69] Those men who took the second option were placed in one of 46 groups classified by year of birth and marital status. Widowed men without dependent children were grouped with single men of a similar age.

All the hard work that had gone into the completion of the National Register now bore fruit. Based on data extracted from the forms, canvassers were provided with lists of prospective targets who met the relevant age criteria. The canvassers, again all volunteers, were themselves recruited from local parliamentary constituency parties, as it was believed they were best equipped to carry out this task.[70] A letter to the *Herts Advertiser* from the chairman of the local canvassing committee, Percival Blow (a local architect with an extensive practice in the area), gives an indication of the success of the initiative:

> The committee entrusted with the canvass of the St Albans area desire ... to express their sincere thanks to the 97 gentlemen who so kindly came forward and undertook the work of canvassing. When it is realised that about 3,000 men had to be personally interviewed in the short space of three weeks, it will be readily appreciated what a large amount of time the canvassers must have devoted to the work.[71]

Only around 2,320 attested out of an estimated 9,900 men eligible for the Derby Scheme in the St Albans district.[72] Across the country the results were similarly underwhelming. Following the Cabinet meeting on 15 December at which Lord Derby produced his preliminary figures, Asquith ordered a Bill to be drafted to introduce conscription.[73]

Conscription and the military tribunals

With the case made, parliament passed the first Military Service Act in February 1916. Under its terms all single men in England, Wales and Scotland who had reached the age of 18 but were below 42 were deemed to have enlisted. The same applied to widowed men without dependent children. However, this was conscription with a twist, the twist being that any man conscripted into the army had the right to apply for exemption from it. This could be temporary (for example, for a man to sort out his affairs before joining up), conditional (for example, the man would have to stay in his current employment) or absolute. In deciding who should consider these applications the government veered away from judicial or military structures, opting instead for the 2,000 or so tribunals consisting of civic dignitaries previously established in each local registration authority in the country in October 1915 to hear applications for postponement under the Derby Scheme.

One historian has suggested that the tribunals 'were a key, if not *the* key institution of 1916–18'.[74] The tribunal system was the fulcrum in the process of not only military but also industrial mobilisation. It was used extensively: around 40 per cent of some 2,400 St Albans men who had attested under the Derby Scheme or who were liable for conscription took advantage of their right to apply for exemption. The St Albans City Military Service Tribunal was the physical embodiment of the system, meeting on over 100 occasions in the town hall.[75] In light of this it is surprising that the existence of the tribunals is now largely forgotten, primarily because the government ordered the destruction of any associated records in the early 1920s.[76]

With hundreds of thousands of new recruits urgently needed, why did Britain opt for the tribunal system? After all, countries with established traditions of conscription, such as France and Germany, did not offer their citizens anything comparable. There were two key reasons for the decision. Firstly, the system acted as a pressure valve against the threat of industrial unrest. Powerful trade unions were worried that conscription and the rapid drive towards the military economy would cost them hard-won gains of the previous 15 years or so. The government's solution to this problem was simple: representatives of the labour movement had to be appointed to each local and county appeal tribunal. Being engaged in the process, unions would see that workers' rights were indeed being balanced against the imperative that everyone had to contribute at this time of national emergency.[77] Secondly, the government was keen to show that the rights of the individual were being considered. The right to apply for exemption on grounds of conscience was evidence of this,[78] as was the automatic right of appeal to the (Hertfordshire) County Appeal Tribunal (CAT).[79] Around a quarter (256) of the applicants took advantage of this.

There were three key components to the tribunal system. Firstly, there were the tribunal members themselves. As originally constituted in November 1915 to hear Derby Scheme cases, the city tribunal consisted of four local councillors and one magistrate. Hastily convened under orders from the Local Government Board (LGB) with little more than a week's notice, the city council had to find men of 'judicial and unprejudiced mind(s)', so it is hardly surprising that this composition was arrived at.[80] The members were the mayor, James Flint, his predecessor, Bertie Edwards, and the owners of two large businesses: councillor George Day, proprietor of the largest straw hat factory in the city, and councillor Edwin Lee, a boot and shoe manufacturer. The fifth member was local magistrate Walter Reynolds. To cope with the expected growth in caseload following the introduction of conscription in March 1916 the panel was increased from five to nine members: Ernest Townson, another councillor and managing partner of Smith's Printing Co. in Hatfield Road, and Frank Beal, a local solicitor, were two of them. With Townson joining Day and Lee, the tribunal now included representatives of three of the largest industries in the city. All the members were natural choices. They had experience conducting council affairs and several of them managed their own substantial businesses. As much as anyone else they had an understanding of the economic and social needs of the city. These were important attributes for a body which had the unenviable task of balancing the needs of the individual with those of local businesses and the military imperative.

It was also at this point that the two representatives of the labour movement joined the tribunal. These were Henry Mayer and Benjamin Wouldham. Mayer was a pillar of the local court of the Ancient Order of Foresters, a friendly society, and also a foreman at Brushes Ltd in Grosvenor Road; Wouldham was a member of the St Albans & District Trades & Labour Council.[81] Although the matter was considered, it was 'not desirable' to have women appointed to the city tribunal.[82]

The second component of the system were the two *ex officio* members. One was Debenham, the town clerk. He had an administrative and advisory role and acted as the direct link to the LGB for questions of process and clarification. The other was Ernest Gape, the military service representative.[83] Appointed by the local honorary recruiting officer, he had the invidious role of doing 'everything possible to protect the military interests of the nation' and to get as many men 'as may be spared' for the armed forces. The handbook for military representatives stated that 'if [the representative] allows his decision to be influenced by any other consideration than that of the national interest, he cannot be held to be fulfilling the duty for which he is appointed'.[84] At hearings he was able to ask questions of applicants or challenge the facts presented. If the tribunal's final decision was not acceptable to him, he could appeal to the CAT.

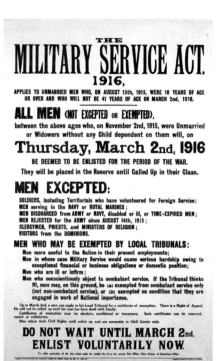

Figure 2.5 Military Service Act 1916 poster setting out exemption terms. © Imperial War Museums (PST 5161)

The last of the three key components were the grounds on which applications for exemption could be made. Men could use one or more of the following six grounds, the first four (Figure 2.5) being the most frequently used at the city tribunal:

1. If it is expedient in the national interests that the man should, instead of being employed in military service, be engaged in other work in which he is habitually engaged; or
2. Ill health or infirmity; or
3. If serious hardship would ensue … owing to his exceptional financial or business obligations or domestic position; or
4. Conscientious objection to the undertaking of combatant service; or
5. If the man is being educated or trained for any work … that it is expedient in the national interests that, instead of being employed in military service, he should continue to be so educated or trained; or
6. If it is expedient in the national interests that the man should, instead of being employed in military service, be engaged in other work in which he wishes to be engaged.[85]

In spite of the many thousands of words written on the topic of conscientious objection, just 2 per cent of the 1,050 men who came before the city tribunal applied for this reason.[86] Similar figures are reported elsewhere in the country.[87] In fact most cases were lodged on the grounds of national interest, often brought by employers anxious to keep skilled – and sometimes not so skilled – men in production.[88] 'Infirmity and ill-health' was one of the grounds used frequently, although for reasons of sensitivity perhaps the least well recorded in the *Herts Advertiser*. Many cases concerned the health of applicants and their alleged mistreatment at the hands of the army's medical boards, the latter under pressure to draw as many men into the Colours as possible, with little regard to filtering out those unable to cope with the physical demands of war.[89]

Others applied because of serious hardship. Several applications appeared frivolous and were rejected. Archibald Harvey of Cornwall Road, for example, needed time to plant his allotment.[90] Others were more serious. In June 1916 19-year-old Cyril Corley of Albert Street was exempted because of tragic family circumstances.[91] Of his three brothers already in the army, two had been killed on the same day.[92] Along with his younger brother, Corley now supported his widowed mother. This respite was only temporary. As military losses mounted, the government required exemptions to be re-assessed. Corley fell victim to this in March 1917 on the successful appeal of Gape.[93] Reports of applications by the city's butchers, bakers and other sole traders, all applying on the same serious hardship grounds, filled the pages of the *Herts Advertiser*.[94] These cases were difficult for the tribunal members to judge. After all, being called up risked commercial ruin and destitution for the applicant's family.

A good example was that of Alfred Thomas Hopkins, aged 29, of Hatfield Road. He was a master plumber and decorator, married with two children. Hopkins's case was first heard at an adjourned hearing on 10 June 1916, when he was given just one month's temporary exemption. This decision was typical, the tribunal members believing it gave a man enough time to settle his affairs and sell his business if necessary. Hopkins appealed to the CAT on 27 June 1916, when his exemption was extended until the end of August. A further appeal to the CAT on 9 September proved futile. Joining the Machine Gun Corps, Hopkins was killed at Passchendaele just over a year later in September 1917. His obituary noted that 'several gentlemen ... have formed a committee with a view to raising a fund so that Mrs Hopkins and her little children may at least be spared the hardships that far too often follow the loss of the breadwinner'.[95] With such support Mrs Hopkins may be said to have been more fortunate than many in her position.

Often with just a few minutes for discussion, these were tough decisions for the tribunal members to make.[96] On several occasions they were unable to decide which of two or more men should be granted exemption and which should not. One of the cases related to William Field, an oilman based in Spicer Street. His two sons, who worked for him, had attested their willingness to serve under the Derby Scheme. Their hearings for postponement were considered on the same day, during which the tribunal elicited from Field that he needed only one son in the business. With nothing to choose between them, the tribunal gave the father the final decision as to which one of his sons could stay and which should enlist.[97]

A further problem for the tribunal members was that official guidance emanating from the LGB was often complex and conflicted. For example, on the one hand they had 'to do all in their power ... to facilitate recruiting'. On the other hand they had 'to secure that the vital industrial and financial interests of the country receive due consideration'.[98] It was also a very public role. From late February 1916 onwards the *Herts Advertiser* assiduously reported most of the tribunal's deliberations, often covering the many contentious cases at length.

It comes as no surprise to learn that the members struggled with their task. In 1919 Henry Mayer recalled the emotional turmoil this unpaid work caused him:

> I particularly remember when men who had made applications
> for release were refused, going home and for hours in the night
> turning the matter over as to the interest and position of those
> men. But the needs of the country were such that nothing but a
> faithful discharge of the duties expected from the Tribunal would
> suffice for its work.[99]

Of all those attending the tribunal, it was Ernest Gape, the military service representative, who had the toughest job. As with the members of the tribunal, in a small place such as St Albans he personally knew men appearing before the tribunal or, if not the men themselves, then their employers. It must have been difficult for these people to come to terms with Gape's need to act in the national interest, which rarely appeared

How I felt before the Tribunal.

Figure 2.6 Contemporary postcard of a tribunal hearing entitled 'How I felt before the tribunal'. © SAHAAS

to coincide with their own. Unsurprisingly Gape suffered a high level of opprobrium for the zealous way in which he conducted his role, which included one death threat. At least after the war he was able to console himself in his belief that the tribunal members and he had worked well together, albeit at arm's length.[100] This was not always the case elsewhere. The members of the Luton Borough Tribunal had threatened to go on strike early in 1917 owing to irreconcilable differences in their relationship with the military representative attached to that tribunal.[101]

Conscientious objection

The scene which comes to mind in the popular imagination when considering the treatment of the conscientious objector at the hands of the tribunal is of a hostile panel of men in thrall to the domineering military representative, all keen to send off the 'conshee' to face dangers from which they, by dint of age and position, were exempt (Figure 2.6). However, more recent research into the deliberations of the Northamptonshire tribunals shows this image reflected a post-war agenda which determined how this unique experience of war was remembered. Too often 'tribunals have been judged largely by the statements [or, rather, outbursts] of individual members rather than the decisions they made collectively'.[102] In part this is a reflection of the nature of surviving sources. With so many tribunal records destroyed, it is newspapers which gave access to the tribunal room; by their nature they tended to feature the unusual and the extreme rather than the commonplace and typical. Equally, though, it was those who had organised against the war, groups such as the No Conscription Fellowship, which in many ways dominated the discourse of the post-war years. They focused on that balance between personal conviction and duty to the state, for whom choleric retired colonels and their angry outbursts were all grist to a political mill.

How did the city tribunal treat the 23 men who applied to it for exemption on the grounds of conscience? As Table 2.1 shows, those who claimed exemption from conscription came from a wide range of occupations. Applications were framed in religious, rather than political, terms. In this, the local experience differed from that of some other parts of the country, such as Huddersfield, where a strong labour movement saw many more applications on grounds of political belief and provided a network of support for those who chose to resist conscription.[103] One St Albans applicant, John Teasdale, claimed to have been a member of

Table 2.1 Men applying for exemption from conscription on grounds of conscience at the St Albans City Military Service Tribunal, 1916–18.

Name	Address	Age	Occupation
Harry Edward Beaumont	35 Worley Road	35	Basket maker
William N. Burridge	16 Folly Avenue	36	Assistant Inspector of Messengers, Post Office
Ernest Frank Conquest	1 Forester's Villas, East Common, Harpenden	36	Nurseryman, J & J.E. Watson
Frederick James Dangerfield	52 Granville Road	34	Technical representative, Hazell, Watney & Viney Ltd.
Horace Llewellyn Davies	59 Lattimore Road	25	Machine operator, Salvation Army Printing Works
Edgar Percy Faux	'Somerville', Clarence Road	20	Not known
William Fraser Frew	2 Brampton Road	28	Assistant Examiner of Patents, H.M. Patent Office
Oswald Godman	8 Oswald Road	35	Postman
Charles Alban Hale	'Linacre', Clarence Road	18	Commercial traveller
Albert George Hammond	2 Ladysmith Road	20	Shipping clerk
Ernest Hickling	2 George Street	34	Manager, Charles Forbes, drapers
Harold Arthur James	27 Bedford Road	33	Organising Secretary, Hertfordshire Band of Hope
George Morrish	46 Ramsbury Road	36	Manager, Morrish & Co., printers
Arthur Victor Punter	23 Ramsbury Road	24	Clerk, War Office, Casualties branch
Albert Frank Rose	13 Thorpe Road	18	Clothier's assistant, Foster Bros. Ltd.
Edgar Rose	45 London Road	49	Owner of a cycle repair shop
Robert W. Rose	45 London Road	18	Cycle repairer
William Henry Stratford	12 Offa Road	21	Aeroplane fitter
John Teasdale	27 Tess Road	n.k.	Civil servant, Post Office
William Thorne	Silk Mill Cottages, The Causeway	19	Draper's assistant
William Robert Tompkins	35 Clifton Street	32	Clerk to H. Smith, King & Gregory, solicitors
Reginald Webb	17 Glenferrie Road	35	Accountant, Railway Clearing House
Frederick White	Holmlea, Folly Avenue	n.k.	Machine minder, W. Cartmel & Sons

the 'Brotherhood of Man' movement for 18 years and argued that 'the fundamental principle of that movement was contrary to militarism'.[104] However, it may be that this phrase appealed to the newspaper reporter as one with which to catch his readership's eye, and was not a true reflection of Teasdale's position. Denominations which were represented among the applicants included Baptists, Plymouth Brethren, Quakers and the Wesleyan Methodists; many men simply referred to their conviction that it was against all Christian teaching to take the life of another. William Tompkins, married with one child, was typical in arguing that 'for him to shed blood and take life would not be right. Warfare was contrary to Christ's express directions.'[105]

The response of tribunal members to such claims focused on trying to test the strength of that conviction by posing hypothetical scenarios of kith and kin threatened by enemies bent on doing them physical harm. Such questioning got to the heart of the matter, but applicants consistently argued that they would not take the life of another. Tompkins responded, 'I don't know what course I would take, but it would not alter the fact that it was not right'; he was granted exemption from combatant service, contingent upon taking up work of national importance.[106]

This outcome of exemption from combatant service was the most frequent decision of the tribunal, with the condition that alternative work of national importance be undertaken. Of the 23 men who appeared before the city tribunal as conscientious objectors, only seven had their applications turned down at this stage. Of these, five took their case to the CAT and of these only one decision was upheld, with four of the men given exemption from combatant service. Some men had already taken steps to secure such work before appearing before the tribunal. Harold James had relocated to Devon, where he had taken up farm work.[107] Robert Rose had already been accepted by the Friends' Ambulance Unit (FAU), a Quaker non-combatant front-line service organisation[108] (Figure 2.7). Other cases were passed to the Pelham Committee, a body established by the Board of Trade in March 1916 to find suitable civilian occupations for objectors.[109]

A further line of questioning seems to have emerged from a sense that this really was a war which was affecting all members of the community, not just those who were heading for the front line. Applicants were asked what sacrifices they had made or were prepared to make given the ultimate sacrifice being made by others on their behalf. Newspaper accounts delighted in the more unusual or comic replies. Reginald Webb had his

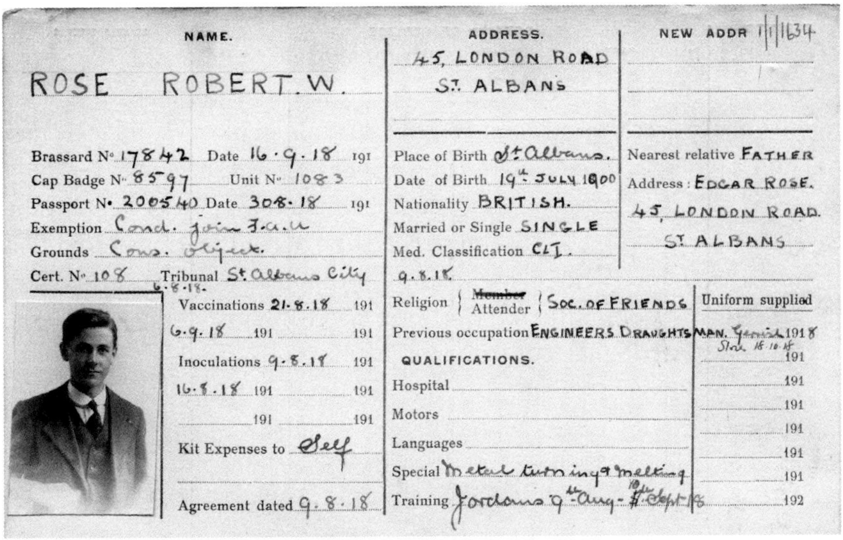
NAME. ROSE ROBERT. W.
ADDRESS. 45, LONDON ROAD ST. ALBANS
NEW ADDR 1|1|1634
Brassard No 17842 Date 16·9·18 191
Cap Badge No 8597 Unit No 1083
Passport No 200540 Date 30·8·18 191
Exemption Cond. join F.A.U
Grounds Cons. Object.
Cert. No 108 Tribunal St Albans City 6·8·18·
Vaccinations 21·8·18 191
6·9·18 191 191
Inoculations 9·8·18 191
16·8·18 191 191
191 191
Kit Expenses to Self
Agreement dated 9·8·18
Place of Birth St Albans.
Date of Birth 19th JULY 1900
Nationality BRITISH.
Married or Single SINGLE
Med. Classification C1 I.
9·8·18
Religion Member / Attender SOC. OF FRIENDS
Previous occupation ENGINEERS DRAUGHTSMAN.
QUALIFICATIONS.
Hospital
Motors
Languages
Special Metal turning & melting
Training Jordans 9th Aug - 11th Sept 18
Nearest relative FATHER
Address: EDGAR ROSE. 45, LONDON ROAD. ST ALBANS
Uniform supplied
191 191 191 191 191 191 191 192

Figure 2.7 Robert Rose's Friends Ambulance Unit personnel card. © Religious Society of Friends (Quakers) in Britain

initial application turned down. When asked by the CAT what sacrifice he had made he replied that he had 'had financial inducements to join the army, but had refrained from accepting them'.[110] Webb was the only St Albans man whose appeal was rejected by the CAT.

Convincing the tribunal members of a deeply held conviction was more straightforward for some than others. Frederick White, who could cite 15 years' membership at Dagnall Street Baptist church, was questioned closely on whether he would defend himself if attacked, but his application was granted; his argument that he was not afraid of death was helped by his acceptance of Gape's suggestion that undertaking the perilous task of mine-sweeping would fit with his conscience.[111] More problematic was the case of William Henry Stratford, a member of the Plymouth Brethren and employed from October 1915 as a fitter of aeroplane piston rings. Had he known of the possibility of exemption he said he would have stayed in his former employment at the Post Office, but he was now prepared to give up his work as a fitter. His application was denied, a decision which may also have reflected his response to Gape's question on taking up work on mine-sweepers that 'he did not think he would be any good at the sea'.[112] At his appeal hearing Stratford was granted an exemption from combatant service.[113]

Even when decisions such as these had been made, there were examples of men returning for further consideration. Oswald Godman was exempted in March 1916 and his case passed to the Pelham Committee.[114] They found him work as a farm labourer. However, his employer would pay him only 16s a week, as he considered him a poor physical specimen; Godman argued that this wage was inadequate to maintain him. After hearing the case, it was agreed by the committee that he should be transferred and trained as a motor tractor ploughman at 25s a week under the supervision of the Tractor Committee at Hertford, a recommendation which was accepted by the tribunal.[115]

Tribunal members were also very aware that their decisions were open to scrutiny by others with different agendas and were not slow to assert their right to be heard or to challenge opinions with which they disagreed. They took their role in the process very seriously and expected others to respect their decisions as being considered judgements worthy of proper acknowledgement. One such judgement concerned William Fraser Frew, an assistant examiner of patents with the Patent Office who appeared no fewer than five times before the tribunal. He was granted exemption contingent upon accepting an engagement in an occupation of national importance, approved by the Board of Trade, within 21 days.[116] However, in the months that followed, Frew continued to work for the Patent Office and the tribunal complained to the Board of Trade that they were not honouring the terms of the exemption. At its review of the case the Pelham Committee concluded that, owing to Frew's poor physique and his experience, he should continue in his job. Unhappy with this, the tribunal asked that Frew should offer some form of personal sacrifice, possibly financial. His response was that he was already making a sacrifice as his career would suffer from his claim under conscience, and his colleagues in the Patent Office, exempt by reason of their work, were not being called upon to make any such sacrifice. The tribunal would not let it rest there and wrote to the committee, challenging their decision.[117] A new judgement on the case saw Frew transferred to work with the Salvage Association, in which post he would help organise the salvaging of vessels and their cargoes.[118]

Volunteer Training Corps

At a very rough estimate, around 50 per cent of all local men eligible to do so chose not to enlist during the voluntary recruitment phase. Even so, there were those who wanted to make a contribution to national defence. The establishment of the Volunteer Training Corps (VTC) met this need. Initially organised on a local basis, groups were established throughout the country, drilling in the parks under the eye of retired soldiers. The War Office was adamant that men should be enlisting in the regular army or the territorials, not staying at home and playing soldiers.[119] In November 1914 a public meeting was called in St Albans by local solicitor Thomas Ottaway. He said the VTC would be for men who were not eligible for the army because of their age or for 'other reasons'. Harold Cossins of Verulam Road noted in his diary that the meeting was 'very well-attended and all

ST. ALBANS, HARPENDEN & HATFIELD V. T. C.

WHIT MONDAY MANŒUVRES.

Excited Attacking Party.—You are all my prisoners!
Excited Defending Party.—Prisoners be blowed. Your lot are all *dead*.
We have been firing on you for the last half-hour!

Figure 2.8 Magazine cutting illustrating the VTC in action at Wheathampsted, 1915. © The British Library Board (LOU.LON 267) *Volunteer Training Corps Gazette*

were very enthusiastic. I should think there would be about 500 members to start with.'[120] He was a little optimistic as, by February 1915, the city's VTC had around 300 signed up.[121]

Eventually, swayed by public opinion, the government reluctantly decided to tolerate the volunteers on the basis that they would at least learn how to defend their country. However, no support in the way of arms, uniforms or money was forthcoming. If men bought their own uniform it must look different from that of the regulars and territorials. If they bought their own rifles, these could not be of the current design.[122] Moreover, they were required to wear, when training, an arm band carrying the letters 'G.R.', which officially stood for Georgius Rex (George V) or, unofficially, 'Grandfathers Rejuvenated', 'Germany's Ruin', or worse.[123]

Despite these restrictions, St Albans's enthusiasm was matched across the county. In Hertfordshire 26 VTCs were set up between October 1914 and May 1915.[124] The local men met in the evenings to learn drill and shooting, using halls and other premises loaned by local supporters.[125] On Sundays and Bank Holidays the volunteers took part in military exercises, for example on Nomansland common to the north of St Albans (Figure 2.8). Cossins recorded one of these sessions as a rather leisurely occasion: 'The weather was lovely, although the sun was perhaps too hot. We took it easily and the ambulance was not required for anyone.'[126] Without any official purpose, at other times the men found themselves tasks such as digging trenches in the grounds of Hatfield House to test the newly designed tanks, patrolling railway lines, checking details on National Registration forms, pulling mangolds and guarding a local anti-aircraft gun.[127]

Matters changed early in 1916 as increasing manpower shortages forced the government to introduce conscription and to take the VTCs more seriously. There was legislation to include them in the country's official military forces, albeit for home defence only; the VTC men were formally enlisted into the army and could discard their hated armbands. Members of military service tribunals across the country were encouraged by the LGB to add a condition to exemptions so that a man whose application was otherwise successful would be required to join the local VTC. In St Albans in 1916 89 men 'volunteered' for the VTC on this basis. The inherent conflict between the coercive nature of the exemption and the overall voluntary spirit of the Corps was apparent in the behaviour of those obligated to join the VTC. It quickly became clear that some exempted men were not turning up at the drill hall on Hatfield Road, or putting in only the one appearance.[128] Veiled threats were made in the local press that those who had not fulfilled the VTC condition would find themselves recalled to the tribunal, which might be less sympathetic next time.[129] However, in the long run there never seems to have been any effective co-ordination between the tribunal and the VTC to overcome the problem of non-attendance.

Further steps to convert the VTC into a more 'professional' volunteer force came during the winter of 1917. Even with this recognition of its importance, local recruitment seems to have reached a low ebb in contrast to the enthusiasm of late 1914. The men who had been sent by the tribunal were having their cases re-examined, with many required to enlist into the army, and further volunteers were not forthcoming.[130] There was also a surprising change of approach by the city tribunal, which did not require any men to join the VTC in 1917. It is not clear why this happened. Perhaps the tribunal members felt their instructions were unenforceable and therefore ineffective. Or was it because they realised that men were working very long hours in their civilian employments, for example on wartime contracts, and such men could not be expected to spend their few leisure hours as a volunteer soldier?

Matters barely improved in 1918, the tribunal obligating just five men to join the VTC, with many more being directed to become special constables instead. This did not go unnoticed by the VTC commander in St Albans. He said he felt that the tribunal had not been supportive and had not sent as many men to the VTC as in neighbouring areas.[131] In spite of the dire military situation following the German spring offensive in 1918, appeals for new recruits met with desultory results.

Following the armistice, men no longer had to attend drills and social occasions were organised just to hold things together. Eventually kit had to be returned, any remaining unit funds disposed of and officers' commissions relinquished. By December 1920 almost all the local VTCs had been disbanded.[132]

Conclusion

What is clear from this chapter is that recruitment fell into two phases. In the earlier recruitment phase the lack of enthusiasm generated by the rallies held in St Albans in 1915 tends to obscure a remarkable achievement. Almost from scratch over a period of 17 months from August 1914 the country created the largest volunteer army ever assembled in the world up to this point.[133] There is a similar problem with the conscription phase. As the military service tribunal system is also now largely obscured, we have forgotten that this was conscription with a twist. Men across the country had the opportunity to avoid compulsory military service. Nearly half of those in St Albans entitled to do so applied for exemption, many meeting with success.

The importance of volunteers on the home front in St Albans also emerges. The members of the tribunal, the canvassers for the Derby Scheme and organisers of National Registration were not paid for their significant contributions, and those who joined the VTC *paid* to volunteer. This theme of unpaid service underpinned life on the home front in St Albans and is explored in several places in this book.[134]

Notes

1. The August Bank Holiday was then always on the first Monday of August.
2. A. Gregory, *The last great war, British society and the First World War* (Cambridge, 2008), p. 29.
3. 'Yeomanry billeted in St Albans', *Herts Advertiser* (*HA*), 8 August 1914.
4. U. Bloom, *Youth at the gate* (London, 1959), p. 48.
5. H.R. Wilton Hall (compiled D. Lapthorn), *Bernard's Heath and the Great War: extracts from the diary of H.R. Wilton Hall* (St Albans, 2009), p. 1, entry for Monday 10 August 1914.
6. Imperial War Museums, documents.4899, H.C. Cossins's private papers, diary entry for 5 August 1914.
7. Bloom, *Youth at the gate*, p. 50.
8. Ibid., p. 52. See also 'An alarming incident. Midnight scare at St Albans', *HA*, 31 October 1914, where the newspaper reported two events close to the riding school where sentries were apparently attacked.
9. T.A. Bickerton, *The wartime experiences of an ordinary 'Tommy'* (n.p., 1964), p. 1. See picture in Chapter 8.
10. HALS, D/ECk F55, Harriet Suzanna Tyrwhitt Drake's diary, 19 August 1914.
11. Bickerton, *Wartime experiences*, p. 2.
12. Hall, *Bernard's Heath and the Great War*, p. 4, entry for 16 August 1914.
13. It is not certain what the maximum number of soldiers based in St Albans at any one time was. The figure may have reached as many as 8,000 in September–October 1914.
14. P. Simkins, *Kitchener's army: the raising of the new armies, 1914–1916* (Barnsley, 2007), p. xiv.
15. The HTF was under the control of the Hertfordshire Territorial Force Association.
16. The Yeomanry consisted mostly of cavalrymen and the 1st Battalion of infantrymen.
17. See Chapter 4. The drill hall site is currently occupied by the Alban City School and the riding school by housing on Edmund Beaufort Drive.

18. Finally ending up at their War Station near Bury St Edmunds, the battalion became one of the first three territorial force units to be sent for service with the British Expeditionary Force. Sailing from Southampton the battalion arrived at Le Havre on 6 November 1914.

19. In November 1915 the gunners arrived at Le Havre in France. After a short period of familiarisation with service conditions on the Western Front, the batteries left for Egypt on 3 February 1916.

20. See Chapter 3.

21. Simkins, *Kitchener's army*, p. 39.

22. J. McDermott, *British military service tribunals, 1916–18: 'a very much abused body of men'* (Manchester, 2011), p. 14.

23. Simkins, *Kitchener's army*, p. 52.

24. *HA*, August 1914 editions.

25. Details of the area covered by the 'District' recruiting office have not come to light. This estimate is based on the 1911 census returns for the St Albans registration district which included the city, Redbourn, Sandridge, Wheathampstead, St Peter's Rural and St Michael's Rural districts. Figures based on recruitment returns published in *HA*, August 1914.

26. Gregory, *The last great war*, pp. 31–2.

27. Ibid., p. 75. The local building trade was particularly affected at this point – see 'Relief for the distressed', *HA*, 29 August 1914. Also see Chapter 5.

28. 'St Albans Gas Company', *HA*, 19 September 1914, p. 7; for the city council, see Chapter 4.

29. HALS, SBR/904, Watch Committee Minute Book, 1912–22, 15 September 1914.

30. HALS, DE/V F1437 1–2, correspondence and papers concerning service of employees of Lord Grimston's businesses during the war, 1914–19, letter to Ernest Gape, 3 January 1916.

31. HALS, PUG 13/1/6, St Albans Gas Company Minute Book, 1914–21, see reports of half-yearly meetings.

32. HALS, BG/STA/17, St Albans Board of Guardians Minute Book, 1913–15, 27 August 1914.

33. Simkins, *Kitchener's army*, p. 75.

34. Ibid., p. 58.

35. Hall, *Bernard's Heath and the Great War*, p. 10, entry for Sunday 30 August 1914.

36. Figures based on 'Call to the Colours', *HA*, 5 September 1914 and 'St Albans doing its duty', *HA*, 12 September 1914.

37. Simkins, *Kitchener's army*, p. 60.

38. 'Your country calls you: memorable meeting at St Albans', *HA*, 12 September 1914. The subsequent discussion of the rally is based on this account.

39. Kernahan was a pupil at St Albans Grammar School. There is no evidence that he was directly involved in recruitment in St Albans.

40. J.C. Kernahan, *The experiences of a recruiting officer* (London, 1915), pp. 28–32.

41. Slade was later reluctant for his son, Hugh Leslie Slade, to be conscripted. He applied on seven occasions to the tribunals in a vain attempt to keep his son at home managing the family-owned hat factory.

42. See Gregory, *The last great war*, pp. 50–52 for an assessment of this.

43. For a general discussion of this point see S. Hallifax, '"Over by Christmas": British popular opinion and the short war in 1914', *First World War Studies*, 1 (2010), pp. 103–21.

44. 'St Albans doing its duty', *HA*, 12 September 1914.

45. K. Grieves, *The politics of manpower* (Manchester, 1988), p. 23.

46. Simkins, *Kitchener's army*, p. 75.

47. H.R. Wilton Hall, *Notes and memoranda relating to St Saviour's church*, Book 5, 1914–16.

48. 'War time notes', *HA*, 12 September 1914.

49. Simkins, *Kitchener's army*, p. 125.

50. See Bickerton, *Wartime experiences*, p. 3. Bickerton certainly had sufficient local affinity to want to join the county regiment.

51. 'Herts men for Herts regiments', *HA*, 29 May 1915.

52. 'The County regiments: Herts Territorials recruiting march', *HA*, 19 June 1915.

53. 'A recruiting meeting and an appeal', *HA*, 29 May 1915.

54. For Smith's Printing Co. see 'Our roll of honour', *HA*, 17 October 1914.

55. Advertisement, p. 5, *HA*, 19 December 1914. For his bankruptcy see 'Motor engineer's failure', *HA*, 26 August 1916.

56. Simkins, *Kitchener's army*, pp. 143–4.

57. Including women in registration indicated the imperative for business leaders to consider the growing importance of introducing women into the workplace.

58. HALS, SBR/871, Urban Authority & General Purposes Committee Minute Book, 1914–20, report to St Albans city council on National Registration (Instructions) Order, issued by the Local Government Board (LGB) dated 16 July 1915.

59. 'Registration. The work in St Albans,' *HA*, 14 August 1915.

60. 'The National Register', *HA*, 21 August 1915.

61. Ibid. The following is an example of the type of problem the enumerators encountered: 'Some domestic servants gave their home address as their permanent address when in fact they should have given their mistresses' address'.

62. Grieves, *The politics of manpower*, p. 21.

63. *HA*, one report in each of 7 August, 14 August, 21 August and 28 August 1915.

64. Simkins, *Kitchener's army*, pp. 120–21, for more about the general initiative to recruit 'bantam' battalions. For advertisement see *HA*, 31 July 1915. It is not clear if this platoon was embodied.

65. Bickerton, *Wartime experiences*, p. 3. See picture in Chapter 8.

66. 'Great recruiting rally', *HA*, 9 October 1915. Longmire Road has since been renamed and is now part of Riverside Road.

67. See pp. 54–7 for a discussion of the Corps.

68. Imperial War Museums, documents.4899, Cossins's papers, diary entry for 2 October 1915.

69. Lord Derby had recently been appointed Director-General of Recruiting at the War Office.

70. HALS, SBR/2960, Lord Derby's recruiting scheme papers, 1915.

71. 'Correspondence: "Lord Derby recruiting scheme"', *HA*, 25 December 1915.

72. 'Lord Derby's scheme', *HA*, 18 December 1915.

73. Simkins, *Kitchener's army*, p. 156.

74. Gregory, *The last great war*, p. 101. Emphasis in the original.

75. The St Albans Rural Military Service Tribunal catered mostly for those living immediately outside the city boundary, e.g. in Sandridge, Redbourn, London Colney. Like the city tribunal, it also met at the town hall in St Albans.

76. McDermott, *British military service tribunals*, p. 1.

77. Ibid., pp. 18–19.

78. Gregory, *The last great war*, p. 101.

79. Along with applicants from the other 32 local tribunals in the county. A further appeal could then be made with leave from the CAT to the Central Tribunal in London. It considered the most contentious cases.

80. HALS, SBR/871, Urban Authority & General Purposes Committee Minute Book, circular from Walter Long of LGB, October 1915.

81. HALS, SBR/1943, Council Out-letter Book (mainly to government departments), 1912–20, letter to secretary of LGB 24 February 1916. For much of its existence, three labour representatives served on the tribunal as, following the resignation of Reynolds in March 1916, a member of the National Union of Railwaymen joined. This was Fred Keech. See HALS, SBR/3384, City Council Correspondence File etc., 1916, letter to Mr J. Lovell, branch chairman of the union.

82. HALS, SBR/871, Urban Authority & General Purposes Committee Minute Book, 10 February 1916. Women were appointed to other tribunals in the county, such as the St Albans Rural Military Service Tribunal and the Hertfordshire CAT.

83. Gape was a member of a family that had played leading roles in the St Albans area since the fifteenth century. He did not have a military background.

84. War Office, *Group and class systems. Notes on administration*, February 1916 (London, 1916).

85. Based on Military Service Act, 1916, s. 2(1). A different order of the grounds has been inserted here for ease of reading.

86. These statistics are extracted from a database of cases created by the Home Front Research Group based on the reports of the *HA* combined with the surviving minute book and three registers (HALS SBR/865, 1813, 1814 & 1815).

87. McDermott, *British military service tribunals*, p. 40. A total of 1.6 per cent of the appeals to the Northamptonshire CAT were by conscientious objectors. In Huddersfield the figure was 1 per cent: see Gregory, *The last great war*, p. 101.

88. See Chapter 5.

89. For example, see 'Military service: "S.A." works employees' classification', *HA*, 28 July 1917, for the case of Benjamin Laver, a 32-year-old printer's compositor from Royston Road. He reported that the doctor from the Medical Board took just three minutes to give him a general examination.

90. 'St Albans tribunal', *HA*, 10 June 1916. This application was heard 18 months before food shortages became a national issue.

91. 'The city tribunal', *HA*, 1 July 1916.

92. Anon, *St Albans roll of honour* (St Albans, n.d.), p. 7. The brothers, Percy Morris and William Archibald Corley of 28 Albert Street, were both killed on 25 September 1915. As far as is known, Cyril Corley survived the war.

93. 'The city tribunal', *HA*, 24 March 1917.

94. See Chapter 6 for a discussion about the problems faced by butchers and bakers in relation to conscription.

95. 'Pte Alfred T. Hopkins,' *HA*, 6 October 1917.

96. Starting at 6pm on Friday evenings, tribunal hearings could often extend beyond midnight, especially in the first half of 1916. In March of that year, there is evidence that only five minutes was set aside for each case to be considered. See HALS, DE/V F1687/3, letters from Lord Grimston to his wife, March 1916.

97. 'St Albans help for the Army', *HA*, 20 May 1916. As far as is known, both sons survived the war.

98. HALS, UDC/4/68/1, Berkhamsted Urban Local Tribunal 1915. See Chapter 5 for further discussion of this conflict.

99. 'A Friendly Societies' champion', *Hertfordshire News and County Advertiser*, 10 December 1919.

100. 'Hertfordshire leaders No. 6, Mr Ernest J. Gape, a record of war work', *HA*, 3 January 1920.

101. 'The tribunal at a dead lock', *Luton News & Bedfordshire Chronicle*, 22 February 1917.

102. McDermott, *British military service tribunals*, p. 39.

103. C. Pearce, *Comrades in conscience: the story of an English community's opposition to the Great War* (London, 2001). Conscientious objector, Harry Willson, refused to attend the local tribunal.

104. 'The St Albans tribunal', *HA*, 25 March 1916. Tess Road has since been renamed and is now part of Woodstock Road South.

105. 'Sultry evening at the tribunal', *HA*, 29 July 1916.

106. 'The St Albans tribunal', *HA*, 25 March 1916; 'Sultry evening at the tribunal', *HA*, 29 July 1916.

107. 'Tribunal decisions', *HA*, 15 July 1916.

108. 'St Albans tribunal', *HA*, 8 August 1918.

109. Ibid.

110. 'Herts appeal tribunal', *HA*, 12 August 1916.

111. 'St Albans tribunal', *HA*, 25 March 1916.

112. 'St Albans military tribunal at work', *HA*, 4 March 1916.

113. 'The appeal tribunal', *HA*, 25 March 1916.

114. 'Tribunal decisions', *HA*, 15 July 1916.

115. 'St Albans city tribunal', *HA*, 8 December 1917.

116. 'Tribunal decisions', *HA*, 15 July 1916.

117. 'The City tribunal', *HA*, 13 January 1917.

118. 'More men for the Army, a conscientious objector', *HA*, 17 March 1917.

119. K.W. Mitchinson, *Defending Albion: Britain's home army, 1908–1919* (Basingstoke, 2005), pp. 71–2.

120. Imperial War Museums, documents.4899, Cossins's papers, diary entry for 16 November 1914.

121. 'Volunteer Training Corps', *HA*, 6 February 1915.
122. J.D. Sainsbury, *Herts V.R.* (Welwyn, 2005), p. 88.
123. 'The "Red Brassards" on the war path', HA, 20 November 1915.
124. Ibid., p. 29.
125. 'St Albans Volunteer Training Corps', *HA*, 6 March 1915.
126. Imperial War Museums, documents.4899, Cossins's papers, diary entry for 24 May 1915.
127. 'Herts Volunteer Regt', *HA*, 8 January 1916.
128. For example, see the case of Hugh Leslie Slade, son of the former mayor. Exempted by the city's tribunal with the VTC condition attached to his certificate, he rarely turned out for drill and was called back to the tribunal to discuss his lapses. See *HA* reports, 21 October and 4 November 1916.
129. 'Tribunal decisions', *HA*, 15 July 1916.
130. 'The Volunteers', *HA*, 26 May 1917.
131. 'St Albans tribunal', *HA*, 14 September 1918.
132. HALS, TAFA/2, Hertfordshire Territorial Force Association Minute Book, 1914–20, 5 December 1920.
133. Gregory, *The last great war*, p. 73.
134. For example, see Chapter 3.

CHAPTER 3

The army in the city

Although St Albans, in common with many British towns and cities before the First World War, had a visible military presence in the form of local Territorial Force units, the city was far from being a garrison town. With the coming of war in August 1914 this would change. The War Office had its sights set on St Albans, a strategy that would have far-reaching implications for the city.

U nder plans drawn up by the War Office in the years immediately preceding the war Hertfordshire was one of the 12 counties under Eastern Command,[1] with St Albans designated as a Permanent War Station for the 2nd London Division. This Territorial Force formation was part of Third Army in the main home defence army, Central Force (see the regional map at the front of the book). Pre-war defence planning was based on an assumption that the probable enemy would be Germany. Although an invasion was considered unlikely on account of the strength of the Royal Navy, British military planners could not discount the possibility of German raids aimed at destroying key military or industrial targets. Beyond such raids the ultimate scenario covered by home defence planning was the landing of 70,000 German troops somewhere between the Humber and Thames, with the aim of making a rapid advance to capture London and overthrow the government. To counter this threat, Central Force was established on the outbreak of war for operations in the east of England.

By 1914 British strategic planners had concluded that the main body of the regular British army needed to be deployed to France in the early days of any war with Germany, leaving home defence duties primarily to the Territorial Force. As these part-time soldiers were less well trained than regulars, many more (195,000 all ranks) were required to ensure that Central Force could defeat a German march on London. To forestall any early German invasion, plans called for Central Force to be concentrated, by the fourteenth day of mobilisation, in positions from which it could bring the invaders to action before London was seriously threatened.[2]

As well as becoming a Permanent War Station, St Albans was also named in the Home Defence scheme of August 1914 as within Third Army's area of concentration, primarily because it was on the main rail line running north from London and was serviced by two branch lines. In addition, the good rail communications through St Albans saw the city, along with Harpenden, designated as Detrainment Area 4 under Emergency Scheme B for the reinforcement of Central Force by troops from Aldershot and the Salisbury Plain training area. In this scheme the detraining capacity of St Albans was given as one troop train per hour. The city was also listed as an 'ammunition station', meaning that its main station had sidings where train carriages carrying ammunition could be 'parked' and their cargo used to resupply troops in the area or passing through, as needed.[3]

Having waved off their own 'terriers' a few days immediately following mobilisation to take up coastal defence duties in East Anglia the people of St Albans did not have long to wait before army uniforms returned to the city's streets, as by mid-August the 2nd London Division had arrived in the district (Figure 3.1). The three infantry brigades of the division, each consisting of four battalions – a total of 4,000 men per brigade when at full strength – based themselves on St Albans, Hatfield and Watford, while the artillery found homes around Berkhamsted, Hemel Hempstead and Kings Langley. Those units known to have an association with St Albans were the eight battalions of 5th and 6th London Brigades (1/17th to 1/24th Londons).[4] The city also housed the divisional headquarters and a number of support units. As the division was still working up to full strength when it arrived it is probable that St Albans initially played host to around 7,000 soldiers, a significant influx for a city of 24,000 inhabitants.

Although these London territorials were to have been a permanent part of Central Force serving on the home front, heavy casualties in France and Flanders during the opening months of the war meant additional troops for service overseas were required immediately. With the volunteers of Kitchener's New Armies just beginning their basic military training, the only significant body of trained men in the UK were the territorials. Much pressure was brought to bear on officers and men in the territorials to sign up for overseas service, and units with a 60 per cent take-up rate became eligible for service outside the UK. Those men expressing reluctance to sign the Imperial Service Obligation, thereby agreeing to serve outside the UK, were withdrawn from their original units. They became the nucleus of second-line territorial units, whose job it would be to take over home

Figure 3.1 Locations used by the military in St Albans from August 1914. © SAHAAS.

Key:

1. Stabling for army horses and mules
2. Artillery Riding School and Gun Park
3. Drill Hall
4. 2nd London Irish Rifles HQ and Military School of Instruction
5. St Albans Anti-Aircraft Defence Command HQ
6. Bricket House Red Cross War Hospital
7. Army Recruiting Office
8. To Gorhambury firing range and training ground
9. St Albans Red Cross War Hospital Supply Depot
10. Pageant House
11. 2nd London Division HQ
12. 1/6th (London) Field Ambulance HQ and cookhouse
13. Army Veterinary Corps
14. Army Service Corps (ASC) HQ
15. ASC transport units
16. To Royal Flying Corps at London Colney
17. To Chalk Hill firing range
18. To ASC transport units at Sopwell House

defence duties and act as a training formation for men who could then be sent to the first-line unit overseas. In March 1915 the option of joining the territorials for home service only was abolished. Pressure on original home service men to sign the Imperial Service Obligation continued until the Military Service Acts of 1916 made overseas service compulsory for any men passed medically fit.

By October 1914 most second-line territorial units had been formed and by the close of the year a large number of third-line battalions and yeomanry (cavalry) regiments were also in existence. The original purpose of these latest units was simply to provide drafts of men for the first and second line, but they were soon incorporated into home defence plans. What followed was a steady turnover of men arriving in St Albans and then moving on to the front or elsewhere, to be replaced by more troops.[5]

In March 1915 the 2nd London Division departed St Albans for France. They were quickly replaced by their second-line formation, the 60th (2/2nd London) Division, and, again, two brigades based themselves around St Albans. These eight battalions – the 2/17th to 2/24th Londons – in turn departed during May for deployment to the Western Front.

Next arrived two brigades from another territorial formation, the 54th (East Anglian) Division, which had previously undertaken coastal defence duties. These latest arrivals comprised four battalions of the Essex Regiment (1/4th to 1/7th), the 1/5th Bedfordshires, 1/4th Northamptonshires and the 1/10th and 1/11th Londons. As with the 60th Division, the association of these troops with St Albans was short-lived as, minus its artillery and divisional transport, the formation departed for Devonport in July in preparation for service at Gallipoli.

Figure 3.2 The 2/4th Lincolnshire Regiment's camp at St Albans in 1915. © St Albans Museums (PX9207_2)

They were followed by elements of the 59th (2nd North Midland) Division. Stationed around St Albans were 176th and 177th Brigades and the divisional headquarters. The units forming the two brigades were the 2/5th and 2/6th Battalions of both the North and South Staffordshire Regiments and the 2/4th and 2/5th Battalions of the Lincolnshire and Leicestershire Regiments (Figure 3.2). The 59th Division had a longer relationship with the city, remaining in the area until April 1916, when units were quickly sent to Ireland after the outbreak of the Easter Rising in Dublin.

From defence to training

The tenure of 59th Division at St Albans coincided with major organisational changes to British home defence. In January 1916 Field Marshal Sir John French, former commander of the British Expeditionary Force, was appointed Commander-in-Chief Home Defence, creating a unified command for home forces for the first time. French's main task was to revise plans for the land defence of the UK and at the same time expand and rationalise the system of training new recruits for the army. Believing it necessary to defeat any German invasion force as it landed, French concentrated his forces along the east coast. As part of this redeployment, Central Force was disbanded in mid-1916 and replaced by Northern and Southern Armies with their headquarters respectively at Mundford in Norfolk and Brentwood in Essex.

French contended with the constantly changing nature and composition of his home defence forces as units completed their training, were classed as efficient and were sent to France. This situation accelerated during the build-up to the Somme offensive on 1 July 1916. His response was to establish the Training Reserve, with a total of 112 battalions divided between 24 Training Reserve brigades.[6] Of these battalions, 60 were available to reinforce Northern and Southern Armies when necessary. As part of this reorganisation, by October 1916 St Albans became home to the headquarters and two battalions of 5th Training Reserve Brigade under Colonel (temporary Brigadier General) G.M. Mackenzie. In terms of home defence these troops, along with two battalions based at Watford, formed an infantry brigade of 5,000 men. At the same time, St Albans continued to be designated an entraining station for units moving eastward to reinforce Southern Army. While on paper such troop numbers appear impressive, it should be remembered that, beyond their home defence commitment, these units were simply a place for the training of new conscripts who, on reaching an efficient standard, were posted wherever the army needed reinforcements. This increasing reliance on barely trained and often poorly equipped troops did nothing to increase the standard of British home defence forces. However, with the German army fully committed on the Somme, at Verdun and on the Eastern Front, the chance of an invasion now seemed remote.[7]

In 1917 further changes in organisation occurred as French sought to streamline the reinforcement system supporting the British army overseas. This time the existing Training Reserve Battalions were converted into either Young Soldiers or Graduated Battalions. The Young Soldiers Battalions took new conscripts through basic training, after which they passed to the latter units. Each Graduated Battalion was organised into four age-related companies through which a conscript passed until he reached the senior company aged 19, from where he could be posted overseas. At the same time as fulfilling a training function, all these battalions were available for home defence duties. In St Albans the changes saw the establishment of Eastern Reserve Centre headquarters under Major General T.D. Pilcher. Within 5th Training Reserve Brigade the reorganisation saw the 23rd Training Reserve Battalion renamed 25th Young Soldiers Battalion and the formation of 26th Graduated Battalion, both based around the city.[8]

In October 1917 all Young Soldiers and Graduated Battalions were allotted to 23 regular line infantry regiments. Graduated Battalions were all numbered either 51st or 52nd, while the Young Soldiers became the 53rd battalion of their allotted regiment. Under this final reorganisation St Albans became home to 53rd (Young Soldier) Battalion, The Queens (Royal West Surrey) Regiment. This unit was part of 4th Training Reserve Brigade, the headquarters of which, along with two battalions, was based in and around Northampton. The 53rd Queens proved to be the last infantry battalion to be stationed in the city during the war.[9]

Air-defence role

As well as being a base for home defence and training units St Albans also served, from late 1917, as headquarters for three batteries of anti-aircraft guns manned by the Royal Garrison Artillery (RGA). Although the threat from Zeppelin airships had greatly diminished by October 1916, in May of the following year German bomber aircraft began raids against London.

These machines posed a totally new challenge to British anti-aircraft defences. To improve matters the London Air Defence Area (LADA) was established on 31 July 1917 under Major General Edward Ashmore. This put in position an outer ring of anti-aircraft guns approximately 25 miles from the capital. These defences were designed to break up bomber formations before they reached London, making the attackers easier to intercept by fighter aircraft of Home Defence squadrons. These defending aircraft were limited to flying in a zone between the inner and outer anti-aircraft gun lines, ensuring that they would not fall foul of friendly fire.[10]

As part of LADA, St Albans Anti-Aircraft Defence Command formed part of the northern outer zone of defence. Commanded by Lieutenant (acting Lieutenant Colonel) H.W. Hamlett, Royal Field Artillery (Territorial Force), guns from 18, 31 and 55 Companies (RGA) were spread out across Hertfordshire, from Bovingdon and Flaunden eastward to Standon. The three companies were equipped with either three-inch 20-cwt or 18-pounder QF (quick-firing) guns.[11] Each unit also had seven or eight searchlights and in 1918 electric height-finding devices were issued. 18 and 31 Companies totalled 189 and 182 officers and men, respectively, while 55 Company numbered 221 all ranks, allowing this unit to crew 13 guns, rather than the seven or eight of the other companies. Headquarters sections of each unit were located with Defence Command headquarters in Donnington House on St Peter's Street.[12]

As the majority of German bomber raids followed relatively direct routes towards London the guns of St Albans Anti-Aircraft Defence Command were not often called into action. During the night of 7/8 March 1918, however, the Germans launched their first moonless night raid with five of their four-engined 'Giant' bombers. Three of these aircraft reached central London, another flew over Golders Green, Mill Hill and Enfield before heading off over Essex, while the fifth bombed Luton and at 12.15am was engaged by guns of the St Albans Command. In total 736 rounds were fired by anti-aircraft guns located at Bridehall, Datchworth, Harpenden, Sacombe, Standon, Welwyn and Wheathampstead. The German raider flew off towards Much Hadham and Great Munden, where it dropped 11 bombs before heading for home.[13]

Also involved in air defence operations were Royal Flying Corps, later Royal Air Force, squadrons based at London Colney. The airfield was established as a Home Defence Night Landing Ground in April 1916 to assist two squadrons in the fight against Zeppelins.[14] Airman 2nd Lieutenant Frank Best described the base at London Colney:

> This aerodrome, where so many scout pilots spent their last weeks in England, lay amongst parkland and large meadows through which the river Colne flows. The neighbouring villages of London Colney, Shenley and Radlett each consisted of only a few houses. The airfield itself must have covered nearly a square mile of ground. At the North it was bounded by Harper Lane, and on the East by Shenley Lane, which was lined on each side by hangars and huts.[15]

The first unit to make London Colney a permanent home was 56 Squadron, which arrived from Gosport in July 1916. Operating a variety of aircraft, the unit worked up to become a fighter squadron in early 1917, flying SE5 aircraft. Serving with this squadron was fighter ace Captain Albert Ball, who, by this time, was already a decorated war hero. While off duty on 25 March 1917, during his time at London Colney, Ball met 18-year-old Flora Young of Bedford Park Road, St Albans. He impulsively invited her to fly with him, and she promptly accepted. On the day 56 Squadron left for France, the couple became engaged, Flora wearing his identification wrist bracelet in lieu of an engagement ring. Ball departed for France with the squadron on 5 April 1917 and was killed a month later in combat.[16]

A training squadron with the same number (56) was also formed to operate at London Colney. With a variety of aircraft, ranging from the outdated BE2 to the recently introduced Sopwith Camel, the unit trained new fighter pilots. In addition to training flights, pilots from the squadron flew against German bombers during 1917 and 1918, although existing reports do not mention any actual interceptions. On 15 July 1918 41 Training Depot Squadron was formed from this training squadron. The new unit was equipped with 24 Avro 504 basic training aircraft and an equal number of Sopwith Snipe fighters, which were used as advanced trainers. It was redesignated a training squadron in October 1919, just a month before its disbandment. Other units based at London Colney included 74 Squadron (1917–18) and the 24th Aero Squadron of the United States Army Air Service (1918). The airfield at London Colney was finally relinquished by the Royal Air Force in early 1920 and the various buildings, including five hangars, were quickly dismantled.[17]

Accommodating the troops

The arrival of large numbers of soldiers in St Albans brought with it a requirement to provide adequate accommodation. In Britain there was a tradition dating back to the English Civil War and enshrined in the Army Act that the billeting of troops in private houses was to be avoided.[18] In line with this, and to prepare for the arrival of 2nd London Division, public buildings in St Albans were requisitioned by the military as accommodation for soldiers within two weeks of war being declared.[19] These included many maintained and private schools, church halls and empty houses. Despite this, and in addition to numbers of soldiers sleeping under canvas in various areas around the city, the demand remained and the systematic billeting of soldiers in private houses began. With the winter of 1914/15 proving to be one of the wettest for decades it became almost impossible to accommodate troops in tents, and billeting in private houses became the only option. In advance of the troops, the billeting officers visited each house in turn to assess the space available. The number of soldiers that could be accommodated was chalked on the front door. When the troops arrived they were marched down the streets, peeling off to their respective billets in twos and threes. One resident, Bernard Smith, remembered an officer and sergeant calling at his family home in Boundary Road to check on how many people lived in the house: 'There was only my mother and father and myself and they said "well you can easily accommodate two soldiers". There was no question of "will you?" it was obligatory.' Barbara Rapson's family in Blenheim Road took in three soldiers, but later on, when they had left, an officer lodged with them: 'He, of course, had a room to himself', perhaps indicating that there was a certain amount of priority given to officers in the more spacious houses in the city.[20] It appears that the army had reconnoitred St Albans in 1913 to identify potential billets. Senior officers and adjutants of the London Irish Rifles spent a weekend in the city that autumn. With no authority to enter houses and other premises, accommodation had to be assessed using other methods, including counting chimneypots.[21]

Accommodation was very basic for soldiers billeted in municipal buildings, schools, church halls and factories, with men crowded into rooms and having to sleep on the floor. Blankets were in short supply, adding to the discomfort.[22] Several of the soldiers billeted in the schoolroom at Dagnall Street Baptist church were reportedly feeling the effects of recent inoculations prior to being posted overseas and, as a result, found the floor a particularly uncomfortable place to sleep. In an act of compassion, Laura Gibbs set to work with other volunteers to manufacture calico-covered mattresses and pillows stuffed with paper shavings from the works of her family's printing business, Gibbs & Bamforth Ltd, publishers of the *Herts Advertiser*.[23]

As the autumn school term approached steps were taken to remove soldiers from school buildings.[24] Not all residents, however, were in favour of this, with the Revd Chadwick of St Peter's writing that the health of the troops should be of paramount importance, especially where schools were being used as messing headquarters. He felt strongly that such buildings should be left at the disposal of the military until they were no longer needed.[25] By 12 September, however, all elementary schools except Hatfield Road Boys, Old London Road Girls and Infants and Priory Park Boys had been handed back to the council, although the privately owned and run St Albans High School for Girls remained in military hands.[26] At the same time the army continued to use the School of Arts & Crafts and Technical Institute on Victoria Street.

Private Harold Chapin (1/6th London Field Ambulance) had the experience of moving billet more than once, going from E. Day & Co.'s straw-hat factory to an unoccupied house about half a mile away. He was then moved again, further away, to 'a gloomy hole – lit by one oil lamp, very damp and draughty'. When in the factory Chapin recalled how the works engineer allowed him to keep his spare clothes in the engine room overnight to allow them to dry, there being no heating in the room in which the soldiers were sleeping.[27]

Troops were accommodated in every quarter of the city, with each battalion having its own messing headquarters. One of the schools in Old London Road, for example, was set up to feed over 1,000 men. On any day of the week 'victualling operations' could be seen in progress in the open air, as in the yard of Day's factory in Marlborough Road and in front of the drill hall on Hatfield Road (Figure 3.3). The *Herts Advertiser* recorded of the latter location:

> There upon the open space in front of the entrance, were benches loaded with huge sides of beef, with bags of potatoes and quantities of other vegetables near at hand. A dozen or more men could be seen busily employed in cutting up the meat and preparing the other eatables ready for the camp boilers nearby.[28]

Figure 3.3 Cookhouse in the yard at E. Day & Co.'s hat factory. © Pat Moore

From Day's factory Chapin wrote home to tell of the heavy work he was doing in the cookhouse, working with three others to feed 240 men a day under difficult circumstances:

> We have only eleven 'dixies' [large iron kettles], every one of which is necessary for each meal and no soda or other means of cleansing them is issued to us. Our full equipment besides the dixies is a set of butcher's tools, a couple of ovens (requiring independent fires over which ordinary kettles can be boiled), a pick-axe, a kettle and an iron girder, found here and invaluable.[29]

Cookhouses were a favourite haunt of local children: Cecil Sharp, a boy scout attached to the 1/6th (London) Field Ambulance, recalled that the soldiers had an abundance of flour and jam and that the quartermaster often gave him some to take home to his mother in New Kent Road. Sharp wondered why he had to go down the side path if he was so honest but, of course, later in life he realised that it was illegal for army stores to be redistributed in this way.[30] There was also a field kitchen at the Corn Exchange in Market Place, where the soldiers handed out soup to local people if they had any to spare.[31]

Those soldiers billeted in private houses were either fed at the central cookhouses or had food prepared by the household with whom they were staying. In the latter case householders were paid an allowance to purchase provisions or the army arranged for the daily delivery of food to the billets. An allowance of up to 3s 4½d per man per day was paid by the army to householders to cover board and lodging.[32] This arrangement must have relieved some of the pressure on the cookhouses. The *Herts Advertiser* reported:

> The distribution of the provisions to the respective billets is a task that is performed *sans ceremonie*. Where there is a side or a back entrance the goods are taken there, otherwise the front door receives the knock or ring. On a hand truck loaned from an adjoining grocer or tradesman or sometimes on a sack barrow, the distribution goes round, and when these methods of transit are unobtainable, a military blanket is used to carry such solids as bread, tins of jam, and pieces of meat – one pound of meat per man. The housewife or servant opens the door and if it is

a distribution of tea and granulated sugar they invariably arrive
together ... caddies, jars or basins are forthcoming and a generous
allowance made from tea chest and sugar box.[33]

In contrast to the catering arrangements made for the troops, the War
Office made no special provisions for the soldiers to wash clothes, and it
was reported that at schools and other public institutions where troops
were quartered the unusual sight could be seen of men's shirts and socks
dangling from the windows. Notices quickly appeared at numerous private
houses offering washing and sewing services for soldiers.[34]

The need to keep soldiers at a high state of efficiency was vital if they
were to remain ready to face the enemy. This was particularly true for the
territorials and later the training battalions that were located in and around
St Albans. Although route marches and drill required little in the way of
special facilities the same was not the case for tactical manoeuvres or rifle
practice, both requiring significant areas of land where interference with
local civilian activities would be kept to a minimum. With two brigades
of infantry arriving in the St Albans area in August 1914 it was obvious
that the rifle range at Sandridge, used pre-war by the local territorials,
would be far from sufficient. Among the new ranges constructed were
two on land owned by the Gorhambury estate, which was also used for
army manoeuvres and battle practice. The troops became a regular sight
marching to and from the training areas (Figure 3.4). Although a standard
British army rifle range of the period was 600 yards in length, with an
earth bank known as a butt behind the targets, an area 250 yards to either
side of the butts, widening out to 500 yards at a distance of 2,000 to
2,500 yards behind the butts, was included in the range. This was known
as the 'danger area' and comprised the space into which any over-shot
rounds or ricochets would fall.[35] The layout of the two ranges on the estate
meant that soldiers fired towards each other. One was on land behind
Gorhambury House, while the other was located at Chalk Hill, off Watford
Road, between St Albans and Chiswell Green. This meant that when firing
was in progress the St Albans–Hemel Hempstead road had to be closed to
traffic, as it ran through the danger area.

The closure of this road caused considerable inconvenience, especially
as, in the beginning, warning notices were posted only on approaches
to the road at the edge of the city. In November 1915 the local chamber
of commerce requested that a red flag and notice be displayed on the

Figure 3.4 The 2/4th Lincolnshires marching through St Michaels Street. © Imperial War Museums (Q 53790)

fountain next to the clock tower whenever the ranges were in use.[36] Despite these warning signs and military guards posted on the road, some road users ignored orders. Mrs Hireson of Bluehouse Hill was summonsed for contravening the Defence of the Realm Act (DORA) (No. 2) 1914 and the Bye Law No. 3 of the Military Land Acts 1892 and 1903 for attempting to cycle through the Chalk Hill danger area when told to stop by a soldier. He pursued her on his bicycle and claimed in court that bullets were whistling about when he stopped Mrs Hireson, who was fined 10s.[37] Two pedigree sows belonging to J.R. Arris of Hill End Farm, immediately to the west of the Gorhambury range, were not so fortunate. They were shot, as was a heifer that strayed into the line of fire.[38]

Transport units of the Army Service Corps (ASC) were located at Sopwell House until May 1916 and at the old rubber works on London Road throughout the war, the latter premises being vacated in August 1919.[39] Here the ASC had installed a bakery, blacksmiths' workshop and petrol store to supply the mechanical transport units that were based there. The ASC also rented ground and buildings at Verulam Golf Club. The dining room was requisitioned to act as a mess for ASC bakers, while the army also occupied the caddie master's office and other rooms. Part of the first fairway became a vehicle park and in May 1915 the club claimed £124 from the army in compensation for damage caused by ASC activity. However, fears that the entire golf course would be taken over as a military camp did not materialise.[40]

Strangely, in the midst of all this requisitioning and hiring of buildings there is very little evidence of the use made of the two major pre-existing military buildings in the city, namely the infantry drill hall and artillery riding school and gun park. Mention has already been made of the use of the Hatfield Road drill hall as a battalion cookhouse. Records show that in 1916 the local Volunteer Training Corps started to use the hall for its original purpose and continued to do so until disbanded.[41] The function of the artillery riding school during the war remains a mystery, as no mention of its use can be found either in records of the Hertfordshire County Territorial Force Association or in the pages of the *Herts Advertiser*.

St Albans's own war horses

With the army greatly reliant on horse transport, there was a need for veterinary facilities and remount depots to ensure the required number of animals were available to each unit. As part of these arrangements St Albans became the location of a horse hospital for Eastern Command. It was run by the Army Veterinary Corps (AVC) and located at the foot of St Stephen's Hill. In September 1916 more than 400 horses were being treated for a variety of ailments and diseases. At this time, cases of mange were so numerous that AVC personnel here became expert in its treatment. The hospital dealt with sick and injured horses until the animals were healthy enough to be sent to a remount depot, from where horses were reassigned to units. With so many horses on hand it is perhaps not surprising that the hospital began a sideline of the sale of manure at 2s a load, making a weekly profit of £5–6.[42]

In total the hospital covered 84 acres and included a large forge where the staff trained new farriers, six 'loose boxes' where horses could be placed in slings, a pharmacy containing all types of medicine and medical instruments, a disinfecting chamber for the thorough cleansing of harnesses, equipment and uniforms, and a large storeroom. In addition, the staff had a canteen and recreation rooms in a small building loaned by the gas company. Much of the facility was taken up by extensive open-air grounds, including glebe land rented from St Stephen's church, in which the treatment and convalescence of less serious cases was undertaken. The hospital even had its own kitchen garden, which ensured that all staff had the benefit of fresh vegetables at meal times.

Newspaper reports indicate that from 30 August 1914 to September 1916 the hospital admitted and treated 3,732 horses, of which 90 died, 162 were destroyed and 190 sold. The remainder had recovered and been sent to remount centres. During the same period 31 sergeants qualified and were sent to various regiments, three mobile veterinary sections were trained and dispatched overseas, 16 men were supplied as grooms to officers and 20 cold-shoers[43] qualified, with a further six still on a course of instruction. The hospital achieved all this with a staff of 185 all ranks. However, in March 1915 only 80 men were available to deal with an influx of over 1,000 horses needing treatment. Such strenuous work caused the commanding officer, Major Elliot, to be invalided out suffering from a breakdown.

The military hospital

The arrival of the army in the city during August 1914 also brought with it a need to provide adequate medical facilities for sick men and those injured during training. On 8 August the local Voluntary Aid Detachment (VAD), 38th Herts, was mobilised. The 38th Herts was established in St Albans in 1911 by Lady Verulam and Lady Thomson, who were also vice-presidents of the St Albans branch of the Red Cross.[44] In common with all VAD units, it was administered as part of the Territorial Force and the commandant of the 30-strong contingent was Lota Boycott, a trained nurse. The VAD nurses received training in first aid and home nursing and worked at the St Albans and Mid Herts Hospital to gain practical experience. In common with other VADs, the majority were middle- and upper-class women.

Bricket House in Bricket Road, a residence and domestic economy teaching centre connected to St Albans High School for Girls, was placed at the disposal of the 38th Herts for conversion into a temporary hospital. A letter from Lady Verulam in the *Herts Advertiser* on 8 August 1914 called for funds and requested bed linen and other equipment. Much of the material required was gathered in through a scheme set up in 1911 whereby people in the city promised to provide items in times of national emergency.[45]

In September 1914 the hospital was taken over by the 6th (London) Field Ambulance as a 15-bed field hospital to replace tented beds set up at Old London Road. Although administered by the army, local VADs continued to assist at the hospital. Matters changed in early December, when Bricket House was mobilised by the War Office as a hospital with 40 beds specifically for troops stationed locally. From this point the nursing and household staff came from 38th Herts under Mrs Boycott, who appointed a resident sister-in-charge and two trained nurses. The VADs were organised into three nursing shifts, with the remainder taking on

Figure 3.5 Silvia, Betty and Gwendolen Glossop of the Voluntary Aid Detachment.
© Diana Bennett

household and kitchen duties.[46] The commandant also started a sewing room where local women came to mend hospital linen and items of kit belonging to patients. Members of well-known St Albans families served with the VADs. Lady Grimston, the Countess of Verulam's daughter-in-law, volunteered at the hospital part-time throughout the war and all three daughters of Canon Glossop and his wife Frances served there from August 1914 (Figure 3.5). Silvia, the eldest, worked part-time in charge of the cooking: she was so successful that the commander of a locally based field ambulance unit sent some of his men to her for instruction. Silvia left in 1916 to cook at a military hospital in France. Her sister Gwendolen remained at the hospital throughout the war and by 1918 was a staff nurse in the operating theatre.[47] Christine Green, younger daughter of Alderman William Green, also worked at the Bricket House Red Cross Hospital as a cook from 1915 and Kathleen Gape, wife of Ernest (the military service representative on the St Albans City Military Service Tribunal), also took on a part-time role in the hospital throughout the war. Working alongside the VADs were medical officers of the Royal Army Medical Corps (RAMC), who attended the patients throughout the war years apart from three months in 1915, when local doctors took over. From May 1916 Major Grossart Wells, a local doctor, was in surgical and medical charge of the hospital.

From the start there was fundraising for and gifts were given to Bricket House to ensure that the hospital continued to function. Although such private support was important, the hospital accounts for 1917 show that well over half the total income came in the form of government grants.[48] Total income for that year, including an estimate for gifts, was just over £2,450; Figure 3.6 shows the percentages of income from different sources.

The largest amount raised from a public entertainment, £140, was a share of the proceeds from a fête held in Samuel Ryder's garden in Upper Lattimore Road. A similar amount came from entertainments put on specially to raise funds for the hospital. The remainder was from collections made at public events such as football matches and gifts from the Mayor's Waste Paper Fund. In addition, just over £140 came from individual donations, which ranged from £10 given by Walter Reynolds, who audited the accounts, to 1s ½d from Michael Hesketh Prichard, aged about eight. There was also a grant from the Hertfordshire branch of the British Red Cross Society of just over £200. It is interesting to note that the overall amount provided by the British Red Cross was almost the same as the amount donated by the people of St Albans to the society over the same period.[49]

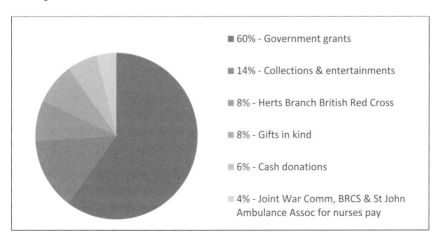

■ 60% - Government grants

■ 14% - Collections & entertainments

■ 8% - Herts Branch British Red Cross

■ 8% - Gifts in kind

■ 6% - Cash donations

■ 4% - Joint War Comm, BRCS & St John Ambulance Assoc for nurses pay

Figure 3.6 Sources of income for Bricket House Military War Hospital in 1917.

By far the largest item of annual expenditure for the hospital, over £1,000, was for provisions. This was somewhat offset by gifts of foodstuffs, although the only items known to have been given in 1917 were vegetables grown in the flower borders at Clarence Park. However, if a letter of thanks in the *Herts Advertiser* of 8 August 1915 for gifts the previous month of eggs, milk, pigeons, soup, cakes and jam – as well as an assortment of fruit and vegetables – is indicative, public support for the hospital was substantial throughout the war. The Joint War Committee of the British Red Cross Society and the St John Ambulance Association paid the salaries of the two professional nurses employed at the hospital. Judging by a staff list in the Red Cross archives, most nurses stayed for a very short period, sometimes only weeks. Nurse Lillian Parsons was unusual in that she stayed for 12 months from February 1917.[50] It is difficult to say why nurses remained at the hospital for such short periods of time, but it is known that qualified nurses often found it difficult to work with VADs, as many of the former felt the involvement of these unqualified members of staff in nursing work undermined their professional status. In addition, some nurses believed that the upper- and middle-class VADs would not be up to the hard work expected of them in a hospital. At Bricket House professional nurses would have been greatly outnumbered by VADs and this may have had a hand in the high rate of turnover in qualified nursing personnel.

From late 1916 general medical supplies for the hospital came via the St Albans Red Cross War Hospital Supply Depot in Market Place, which, as well as supplying Bricket House and the County of Middlesex War Hospital at Napsbury, also sent items to other hospitals in England and France. During the influenza epidemic, which started in October 1918, the depot sent 30 pneumonia jackets to Bricket House. These were padded jackets designed to keep the heat in and assist with breathing. The hospital was badly hit by the epidemic, with 17 patients dying and many of the personnel affected. Volunteer RAMC orderlies lent a hand by taking over some of the night duties. VADs who had left the hospital returned to help and a number of local women also came to assist, including Frances Glossop, who volunteered as a part-time nurse in October 1918.[51]

By the time the hospital closed at the end of January 1919 almost 2,300 in-patients had been treated at Bricket House, 300 operations carried out and over 2,000 out-patients seen as well as disabled men receiving massage. When the equipment had been dispersed the treasurer was able

Figure 3.7 The YMCA centre in Spicer Street. © YMCA. Image: Cadbury Research Library: Special Collections, University of Birmingham

to donate £770 to the Hertfordshire Demobilisation Committee. For their work in running Bricket House Lota Boycott and Lady Thomson were awarded MBEs.[52]

Entertaining the troops

As well as medical provision there was also a need to maintain morale among the men through the provision of entertainment and recreational facilities for the off-duty soldier. To this end the YMCA quickly erected several tents around the city. Within a fortnight additional arrangements were being made by the council and several churches to provide 'facilities for brightening the lives of the soldiers now quartered with us, and [offer] them inducements for spending their time more profitably than by walking about the streets and lanes when off duty'.[53] Of course, what is really meant by this statement is that it was hoped the facilities would keep many of the soldiers out of the local public houses. In addition to recreation rooms, the YMCA offered a regular programme of evening entertainment. These concerts and lectures relied greatly on local talent, and perhaps enthusiasm flagged slightly after a year of war, as the *Herts Advertiser* gave good coverage to a plea from the YMCA for 'volunteers from the city to organise concert parties or some form of entertainment ... in order to relieve the pressure on the canteen tent' (Figure 3.7).[54]

Figure 3.8 Mrs Dearbergh with her gift from the 1/7th Essex Regiment. © Hertfordshire Archives and Local Studies (DE/X1030/4E)

Recreation rooms for troops were also established at several churches, including Trinity, St Saviour's, Spicer Street and St Paul's, run by members of the congregations. One of the first to act was St Saviour's, which, in late August 1914, erected two tents on the vicarage lawn: a large one used for reading, writing and entertainments, with a refreshments counter, and a smaller one for games. In those early weeks the ladies of the church, with input from soldiers, put on concerts nearly every evening, and the churchwarden provided cinematic entertainment for audiences of up to 300 soldiers.[55] By October the facilities at St Saviour's were proving so popular that the church put out an appeal for daily newspapers, which boy scouts collected from donors' houses each afternoon. St Saviour's new parish hall opened in November 1914, but the following May the army requisitioned part of the building, an arrangement that stayed in place until March 1918. Despite this, the ladies of the parish found space to run a canteen for soldiers. Profits made from the canteen were used to purchase New Testaments, presented to members of the 2/6th South Staffordshires in 1916.

At the beginning of the war the council and the military agreed that Pageant House, at the junction of Victoria Street and Upper Marlborough Road, should be utilised as a social club for soldiers rather than be used for billeting. The basement was turned into cloakrooms. On the ground floor there was a large refreshment room, reading and writing rooms and two games rooms. Space on the first floor was allotted to non-commissioned officers (NCOs) and the top floor was used for concerts and games. The building was fitted out at nominal or no cost by local businesses and a call for the permanent loan of such items as wicker chairs and large pot plants ran in the *Herts Advertiser*.[56] Pageant House was run by a joint committee of civilian and military representatives under Captain T.C. Macauley of the Church Army and was heavily dependent on financial support from the public through collections and donations.

A military recreation room called 'The Trumpet' was set up in Union Lane (now Normandy Road) for troops billeted in the area by Frederick and Amy Dearbergh, whose home, Osterhills, was nearby. An old pub sign from a former Holywell Hill drinking establishment was found when turning out the building – a materials store belonging to building contractor J.T. Bushell – to make room for the soldiers, hence the unusual name. When the 1/7th Essex departed they presented Amy with a trumpet with thanks for the help she had provided (Figure 3.8).[57] Local people did their best to entertain the troops in different ways. A correspondent in the local press suggested in August 1914 that residents should invite a few soldiers to visit on Sunday afternoons: 'The men are most grateful for the quiet time they can spend reading, writing and smoking. I find they also enjoy a good tea.'[58]

As mentioned above, the writing of letters to family and friends was a regular occupation for many soldiers away from home for the first time and the provision of writing rooms and stationery quickly became a central task for welfare organisations and philanthropic individuals. The mayor, Horace Slade, personally supplied stationery for soldiers in the weeks after the outbreak of war. The following year Trinity church followed suit and in November reported posting 31,000 soldiers' letters during the year.[59] The much-frequented YMCA centres in St Albans posted, in just one week, 4,500 letters on behalf of soldiers.[60]

The public library opened its doors on Sundays just for the soldiers. The importance of the library as a recreational space for the troops was stressed when the War Office proposed taking over the building for billeting purposes in November 1914. The council won the argument at a time when most public buildings in the area were requisitioned to house troops.[61] The popularity of the reading room among soldiers is indicated by the fact that in April 1915 the library had 310 military members, many of them from the professions.[62]

In contrast, physical exercise could be had at the local swimming baths, made available to the troops for set periods every day.[63] From March 1915 officers billeted in the area could take advantage of a generous offer to play a round of golf for half the usual fee at the Verulam Golf Club. NCOs and other ranks could play too, provided they were members of recognised clubs. Access to the course was restricted because the ASC was in occupation, as mentioned earlier.[64] This new source of income somewhat made up for a dramatic drop in club membership caused by the war, which placed the club in serious financial difficulties.[65] Cricket and football matches were arranged on a casual basis between different military units, schools or other organisations. Private William Stocker of the RAMC, stationed in St Albans at the beginning of 1915, was a keen football player. In a letter to his girlfriend he wrote about a game played against the London Irish Rifles that his team won 4–2, adding 'We are the first to beat the Irish Rifles.'[66]

Many local people welcomed the chance to watch military sports, as local clubs were no longer staging events owing to the war. When sports arranged for Whit Monday 1915 in Clarence Park were cancelled at the last moment after units of the 2nd London Division received orders to move, Horace Slade stepped in and with a committee of officers from several battalions arranged a sporting programme, which was much enjoyed by a crowd of over 6,000 people. The men and officers took part in all sorts of races, on foot and bicycle. Following a tug-of-war, proceedings finished with four rounds of boxing, these being the semi-finals and final of the Brigade Championship Cup.[67] Two weeks later a sports programme was given at the home of the Dearberghs, with Frederick helping to organise the races and his wife Amy providing the tea and most of the prizes. Events that day included a horse race for officers, handicapped by having to ride bareback on transport horses, a pillow fight and a race in which each participant had to find his footwear from among a pile of boots, put them on and run back to the finish line.[68]

By 1916 soldiers – either in groups or individually – were taking part in numerous local entertainments, often to support war charities. Their duties as soldiers, however, always took priority. In March 1917 several soldiers were ordered to withdraw from a planned concert as there was an outbreak of measles in the city.[69] The following week, however, the men in khaki were given the all-clear to participate in a St Patrick's Day concert at the Liberal Club. The troops performed at the Abbey Institute, YMCA centres and the Patriotic Club, gave lectures and led church services. Drumhead services were held in the better weather and in winter months there were church parades, usually at churches near to where the regiments were billeted. The London Irish Rifles were housed at St Albans High School for Girls and marched, with regimental band playing, to the Roman Catholic church in Beaconsfield Road to attend a military mass in October 1914.[70]

With two military hospitals in the immediate area, entertainment was also provided for wounded soldiers. For example, in 1916 Elizabeth Chegwyn, headmistress of Birklands School for Girls on London Road, invited two parties of soldiers from the County of Middlesex War Hospital at Napsbury for an afternoon. On the first occasion 30 men attended but unfortunately it rained and they were confined to taking tea in the gym and listening to a concert performed by the girls. The second party of 50 men were favoured by better weather and after tea, at the soldiers' request, a game of cricket was played. To make an even contest the soldiers bowled underarm and batted left-handed. The result was a win for the girls, 29 runs to 26. In addition, bowls and clock golf were played and the soldiers were loath to leave when the cars came for them.[71]

In 1916, when Kathleen Ryder, daughter of Samuel, celebrated her twenty-first birthday with a garden party, convalescent soldiers from Bricket House and Napsbury were among the guests.[72] On another occasion 30 military patients from Napsbury were given a tour of the cathedral, the Salvation Army's musical instruments factory and Day's hat factory, where they saw military sun helmets being manufactured. The outing ended once again with tea and a concert by the pupils of Birklands.[73]

The proximity of St Albans to the capital allowed off-duty soldiers of the 2nd London Division in particular the chance to spend free time visiting home if they could get a weekend travel permit. On a Sunday night trains would be crowded with men returning to their billets. Not all could be given leave, however, and there are reports of hundreds of friends and family making the trip to St Albans from London by bus and train. Unaccompanied women could find safe lodgings, as Private Stocker mentions the existence of a YWCA on Victoria Street in a letter to his girlfriend when asking whether she could visit St Albans for the weekend.[74]

The soldiers and their visitors had money to spend, giving the local economy a valuable boost. 'Tommy' spent his money on 'tobacco, eatables and other refreshments, newspapers and innumerable knickknacks'. The local hairdressers also did a good trade, and:

> a visit to the little huckster shops in the back streets, where
> large numbers of the men are billeted, at about supper time,
> will provide an object lesson as to Tommy's tastes ... he shows
> a strong penchant for bloater paste, jams and marmalades, cold
> ham, kippers and bloaters, tinned salmon, saveloys, and tell it
> not in Gath, German sausage. As the army commissariat does
> not include fish on the military menu, Tommy naturally displays
> a fancy for the fried variety with chipped potatoes so liberally
> on sale nightly in our midst. Penny bazaars, where needles,
> cotton, plates, buttons, cups, glassware, paper serviettes, and a
> score of other little bachelor and domestic requirements can be
> purchased, are also well patronised by the men in khaki.[75]

Not all soldiers spent their money in the shops, cafes and pubs of St Albans, as there were pleasures of a more earthly kind to be had in the city. The area near the army veterinary hospital was reportedly a popular haunt of prostitutes. Here two women, the wives of serving soldiers, were arrested and found guilty of immoral behaviour. They were sentenced to 14 days' imprisonment and as a result their children were placed in the care of the workhouse.[76] In another case two women were charged with keeping a disorderly house in Sopwell Lane where soldiers were reportedly allowed to stay overnight and were supplied with beer despite the property being unlicensed. Found guilty, the two women were sentenced to three months' hard labour. At a magistrate's hearing one of the defendants was asked about her activities and replied 'how do you expect me to exist on 31s a week?' When it was pointed out that she had existed, at the most, on 20s a week before her husband went to war, she had no answer. It was noted that before the war she had kept a good, clean home and that her children were well cared for.[77]

Although no records appear to have survived regarding numbers of soldiers visiting prostitutes in St Albans, the Orderly Book for 74 Squadron at London Colney records that between December 1917 and March 1918 three officers and two NCOs were either sent to or returned from hospitals known to specialise in venereal disease cases.[78] There is no direct evidence linking these cases to St Albans, but the city was the nearest large urban area to the airfield and RFC personnel were known to frequent its cafes, restaurants and bars, and perhaps some unlicensed premises too.

Figure 3.9 Waiting for King George V to pass on his way to Gorhambury to review the troops, 1914. © Hertfordshire Archives and Local Studies (NE980/AA/14a)

Enthusiasm for the military

The enthusiasm shown by the people of St Albans towards the troops was widespread. There was much excitement at the visits of King George V and Lord Kitchener to review units of 2nd London Division on 18 and 29 September 1914, respectively (Figure 3.9). The large crowds that gathered on these occasions were not unique: on 23 August 1914 a military band concert in Market Place had to be called off as the crush of people made it impossible for the band to play.[79] Likewise, when some of the London battalions left to undertake training in November 1914 a number of people turned out to wave them off from the Abbey station. There was a great deal of noise and commotion at their departure and afterwards:

> The old city has looked very slow with so many of these bright and hearty young soldiers away during the week and certainly when the day comes for St Albans to cease to be a garrison town, as it certainly is at present, it will be a sad day for the local community. *Tipperary* nowadays raises a lump in the throat of the most hardened Britisher but rendered by a military band playing troops to a railway station it seemed to strike home with extra force and many in the crowds near the railway station were by no means unaffected.[80]

Good relations between the army and local people were fostered by the assistance provided by soldiers in times of crisis. One example of this occurred in September 1914, when the garage occupied by Herts Motors on London Road caught fire. Soldiers billeted in nearby Paxton Road were quick to take up the role of fire fighters, forming bucket chains along the passages of the houses to get a supply of water to the rear of the burning garage. Other soldiers assisted residents of adjacent properties to remove furniture and other belongings, including chickens, to places of safety.[81] Local people were credited with taking a keen interest in the troops billeted in the city and, as with their own men who had gone to bear arms, when the time came for them to leave 'the good wishes of the people at home have gone forth with them to the battlefield'.[82]

This was particularly true of the men from battalions of the 2nd London Division, the first troops to arrive in St Albans. As early as November 1914 the vicar of St Saviour's Church declared the 1/24th Londons 'seem like our own soldiers'.[83] Such sentiments of public affection endured beyond the time when the battalion deployed to France. In July 1915 the vicar of St Saviour's ordered 500 chocolate bars to be sent to survivors of the 1/24th Londons, receiving thanks with a note that they had spent 16 days in the front line.[84] Assistance to the unit from the parish continued as a working party was set up to make socks, flannel vests, scarves and mittens for the troops that winter.[85]

It was reported in the local press that in many homes in St Albans there was keen grief at the losses, 'many of the young soldiers having come to be regarded by their hosts after so long a residence amongst them almost as members of the family'.[86] St Saviour's held two memorial services in 1915, for the dead of the 1/24th Londons and for the 1/17th Londons and 1/4th and 1/7th Essex regiments, all of whom had been billeted locally.[87] The surviving soldiers of the regiments, especially from 2nd London Division, did not forget their time in St Albans and kept in touch with the families they had got to know.[88]

For men heading to war St Albans proved to be a welcoming staging post on their path from civilian to soldier. A neat summary of the feelings of soldiers towards the city and its inhabitants is found in the pages of the history of the 21st Londons (1st Surrey Rifles), of whose battalions both the 1st and 2nd spent time in St Albans:

> We cannot attempt to describe life at St Albans without immediate mention of the hospitality and kindness of its citizens in general and our billet-owners in particular. Thanks to their public spirit and splendid arrangements everything possible for our military training and our general comfort was offered and by their ceaseless private efforts many joys were added for the benefits of men, numbers of whom were, alas, destined to taste them there for the last time.[89]

Notes

1. The twelve counties were: Bedfordshire, Cambridgeshire, Essex, Hertfordshire, Huntingdonshire, Kent, Middlesex, Norfolk, Northamptonshire, Suffolk, Surrey and Sussex.

2. See K.W. Mitchinson, *Defending Albion: Britain's home army, 1908–1919* (Basingstoke, 2005), for a full account of British home defence planning before and during the First World War.

3. The National Archives (TNA), WO 33/729, *Emergency Scheme B – Reinforcement of Central Force North of the Thames by Troops from Aldershot/Salisbury Plain Training Centre*, 1915.

4.   E.A. James, *British regiments, 1914–1918* (London, 1978), lists all eight battalions as being in the St Albans area between August 1914 and March 1915.

5.   Ibid. This footnote also applies to the following text.

6.   Mitchinson, *Defending Albion*, p. 142.

7.   TNA, WO 33/782, *Composition of the Headquarters of Home Forces*, October 1916; WO 33/812, Distribution of Home Defence Troops (corrected to 1 March 1917).

8.   As there is no mention of the 26th Graduated Battalion after August 1917, when it is listed as forming at St Albans, it is probable that the unit was either quickly disbanded or absorbed into another training battalion.

9.   The information on training units based in and around St Albans during 1917–18 was drawn from James, *British regiments* and various documents held under TNA WO 33 including WO 33/837, *Distribution of Home Defence Troops and Reserve Units at Summer Stations, 1917*; WO 33/843, *Composition of Headquarters Home Forces*, October 1917.

10.   See E.B. Ashmore, *Air defence* (London, 1929), for the full story of the development of the London Air Defence Area during the First World War.

11.   The latter guns were probably QF 13-pounder 9-cwt guns. This was an 18-pounder field gun modified to fire a 13-pounder shell. It was one of the standard British anti-aircraft guns of the First World War.

12.   Donnington House is now called Mallinson House.

13.   Imperial War Museums (IWM), 17/3 (141) 0, Aeroplane Raids 1918 – Reports compiled by the Intelligence Section, GHQ Home Defence, May 1918.

14.   The squadrons were 36 (Home Defence) and 44 (Home Defence).

15.   Royal Air Force Museum (RAFM), X001–3532, Personal diary: *A short life and a gay one: diary of Frank Best, 1893–1917*. The book was written some time after the war, most probably by R.D. Best, brother of Frank Best, based on the diaries and letters of his late brother.

16.   C. Bowyer, *Albert Ball VC* (Manchester, 2002), pp. 156–7, and <www.gracesguide.co.uk/Albert_Ball> accessed 9 February 2016.

17.   M. Chorlton, *Forgotten aerodromes of World War 1* (Manchester, 2014), pp. 82–3.

18.   War Office, *Manual of military law* (London, 1914). See pp. 179–82 for history of billeting and pp. 475–82 for terms of billeting under the Army Act.

19.   'In the hands of the military', *Herts Advertiser* (*HA*), 15 August 1914.

20.   D. Broom, *My St Albans memories: an oral history of life and times in St Albans* (St Albans, 2001), pp. 77–8, pp. 85–6.

21.   London Irish Rifles Association, Chapter 1: Mobilisation, Training and First Actions, August 1914 to March 1915, <www.londonirishrifles.com> accessed 16 February 2016.

22.   'The mayor appeals for blankets', *HA*, 3 October 1914.

23.   'Beds for Tommies', *HA*, 3 October 1914.

24.   HALS, HCC HEd/5/19/1, St Albans City Local Education Sub-Committee Minutes, 1913–21, September 1914.

25.   'The troops and the schools', *HA*, 5 September 1914.

26.   'Schools and the military', *HA*, 12 September 1914.

27.   H. Chapin, *Soldier and dramatist: being the letters of Harold Chapin* (London, 1917), pp. 48, 53, 55.

28. 'Feeding the troops', *HA*, 22 August 1914.

29. Chapin, *Soldier and dramatist*, p. 36.

30. Museum of St Albans Library, Oral History (Tape 5), unpublished interview, recorded by Broom, *St Albans Memories*.

31. Ibid.

32. P. Simkins, *Kitchener's army: the raising of the new armies, 1914–1916* (Barnsley, 2007), p. 246.

33. 'Troops at St Albans. An insight into billeting', *HA*, 6 February 1915.

34. 'Local war news', *HA*, 5 September 1915.

35. War Office, *Musketry Regulations Pt.2 – Rifle Ranges and Musketry Appliances* (London, 1910).

36. HALS, SBR/871, Letter from Stanley M. Robinson, Secretary of the St Albans Chamber of Commerce in Report of Highways and Plans and Nuisances Sub-committee, 23 November 1915.

37. 'Defying the bullets. Fearless but unwise cyclist at St Albans', *HA*, 21 July 1917.

38. HALS, DE/V E170, Correspondence and papers, April–September 1915, 27 September 1915. HALS, DE/V E171, Correspondence and papers, October 1915–March 1916, 1 November 1915.

39. HALS, DE/V E180, Correspondence and papers, March–September 1919, 16 October 1919.

40. Verulam Golf Club Ltd, General Committee Minute Book, 1912–18.

41. The VTC was formed in November 1914: see Chapter 2.

42. 'The horse hospital – what the AVC is doing at St Albans – an Advertiser view', *HA*, 2 September 1916. Following section relates to same footnote.

43. Cold-shoeing is a method of fitting horse shoes without heat.

44. K. Acland, 'A town voluntary aid detachment', *Journal of the Royal Army Medical Corps*, 51/2 (1928), p. 121.

45. 'Voluntary aid. Appeal for funds', *HA*, 8 August 1914.

46. Acland, 'A town voluntary aid detachment', p. 122; 'Bricket House Record of Valuable War Work', *HA*, 8 February 1919.

47. British Red Cross Archives, hospital record card no. 493, Bricket House Red Cross Hospital, St Albans.

48. HALS, DE/V Q58, Correspondence, papers and leaflets including St Albans and District British Red Cross accounts, 1917, Red Cross accounts for 1917 including Bricket House.

49. British Red Cross Archive, hospital record card no. 493, Bricket House Hospital, St Albans.

50. Ibid.

51. Ibid.

52. Acland, 'A town voluntary aid detachment', pp. 122–3; 'Bricket House Record of Valuable War Work', *HA*, 8 February 1919.

53. 'Entertainment for the troops', *HA*, 29 August 1914.

54. 'Entertaining the soldiers', *HA*, 21 August 1915.

55. 'Entertainment for the troops', *HA*, 29 August 1914.

56. 'Pageant House open', *HA*, 5 September 1914.

57. 'The call of the trumpet', *HA*, 17 October 1914.

58. 'Correspondence: "a suggestion"', *HA*, 29 August 1914.

59. 'Trinity soldiers' recreation room', *HA*, 13 November 1915.

60. 'Entertaining the soldiers', *HA*, 21 August 1915.

61. 'St Albans Library – quarterly meeting', *HA*, 23 January 1915.

62. 'St Albans Library', *HA*, 24 April 1915.

63. 'Soldiers at the baths', *HA*, 29 August 1914.

64. Verulam Golf Club Ltd, General Committee Minute Book, March 1915.

65. HALS, DE/V E173, Correspondence and papers, July–November 1916, Letter from Verulam Golf Club to Lord Verulam, 6 November 1916.

66. William Stocker, *Letters of Private William Stocker*, 1/5th (London) Field Ambulance (in private hands).

67. 'Military sports at St Albans', *HA*, 29 May 1915.

68. 'Sports at Oster Hills', *HA*, 12 June 1915.

69. 'Successful railway concert at the Abbey Institute', *HA*, 17 March 1917.

70. 'Troops at St Albans', *HA*, 24 October 1914.

71. IWM, E.J.1106, Birklands School Magazine, Summer 1916. Clock golf is a lawn game in which players putt to a hole in the centre of a circle from successive points on its circumference. Source: Oxford Dictionary.

72. 'Social events of the year', *HA*, 30 December 1916.

73. 'Soldier patients entertained', *HA*, 11 December 1915.

74. Stocker, *Letters*.

75. 'Troops at St Albans', *HA*, 12 September 1914. Note: Gath was one of the five principal cities of the Philistines.

76. HALS, PS21/2/22, Petty Sessions Register 1915–19, 8 January 1917.

77. Ibid., 31 May 1917.

78. RAFM, X006–7001, Orderly Book of No.74 Squadron (RFC), December 1917–March 1918.

79. 'Visiting day', *HA*, 29 August 1914.

80. 'Troops at St Albans', *HA*, 7 November 1914.

81. 'Great St Albans fire', *HA*, 12 September 1914.

82. 'Review of local events: matters military', *HA*, 1 January 1916.

83. HALS, DP96A/11/2, St Saviour's parish magazine, November 1914.

84. Ibid., August 1915.

85. Ibid., November 1915.

86. 'The London regiments. Heavy casualties reported', *HA*, 5 June 1915.

87. 'Memorial services', *HA*, 4 December 1915.

88. 'A narrow escape', *HA*, 15 May 1915.

89. *War Record of the 21st London Regiment (1st Surrey Rifles) 1914–1919* (London, 1927).

CHAPTER 4

Everyday life in wartime

At home, school, in the workplace and even at brief moments of leisure the war pervaded every aspect of daily life for the men, women and children of St Albans. They opened their doors to strangers in khaki, sewed and saved, organised fêtes and flag days, crept around in darkened streets, kept the curtains tightly closed lest a chink of light attract a Zeppelin bomb, and venerated their fighting men in life and death.

In drawing a picture of the daily lives of the people of St Albans during the war it is impossible to ignore the importance of the *Herts Advertiser*. It is perhaps hard to perceive a time when people queued anxiously to buy a local weekly newspaper to find out about the latest war news as it affected them. However, this is how influential, trusted and vital the newspaper was throughout the war years and how invaluable it has been in providing a record of those times. From its tightly packed columns we know that the realities of war on the home front were spelt out for the people of St Albans before a single shot had been fired by British troops.[1] Writing on 15 August 1914, editor Frederick Usher stated: 'Those of us who are spared the horrors of actual participation in the work at the fighting lines have duties not less pressing and we must see to it that no selfish motives shall clog the wheels of the machine at home.'[2]

Billeting officers had already called: a new experience for the people of St Albans, many of whom were at first inclined to view their enquiries as an interference with the sanctity of the home. Rifleman Patrick MacGill was one of those soldiers billeted in St Albans in 1914. In a memoir he wrote:

> It was not until we were unceremoniously dumped amidst the peaceful inhabitants of a city that slumbers in the shadow of an ancient cathedral that I felt I was in reality a soldier. Here we were to learn that there is no novelty so great for the newly enlisted soldier as that of being billeted, in the process of which

Figure 4.1 Soldiers enjoying a bit of free time in Upper Culver Road. © Andy Lawrence

> he finds himself left upon an unfamiliar doorstep like somebody
> else's washing.[3]

While all was bustle and excitement in the newly garrisoned city
(Figure 4.1), reports of what was happening at the front were scarce. At
the end of August Usher wrote:

> The censorship at the front is now so strict that comparatively
> little news has reached us from the great battlefield of Europe
> since we went to press with our last edition ... We know that
> heavy fighting is going on along the whole line but we are not
> permitted to know the results from day to day.[4]

A small advertisement published in September 1914 invited readers to
forward to the editor copies of any letters received from local men fighting
at the front that included details of their experiences. Many letters were
received in response to this appeal, including some sent directly to the
editor from the men themselves.[5] These accounts provided telling insights
into the war as lived by local fighting men. For example, this letter from
Herbert Brazier with D Company of the 1st Bedfordshire Regiment, sent
from the front, describes how

We are having rather a rough time of it just now; there are plenty of German shells flying about. We drove the Germans out of a village on the 14th and were heavily fired on by shells and Maxim guns but we managed to take up a position and entrench at night. The next day we were shelled by the German 'Jack Johnsons', as we call them, or the 'Black Marias', so we were forced to retire out of the village about 600 yards. There we took up another position, after working all night, digging ourselves in. We had many killed and wounded, and about thirty captured. The Germans were very kind to the wounded; they dressed their wounds and gave them wine to drink. We had to leave these [men] behind, because they were down in cellars in the people's houses.

Private Brazier went on to describe how D Company hung on for a couple of days and managed to recapture the village after the British artillery bombarded it, adding that 'there were a fine lot of lads in the regiment and when they heard the shells coming they all started to sing'.[6] These homespun reports, together with the latest official news, heavily censored by the government, and details about enlistments, casualties, deaths, missing and prisoners of war (POWs) among local servicemen made the newspaper essential reading. The term 'Roll of Honour' came to hold very significant meaning as the war progressed. The title first appeared in the *Herts Advertiser* above a list of names of those who had answered the call to the Colours. Workplaces, schools, clubs and local villages all supplied to the newspaper names of those who had volunteered or otherwise been called up.[7]

In September that year the archdeacon of St Albans the Hon. Kenneth Gibbs called for churches to post a 'Roll of Honour' listing every man from the parish serving in the forces, to be erected 'conspicuously ... near the main door' of every church. These became the focus for prayers of intercession. The archdeacon clearly intended that the church rolls should be kept current, indicating the status of those listed: for example, 'at the front', 'wounded' or 'Died for King and Country'.[8] Records show that Christ Church in Verulam Road, St Saviour's and St Peter's displayed such lists.[9] It is almost certain that, following the Battle of the Somme in 1916, when many local men lost their lives, 'Rolls of Honour' in the form of war shrines began to appear on the city streets, beyond the confines of the

Figure 4.2 Dedication of Cannon Street war shrine, 1917. Mrs Warner, whose son won the VC, is pictured to the left of the shrine. © Hertfordshire Archives and Local Studies (DE/X1030/1/131)

parish churches (Figure 4.2). There were at least 27 in St Albans, including five in Christ Church parish and 15 in the Abbey parish, made by boys at the technical school in Victoria Street. The street shrine movement began in Hackney, led by evangelical members of the Anglican clergy as part of the 'National Mission for Repentance and Hope', which was organised in response to criticisms made in the press in early 1916 about the Church of England's role in providing spiritual guidance at such a critical time.[10]

Revd Alexander Barff, the incumbent at St Paul's church in Hatfield Road, described the aim of the mission as a call from the Church to the nation to turn to God in sincere repentance. Its message was of the sure hope of God's deliverance for such a repentant people: 'God's word gives sure ground for this great hope.'[11] Barff regularly held street services and a report in the *Herts Advertiser* provides further confirmation of the way the shrines were venerated in the community: 'Another of the impressive intercession services which are being conducted by the clergy of the Abbey Church at the respective "Rolls of Honour" in the parish was held on Friday in Prospect Road.'[12]

Before the war photographs were few and far between in the pages of the local newspaper, but there was a noticeable change in August 1914. Frederick Usher was a keen photographer and honorary secretary of the

St Albans Camera Club, so it is probably no coincidence that the *Herts Advertiser* increasingly told the story of the war in pictures as well as words. This development started with photographs of billeted troops in St Albans participating in military exercises. Photography was an expensive hobby at that time, but a professional photograph taken at a studio was within the means of working-class people and these pictures, often in postcard form, taken of men smartly dressed in uniform before going off to war, also started to appear in the local press. Sadly, they were usually published to mark the loss of a young life, as in the case of 23-year-old Bandsman Cyril Charles Godman, one of the 736 men killed on *HMS Bulwark* when it exploded on the river Medway in November 1914.[13] When men were posted missing their photographs were sometimes included too, as in the case of Private Thomas Bickerton (see Figure 8.6). The paper reported how the Army Records Office had 'intimated' the distressing information to his parents in May 1918. His picture was published along with a request that 'any news from any of the men in his regiment will be gratefully received'.[14] In fact, Bickerton had been taken prisoner at the end of March 1918 and it appears that his family received news of his capture almost three months later, through official channels.[15]

The creation of simple war shrines and the posting of 'Rolls of Honour' show that commemoration did not just take place after the war but was an ongoing feature of daily life for the people of St Albans, supported and encouraged by the press and, of course, the Church.

Living under military rule

The citizens of St Albans quickly had to adapt their way of life to a whole raft of new legislation imposed under the Defence of the Realm Act (DORA), passed four days after war was declared. The Act gave the government and the military unprecedented, wide-ranging powers and control over the lives of people and property. Billeting in people's homes and the requisition of buildings and land came under DORA, as did censorship and strict controls over an individual's right to freedom of speech, including dissent from the popular, patriotic fervour expressed by many in the early days of the war. The all-encompassing restrictions also covered lighting in the home and on the street. As a garrison town, a blackout was imposed on St Albans that lasted throughout the war. It greatly limited the ability of people to go about their business and affected shops, businesses, places of entertainment and the timing of church services.[16]

In the early days of the conflict there were fears about a possible German invasion and the threat of aerial attack by enemy airships and planes, as noted in Chapter 3. Householders had to ensure that no lights were visible through the curtains and enterprising local shops obliged by selling well-advertised 'Zep' (for Zeppelin) blinds. Although not fully reported at the time, local people would have been aware through word of mouth about the bombing of Hertford in October 1915. Nine people lost their lives following a Zeppelin attack, exposing the home front's vulnerability to an entirely new form of warfare.[17]

The Aliens Restriction Act was another piece of legislation passed at the start of the war. Its main purpose was the removal or detention of spies and, although St Albans was no hotbed of intrigue, a number of arrests were made. In addition, as attitudes hardened against 'the enemy' in 1915, this led to one or two unpleasant incidents in St Albans, although nothing on the scale of the anti-German riots that erupted in London and other major cities. Under the Act, all foreign nationals aged over 16 had to register with the local police, providing a photograph and their name, address, marital status and place of employment. The legislation also permitted the deportation of aliens and restricted where they could live. British wives of foreign nationals also had to register as aliens. Eleven days after war was declared two young Austrians were arrested in St Peter's Street while in the city looking for work – one for failing to register and the other for travelling without a permit, which any foreign national was required to have if they wanted to travel five miles beyond where they lived. The magistrates sentenced them to six months' imprisonment with hard labour.[18]

In the autumn of 1914 the *Herts Advertiser* carried several reports of foreign nationals summonsed for not having registered with the police. Some were of German origin but had lived in Britain for many years. Thus publican Henry John Schafer, alias Clark, of Verulam Road, had been brought up by an aunt in England, taken the surname of his godfather and served in the British army for 18 years. The magistrates judged that he had committed a technical offence and fined him 10s and his wife 1s, saying they hoped the couple would take steps as soon as possible to become naturalised and so keep themselves clear of further trouble.[19]

Around the same time the head constable George Whitbread made a number of arrests of alien residents following instructions from the Home Office. These were Germans and Austrians of military age, including businessmen, clerks, artisans and waiters. They were shown 'all consideration possible under the circumstances' and later moved to an internment camp in Wakefield. The news was reported in October 1914 with the comment:

> The arrest and removal of all Germans and Austrians of military age, the segregation of all suspicious aliens and the expulsion of all such from the coast and from areas of military importance, is an unpleasant undertaking which conflicts with our English ideas of freedom and hospitality ... Many innocent Germans may have to suffer inconvenience and loss, but they have the Kaiser to thank for the trouble which has been brought upon them.[20]

Rumours about spies were rife at this time. People with foreign-sounding names and individuals asking too many questions or showing a little too much interest in the comings and goings of the troops in St Albans all came under suspicion. During the first few months of spy mania it looked as if St Albans might be able to chalk up its own success in spy catching, but the 'culprit' turned out to be J.P. Moss, sporting editor of the *Daily Mail*. He came to the city to follow up a story concerning the troops but ended up making the headlines: 'I was apparently taking too close an interest of what was going on around me, for a vigilant corporal suddenly challenged me as to my business.' As a result, Moss was marched by military escort to the guardroom and then by the military police through the streets of St Albans – an experience he described as 'an ordeal'. The matter was soon cleared up and he was a free man again.[21]

The sinking of the *RMS Lusitania* on 7 May 1915, reports of the use of poison gas on soldiers at the front and the growing numbers of casualties all served to harden anti-German feeling, and turned former workmates into enemies. It led to several incidents in the city involving the abrupt dismissal of some employees. Referring to the sinking of the *RMS Lusitania* as 'the greatest crime', the *Herts Advertiser* was quite vitriolic in its claim that people's 'eyes have been opened at last, and they realise, every man of them, that we are at war – grim, deadly, merciless war – with an enemy who is without heart, without honour, without virtue of any kind', adding that many people in the country had needed such a 'drastic physic to correct the malady of their satiated content and selfish indifference'.[22] It was editorials like this that clearly demonstrated the paper's strong patriotic stance throughout the war.

The first of the incidents referred to above involved employees at John Freshwater & Co. Ltd's shoe factory in College Street. They had downed tools in protest against a fellow employee who they claimed had expressed pro-German sentiments during a discussion about the fate of the passenger ship. A deputation 'waited upon the manager', lodging a complaint and declaring that if the service of the man was retained they would decline to resume work. The man was well-thought-of as far as his work was concerned, but nevertheless he was let go with two weeks' pay in lieu of notice.[23] The second case involved E. Oscar Winkler, a German Dane, working for the Deep Well Tool and Boring Company Ltd in Sandridge Road, which at that time was busily engaged on government contracts. The newspaper report stated that the agitation against the presence of Winkler and three workers who were Austrian–Poles had become 'growingly bitter'. The report went on to state that the feeling of the employees was so intense that there might be a cessation of work unless the matter was satisfactorily arranged. The men were persuaded by the management of the loyalty of the Austrian–Poles to the cause of the allies, but failed to make a convincing case for Winkler, who was subsequently sacked.[24] He put his case in a letter published in the following week's paper, stating that he was German 'merely by virtue of conquest and annexation, and have inherited from my ancestors the longing for an independent Schleswig-Holstein under Danish autonomy, similar to the political aspirations of the Polish race'. He pointed out that he had been released from internment after four weeks following a full investigation of his case. He also remarked: 'The demand of the men for my discharge after three years of satisfactory service is due to a misguided patriotism for which my English wife and child will have to suffer.'[25]

People who were wrongly or mistakenly referred to as German sometimes took steps to have such 'slanders' publicly corrected. The following letter, published in the form of an advertisement on the front page of the *Herts Advertiser*, was from William Woolger to the solicitors Messrs Stanley Robinson and Commin:

> I admit that I called your client Mr W.H. Swinton of The Midland Station Hotel 'a German' and that same is utterly untrue. I repeated it having heard others say so. I sincerely regret having done so and tender my sincere apologies and regret for the annoyance [caused] to your client and undertake never to repeat

such a statement in the future. You are of course at liberty to publish this letter so as to endeavour to undo any mischief, which may have been caused by my unguarded statement.[26]

Any resentment people in St Albans continued to feel against Germans went largely unreported, although at the end of the war a local woman was hissed at in the street for giving a cake to a German POW, an incident described as 'not surprising' in a letter to the editor published on 7 December 1918.[27]

Save, save, save

It cost billions of pounds to fight the First World War, resulting in a massive debt that has only recently been repaid.[28] At the time the chancellor of the exchequer, David Lloyd George, speaking in the House of Commons on 5 August 1914, said: 'In this tremendous struggle, finance is going to play a great part. It will be one of the most formidable weapons in this exhausting war.'[29] In January 1916 the *Herts Advertiser* reported that government expenditure on the war was approaching £5 million a day:

> Next year the total expenditure will probably exceed £1,800,000,000, which, with taxation at the present level, would involve a deficit of over £1,400,000,000. The Financial Secretary to the Treasury [Edwin Samuel Montagu] stated that this gigantic sum must be drawn almost entirely from the pockets of the nation in the form of tax or loan.[30]

These figures – shown in the newspaper with all the zeros as above – must have seemed almost incomprehensible to working people who at that time earned just a few pounds a week. Income tax rates more than doubled during the course of the war and wage inflation meant that a higher proportion of the population reached the payment threshold, tripling by 1920. In all, the government's tax income rose from just under £300 million in 1914 to over £1 billion in 1919. Nevertheless, war expenditure outstripped it three to one. The shortfall in 1916 alone was twice the size of the total national debt before the war.[31]

In April of that year the government established the National War Savings Committee, whose purpose was to promote the sale of War Savings Certificates through local associations, targeting in particular the working classes because of what the Bank of England referred to as their 'remarkable prosperity' at that time.[32] The certificates went on sale in June 1916.[33] The following month a 'war savings week' was held in St Albans and on 22 July the local paper reported that 'the gospel of national thrift has been preached from a great variety of pulpits, beginning literally with the churches and embracing practically every kind of community – office, factory and workshop'.[34]

From a slow start, 34 war savings associations were established in the St Albans area, with over 4,700 members (nearly 20 per cent of the population).[35] They were affiliated to the Central War Savings Committee and run by a volunteer secretary whose duties included making out certificates, taking monies from collectors, paying into the Post Office and purchasing certificates.[36] St Saviour's was the first church to set up an association in St Albans,[37] while the most successful locally, in financial terms, was the East Ward Savings Association in Fleetville. Savers could buy 6d coupons or stamps and put them towards purchasing certificates, which cost 15s 6d each, offering a return of 29 per cent over five years.[38] A large war savings clock was erected on the front of the town hall, the hour and minute hands giving the latest update on the number of certificates sold.[39] Throughout this period war savings certificates, war loan stock and war bonds were on offer, but in order to stimulate continuous investment, which the government was relying on to fund the war, there were frequent campaigns, usually instigated at a local level, to draw in the public and their cash.[40] One such was the Victory Loan campaign, launched at the beginning of 1917. The prime movers of the war savings movement in St Albans were Albert and Edith Garrett, who ran the East Ward Savings Association. They took over as honorary secretaries of the central [St Albans] war savings committee and spearheaded the Victory Loan campaign. It was a task Edith Garrett described as 'not always easy', as they were often rebuffed by people who told her they 'objected to the war, to the government and the government's methods'. She said those who objected to the war savings schemes were those who were 'doing well out of the war but seemed unwilling to put their hands in their pockets to help their country'.[41]

At the end of February 1917 the newspaper was able to announce that the people of St Albans had invested £275,000 in Victory Loans, claiming that this splendid record compared favourably with sums raised in many neighbouring towns:

for it must be remembered that in the cathedral city at the present time matters financial are not nearly so flourishing as they are in those centres where there is a large employment in the manufacture of munitions or where troops in large numbers are quartered. On the contrary, there are circumstances, which have led to a very considerable diminution of income for some sections of the community, who find it exceptionally difficult to meet the gradual creeping up of prices of essential commodities.[42]

The pockets of the people of St Albans were continually targeted throughout the war. In March 1918, during Business Men's Week (also called Boom Week), the aim was to raise £65,000 to provide capital for the purchase of 26 aeroplanes for the war effort. Under the headline 'Bravo St Albans!' it was reported that: 'The war saving enthusiasm in St Albans would appear to be boundless; and what is better still, that enthusiasm is eminently practical, as witness the splendid achievement of the city thus far.' The fund was boosted enormously by a £25,000 donation from the mining magnate Jack Barnato Joel of nearby Childwickbury and raised £76,639 following a campaign that saw promotional leaflets dropped from planes flying low over the city by 'daring bird-men'. The daredevil pilots from the Royal Flying Corps based at nearby London Colney also performed an aerobatic display over the city, a spectacle witnessed by over 7,000 people gathered in Market Place.[43]

Even after the war ended appeals continued to be made to invest in war bonds and war savings certificates. 'St Albans Thanksgiving Week' ran from 2 to 7 December 1918, this one event alone raising £133,000[44] (Figure 4.3). This was in addition to over £500,000 raised by the people in and around St Albans by the summer of 1918 through the purchase of war savings certificates, loans and bonds to support the war effort.[45]

It was not just by digging deep to find money to buy government bonds and certificates that people supported the war effort. Goods and materials were in very short supply because of the German blockade of ports and because the country had become so reliant on imports in the pre-war years. In August 1915 the Parliamentary War Savings committee issued a long list of ways in which people could save, including the following: 'No one should build a house for himself at this time; moving (unless to a cheaper house) should be avoided; the purchase of jewellery should be

St. Albans Thanksgiving Week

DECEMBER 2nd—7th.

Show your Gratitude for what the Guns have done for You.

In many a desperate fight it was to THE GUNS that our advancing armies looked to blast the way to Victory. And it is to YOU that your country now looks for that financial support which is to-day as necessary as artillery support was in the day of battle. Lend your money to the nation. Buy the biggest Bond you can, or put the biggest sum you can into War Savings Certificates.

Every week
your country still needs
£25,000,000

from the sale of National War Bonds. For months to come every patriotic man and woman must continue to save and lend. Week by week immense sums will still be required to feed, clothe and equip the millions of men in our armies, and to bring home those who can be spared from the post of duty at the earliest possible moment.

Gun Week is your opportunity to help in that great home-coming of the Victors. Invest your savings, your earnings, your profits, your dividends—the cash in your pockets, the balance at your bank. Buy War Bonds. Buy War Savings Certificates.

LEND
all you can

15/6 Invested to-day, becomes in five years £1. In ten years **26/-**

No other Investment Pays so well as, or is so safe as

WAR SAVINGS CERTIFICATES
AND
NATIONAL WAR BONDS.

Buy your Certificates and at the Town Hall and take them to the Gun in St. Peter's Street to be stamped by THE MEN BEHIND THE GUN.

Figure 4.3 The planned war savings gun week was turned into thanksgiving week in December 1918. © Hertfordshire Archives and Local Studies

discountenanced.' The committee issued leaflets setting out how people could save on essential foods such as bread. It also published a whole series of money-saving suggestions for men, from shaving themselves to avoiding smoking in strong winds.[46]

Thrift and economy were everyday companions for the poor, but the comfortable middle classes also had to learn to go without as costs rose and many goods were in short supply. Everything from old newspapers to potato peelings had a value. As Florence Petty stated in a book first published in January 1917, 'Every good cook or housekeeper is, in these days, a good patriot.'[47]

Giving a helping hand

Almost 18,000 charities were established during the war, resulting in new laws to regulate the sector. In 1916 the War Charities Act was instituted, making registration for public appeals compulsory.[48] The causes that people in St Albans took to their hearts were many in number but first and foremost were the families of soldiers, the men at the front and the wounded. One of the first organisations to step in and provide help for families was the Soldiers' and Sailors' Families' Association, established during an earlier conflict. The honorary secretary and treasurer of the St Albans division was Ernest Gape.[49] By the second week of the war the association was already helping families in need, preventing, in the words of Gape,

> a fearful amount of hardship and distress that would otherwise have been incurred among the families and children and dependants of soldiers suddenly called up on 4 August, when no preparation had been made by the country for separation allowances and such like.[50]

The association was merged into the Naval and Military Pensions Committee in July 1916 and the work then came under government control and regulation, with funds provided by the Ministry of Pensions. This same committee was responsible for war disability pensions, which became statutory in 1917. This development was an important acknowledgement by the State of its duty of care to the men who had suffered physical or mental injury in its service. Some 27 per cent of men who fought in the war received a pension or gratuity from the government for disabilities attributable to their war service.[51] The people of St Albans were described as 'Samaritans' in the local press, particularly with regard to the way that the wounded soldiers returning from the Somme and other battles were supported:

> In men and in money the ancient city has vied successfully, in proportion to its population, with any town in the kingdom, and today its people are shouldering quite cheerfully and willingly another responsibility, that of bringing happiness to the brave fellows who, having fought on the blood-stained battlefields in our different fighting zones, are now disabled and in need of helping hands and warm, homely hearts. Rich and poor alike vie with each other in trying to reduce the inconvenience to which the wounded are subject ... every week the number of persons who seek to do their bit is increased.[52]

Many British POWs suffered despite the best efforts of those on the home front. The mayor set up the Prisoner of War Help Committee in 1915 with the aim of sending every known prisoner from St Albans not provided for by their regimental fund a 5s parcel, together with 4 lbs of bread (sent from Berne in Switzerland), every week. POWs were helped, too, by the St Albans Red Cross Working Party, an organisation that made 'comforts' for the troops – those at the front, the wounded and British POWs. The work was undertaken entirely by volunteers and was chaired throughout the war by Jane Alice Slade, wife of Horace Slade, mayor of St Albans in 1913–14. It was reported in 1916 that in just ten months the working party had made 3,750 garments for soldiers at the front. The work was funded entirely by donations.[53]

Another organisation helping POWs was the Hertfordshire Regiments' Prisoner of War Help Committee. By October 1917 it was supporting 151 prisoners, 14 from St Albans. The cost of each man, including bread, tobacco and cigarettes, was £3 a month. There were, of course, appeals made to support loved ones in other regiments, and all such aid was coordinated through the Red Cross.[54]

The plight of the Belgian refugees, thousands of whom had fled to Britain at the beginning of the war, also struck a chord with the nation. Appeals went out to local councils to set up committees to help them and in September, with the support of local churches and notices published in the local press asking for help, around 160 Belgians came to live in the city.[55]

The local relief committee galvanised support for the Belgian families, ensuring that their first Christmas in exile would be as comfortable as possible.[56] Once the immediate crisis was over and despite the support of local churches, the relief committee, the local chamber of commerce and the people of St Albans, it became clear that more practical help would be needed to enable the families to become self-supporting over the longer term. Options were limited, as there was an agreement between the British and Belgian governments that refugees in this country should not be employed in any trade or industry where British labour was available, and any goods made by refugees could not be sold in the UK to avoid any possible competition with British businesses.[57] This must have made things very difficult for the Belgian refugees, but, with the committee's help and their own enterprise, by May 1916 only one family still needed financial support and plans were made to wind up the Belgian fund.[58]

Through a memoir written by Harold E.L. Mellersh we have an insight into the experience of one St Albans family who housed Belgians. Mellersh was a 2nd Lieutenant with the East Lancashire Regiment and his family lived in Clarence Road. They took in Madame Maria Louwage and her four-year-old daughter Vivienne, while her husband, Florent, remained in Belgium fighting with the Belgian forces. Harold, wounded and home on leave from the front in 1916, wrote:

> I had not been home for six months or so. I found a difference. Belgian refugees had been taken in ... 'Madame', so we called her, but it meant nothing of distance or formality – was vivacious, and temperamental and intriguingly foreign ... As for the little girl ... she became a favourite.[59]

Supporting the troops and the Belgians all took time and effort as well as money, and yet rich and poor alike in St Albans contributed directly, through the many new charities or by supporting an almost daily round of fundraising events. The women of St Albans volunteered in their hundreds to work at the Red Cross War Supply Depot, the St Albans Red Cross Working Party, the two local military hospitals and the many YMCA centres, not just for a week or two but for the duration of the war.

Keeping them off the streets

The arrival in St Albans of large numbers of the military in August 1914 gave rise to much anxiety about the moral welfare of the soldiers and the girls of the neighbourhood. A meeting was organised by Edith Jacob, the sister of the bishop of St Albans, to bring together the girls and to place clearly before them their duties and responsibilities in the 'exceptional circumstances in which the country finds itself'. Miss Jacob was supported in this endeavour by Mrs Church, a stalwart of the St Albans YMCA. At a meeting held in the bishop's garden at Verulam House the two ladies addressed an audience of around 270 young women about how they could play their part 'to help and not hinder what is good in the soldiers'.[60]

At more or less the same time as this meeting was held the council, the churches and other organisations, including the local suffragists, started to take steps to address the same issue. As noted in Chapters 3 and 7, the city council rented Pageant House in Victoria Street to the military to provide a large, centrally located social club for non-commissioned officers and men. The men were also being catered for in the many YMCA centres springing up in the city. The local branch of the Church League for Women's Suffrage then stepped into the debate about the girls and the soldiers, ruffling quite a few feathers. The league had about 50 members in St Albans and in a letter published in the local paper reported on the outcome of a meeting it had held to discuss the problem, outlining the following suggestions:

- A club for girls providing 'wholesome recreation and shelter';
- Employment for girls out of work;
- Crèches for children to help the 'poor mothers in the town [who] are distracted with idle children at home, every available space being filled with men. The children are turned out on the streets and are running wild';
- A list of suggestions for mistresses and their maids, including the proposal that mistresses should re-arrange their maids' time off so they were indoors before 8pm.

This last proposal provoked some correspondence.[61] 'Why cast the first stone at us?' wrote one anonymous correspondent, stating that the comments of the league were an insult to the maids and to the men.[62] Another letter-writer, replying to those who were 'so ready to judge the girls', stated that 'while we are treated in a respectful and social way by the soldiers, we shall still continue to be friendly with them and that we think by so doing we are treating somebody's brother as we should like our own to be treated'. She also pointed out that it was wrong to make it 'bad for all' because of 'a few very young and very ignorant "flappers"'.[63]

One of the above suggestions was implemented, although there is no evidence that it was as a direct result of the suffragists' appeal. The YWCA Girls' Patriotic Club opened at 19 Chequer Street shortly afterwards and provided somewhere for the girls to go, its purpose being to 'attract girls of St Albans to more profitable pastimes than roaming the streets in the evenings, and affording the opportunity for social intercourse with soldiers under proper conditions'.[64] The club was almost certainly cosier than the YMCA recreation tent in St Peter's Street, which was described in autumn and winter 1914 as being so cold it was necessary to have regular concert intervals so that the audience could get up and stamp their feet.[65]

It seems more than likely that sexual contact took place between soldiers and local women. The Poor Law Institution infirmary in Union Lane (now Normandy Road) reported that in 1916 21 babies were born at the infirmary, as against an average of 12 a year over the war years – the majority illegitimate. The numbers of babies born at the infirmary then dropped back before starting to climb again, but without reaching the peak of 1916. Miss Spackman, a member of the Board of Guardians, which managed the Poor Law Institution, gave a possible reason for the decline in the number of illegitimate births. Presenting the Girls' Aid Committee report on 29 February 1918, she claimed that the reduction in numbers was due to 'increased opportunities for good wages'. Whether this implies that the girls referred to were now channelling their energies into earning an 'honest' living is a matter for conjecture. The only other fact we have is that in her 1918 report Miss Spackman referred specifically to four single women who had given birth at the infirmary, stating that they remained in residence at the adjacent workhouse 'for the well being of the race'.[66]

Lessons in wartime

It was not uncommon for children as young as 12 to be in full-time employment in this period and certainly by 14 most had started work. The elementary education returns for the spring term 1914 show over 3,900 children on the school rolls in St Albans.[67] In addition, there were 157 girls attending St Albans High School and 245 boys at St Albans Grammar

Figure 4.4 Camp School, one of many schools requisitioned by the army in August 1914. ©
St Albans Museums (PX9754_T4460)

School.[68] Numbers for the other schools in St Albans in 1914 are not
known. Working-class children shared many of the disruptions caused by
the war with those youngsters who attended the fee-paying schools in the
city. However, while school buildings for rich and poor were requisitioned
and all children regardless of class carried out war work, from making
comforts for the troops to growing vegetables, it was undoubtedly the
poorest whose education suffered the most (Figure 4.4).

The school log books for Garden Fields School, then situated in
Catherine Street, and Priory Park School in Old London Road provide a
fascinating insight into the day-to-day lives of the children and staff at the
two schools.[69] They tell a story of teacher shortages, lack of continuity in
educational studies owing to staff turnover and the requisition of school
buildings, the chronic shortage of even the most basic learning materials,
poor school attendance owing to family demands and malnutrition and
illnesses that afflicted children severely in those days.[70]

St Albans Grammar School headmaster Edgar Montague Jones joined
his regiment, the 1st Herts, ten days before war was declared. He wrote
a letter to the chairman of governors explaining his absence and stating
that he had appointed someone to take his place and would arrange to
visit the school from time to time 'to ensure as far as possible the proper
carrying out of the work'.[71] In the city's rate-financed and voluntary-aided
schools 11 teachers had been called up or enlisted by June 1915.[72] War

supply teachers were drafted in to take their place but all schools were under tight financial constraints, set out in a circular from the Local Government Board dated 4 August 1915, which stated that local education authorities had to ensure that elementary schools had 'no excessive staff'. This meant that schools had to amalgamate classes when staff were ill, had transferred to other schools or had left before a replacement could be appointed. The Garden Fields log book for February 1916 states that, with one teacher transferred to another school, another away with influenza and a third at school but too ill to teach, the headmistress Olivia Lamb had three large classes on her hands and was finding it impossible to adhere to the timetable. A teacher from another school came to help but a month later the headmistress herself was too ill to carry on and permission was given for the school to close for a day and a half. There is evidence that at Garden Fields at least all these problems led to lower standards of achievement among the pupils. In November 1916 the log book recorded:

> Some excellent work has been done during the term. The children in Standard 1 can now all read, some quite nicely and are orderly and attentive and interested in their work. I mention this class especially because of its terrible backward condition last September. The other classes are making very fair progress but it will be some time before they recover from the poor staff and other ups and downs of the last two years. At present there is a teacher for each class.[73]

Paper was in short supply from the beginning of the war and the cost of all paper products rose steeply. The company supplying exercise books to local schools was forced to restrict supplies, with the result that some schools had to resort to using scraps of paper, while others ordered slates for junior departments. It was noted in October 1916 that 'Everything is so expensive and so much less is allowed that it seems almost impossible to provide material for the classes.' Children brought in odd pieces of paper from home and exercise books were used only once or twice a week, with the result that 'writing and setting out is becoming slovenly owing to so much work on scraps'.[74] There were also cutbacks on fuel and lighting, resulting in a note in the Priory Park log book in February 1915 that there were no fires at all on one particular day. Three years later, in January 1918, girls at Garden Fields shivered in their classrooms when the temperature dropped to just above freezing, indicating that the heating and lighting situation continued to deteriorate as the war progressed.[75]

Absenteeism was a major factor and many girls were kept at home to look after younger siblings so that their mothers could go out to work. Others had to stand in queues for hours before and after school to try to buy food for their families. The school log for Garden Fields in February 1918 states: 'It is not uncommon for twenty or more girls to come in too late to be marked. They are often very tired and cold, having been standing since 8am or even earlier. Their best work cannot be expected in such circumstances.'[76]

War work of various kinds was fitted into the school day. A large number of the elementary schools in the county were producing useful articles for wounded soldiers. A *Herts Advertiser* report stated that this war work would 'bring the children into closer touch with the conditions that are prevailing in the country now'. In the same report it was noted that 20 boys from Hatfield Road School had recently made splints and also constructed 1,000 hand-grenade boxes at very short notice, 'the lads working most assiduously and seriously at this task, realising that their handiwork was destined to be taken right up to the firing line'.[77]

Schoolgirls were given the sewing tasks, including making comforts for soldiers. In February 1915 the girls at Garden Fields made 120 scarves, 8 pairs of gloves, 10 helmets, 80 cuffs, 10 caps, 153 pairs of mittens, 4 body belts, 58 pairs of socks and 6 chest protectors for the troops and, in addition, sent 11 large consignments of new and carefully mended garments for, it is believed, Belgian refugees. The school was one of 175 out of a total of 249 girls' and mixed infants' schools across Hertfordshire engaged in 'war needlework'.[78]

The girls at St Albans High School had already sacrificed their school buildings in the first year of the war. A school report published in 1919 stated that the girls had contributed 270 feet of pennies for the Queen's Work for Women Fund, invested in war savings, sent parcels of clothing to families in Camberwell who had been bombed out of their homes, started an allotment garden – as most other private and state schools did – and, with former pupils, raised £25 to endow a bed at the King George's Military Hospital in London.[79]

The war overshadowed many young lives, but perhaps children's sheer resilience and their capacity to enjoy life is demonstrated by the fact that quite a few took the afternoon off from school without permission the day peace was declared.[80]

High- and low-brow pastimes

There were many well-established sporting, social, political and religious clubs and societies in St Albans in this period, popular pastimes including stamp collecting and the study of natural history and archaeology. The war and the restrictions it imposed on daily life disrupted many activities, but most clubs and societies soldiered on. The hurdles they faced included declining membership, because so many men had joined up, difficulties booking public halls, as most had been requisitioned by the military, and organising outings, as there were fewer excursion trains. There are indications too that some activities, such as horse racing, were seen as morally wrong at a time of war.

Local businessman Arthur Phillips, of the St Albans Gas Co., was one of those who spoke out against the sport. At a meeting of shareholders in March 1915 he said:

> This morning I read in the newspaper that at a meeting of influential gentlemen, it was decided that this year the great races are to take place. They say there are to be no picnics and no luncheons but surely it can only be the desire for pleasure or the desire to cultivate that inveterate and highly intellectual amusement of betting? ... Why should not these jockeys, these horse trainers, these vendors of race cards, these gentlemen of the betting fraternity, if they are of suitable age, go to the front?[81]

There were more than 100 members of the Hertfordshire Natural History Society in this period and it remained reasonably active, visiting the Zoological Gardens at Regent's Park in June 1915, putting on an exhibition of specimens at the newly extended County Museum in Hatfield Road in February 1916, visiting Kew Gardens in July that year and holding a field meeting at Royston Common that August with members of the South London Entomological Society.[82] One of its keenest members was Arthur Ernest Gibbs, co-proprietor of the *Herts Advertiser*. He was president of the society until his death in 1917.

Gibbs was also a leading member of the St Albans & Hertfordshire Architectural & Archaeological Society, which held its meetings at the County Museum. As the war progressed it became increasingly difficult to secure speakers and organise excursions and in the winter season 1917/18 the society arranged for members to be given free access to the museum's programme of lectures on general technical, artistic and scientific subjects in return for a payment of £5 by the Society.[83] In the summer of 1916 the society had its own battle, with John Wells of Fifth Avenue, New York, the owner of an historic building on the corner of St Peter's Street and Spencer Street. There were plans for the old property to be demolished and for some oak carving to be removed and shipped to America.[84] It was a battle that the society did not win, despite many protest letters.[85]

Children, too, enjoyed some new and interesting pastimes. Scouts were recruited to act as military orderlies, reporting the arrival of troops, collecting soldiers' washing, distributing leaflets for the mayor and acting as patients for the Royal Army Medical Corps to practise on. For this war work they were excused school or allowed time off work.[86] However, schoolboy scouts had to return to their studies in November 1914 under orders from the War Office, although they could continue to help during the holidays.[87] For girls there was the Girl Guides Association, established in 1910, although it was not until 1916 that the first company was formed in St Albans at St Paul's Church. Interestingly, there was a guide company at Ryder's seed merchants, which employed a large number of girls. All the guide companies in St Albans grew potatoes and gathered all sorts of scraps to raise money for good causes and company funds.

There was definitely a class divide in the pursuits, pastimes and hobbies of the period, with cinema seen as a rather low-brow, working-class form of entertainment. Its power to stir up patriotism and support the war effort was not immediately recognised by the government, although the *Herts Advertiser* appears to have understood its potential as a means of mass communication from the start of the war.[88] The St Albans Cinema in Chequer Street (later known as the Chequers) and the Poly Picture Palace in London Road opened six days a week, changing their programmes mid-week. As well as the main feature, there was usually a serial, sometimes running for 20 episodes. Melodramas, detective stories, the classics – such as *David Copperfield* – and of course comedies featuring rising stars such as Charlie Chaplin were the order of the day and invariably described as 'sensational'. On 8 August 1914 the usual page one advertisement for the St Albans Cinema carried the message: 'Through the kindness of the *Herts Advertiser* we are showing all the latest war news.' The first official war pictures were shown in July 1916 and described as 'anything but cheerful as they reveal scenes of desolation about the countryside of Flanders, which speak volumes for the dreadful work of devastation accomplished by the guns of the Huns'.[89] In September 1916 it was announced that the current week's war series included a film of the last visit to the trenches by the late Lord Kitchener, 'a picture that cannot be looked upon save with the eye of emotion'.[90] The following month it was reported that 7,000 people had seen the 'sensational' war film *The Battle of the Somme* in St Albans the previous week.

In November 1917 a film with a local connection was screened. *Boy Scouts – Be Prepared* was made partly in St Albans and is believed to have included some local boys. The mayor, James Flint, arranged for a matinee performance of the film in aid of the Boy Scouts Fund, during which all six episodes were shown.[91] Cinemas were sometimes referred to as 'flea pits' and in November 1918 the St Albans Cinema included in its regular weekly advertisement the following message: 'The theatre is disinfected daily with Jeyes Fluid and English Lysol.'

As well as the magic of the silver screen, showing silent pictures to piano accompaniment, St Albans had the County Hall Theatre, which attracted professional vaudeville-style acts from the London theatres. The building was requisitioned by the military authorities in 1914 and for a period was used for military concerts and boxing tournaments. The army

Figure 4.5. Soldiers outside the County Hall theatre, St Peter's Street, requisitioned in 1914.
© Hertfordshire Archives and Local Studies (4234.18 #025)

vacated the premises in April 1915, at which time the lessee Sidney Foster reapplied for a theatrical licence. The theatre formed part of the County Constitutional Club in St Peters Street, with access via a passageway to the right of the club (Figure 4.5). Revues and variety shows, as well as amateur productions and fundraising concerts, were put on throughout the war. A tax on places of entertainment must have added to the problems of making theatres and cinemas pay their way in wartime, but the ever-enterprising Foster turned such setbacks to his advantage. He quoted the chancellor of the exchequer in an advert for the theatre in 1916: 'By all means let people go to entertainments; it is good for them and good for the Exchequer', reminding readers that the entertainment tax rate added 2d to 3d to the cost of a seat.[92]

All these many high- and low-brow activities must have helped to take people's minds off the exigencies of the war, at least for an hour or two. As Neville Chamberlain, then Director of National Service, is believed to have said, 'Amusement is of national importance.'[93]

The role of the church

The more serious issue of the righteousness of the war was something the churches in St Albans had to grapple with. In general terms churches of different denominations believed it was a just cause because neutral Belgium had been invaded. There were, of course, prayers for peace, but for hostilities to end only when the allies had won. There was little apparent dissent from this view, although in late spring 1915 the Quakers in St Albans did give a platform to a speaker who said that if Germany could be persuaded to withdraw from Belgium Britain should make peace. However, there was considerable opposition from those present.[94]

In early June 1915 many clergy from the diocese, six mayors and a large congregation attended a service of intercession at the cathedral. The bishop said an act of penitence and in his sermon emphasised that everyone must do their utmost for the cause in gratitude to the fighting men.[95] At a similar service in June 1918 the nonconformist ministers joined the clergy procession, including Sister Rachel, pastor of the Primitive Methodist Church.[96] The clergy supported the war in different ways. The vicar of St Peter's called for greater Christian commitment and stated repeatedly that money should not be wasted on alcohol and that it should be illegal to offer drinks to soldiers, a view which later became law.[97] The Revd Alexander Barff of St Paul's in Fleetville was concerned with food production and fuel wastage. Several times he and the congregation processed round the parish to bless allotments. During the war years he held church services in the streets of serving soldiers and, on a practical level, offered to introduce potential allotment cultivators to holders whose husbands were in the forces.[98] The practical Revd Leonard Westall of St Saviour's in Sandpit Lane was involved in setting up working parties so that every man from the parish serving at the front received a parcel that included warm clothes. Twice, when regiments that had been stationed in the parish suffered heavy losses in the fighting, Westall held memorial services, making every effort to maintain a correct record for the church's 'Roll of Honour' of those that had enlisted.[99]

The spiritual well-being of serving men was not forgotten. A committee of church ladies raised enough funds to purchase 7,000 specially printed bibles called 'Active Service' testaments. These were handed out at church parades and distributed from the town hall. There the ladies wrote each soldier's name and number inside his copy, handing the testaments over with words of encouragement. They were clearly popular, particularly the hymns at the back, as one officer wrote from the front requesting more copies.[100]

Not forgetting the poor

The Poor Law rate funded St Albans Poor Law Institution, including the workhouse and infirmary situated in Union Lane (Figure 4.6). It was overseen by an elected Board of Guardians representing the parishes of Redbourn, Sandridge, Harpenden and Wheathampstead and the St Albans' parishes of the Abbey, St Michael's, St Peter's and St Stephen's. In 1914 the guardians were supporting around 500 men, women and children, including inmates of the workhouse and a shifting population of vagrants and patients being treated in other institutions, including mental asylums. Men and women aged over 60 made up 53 per cent of the population of the workhouse according to the 1911 census and children under 14 accounted for 10 per cent of the total. These two groups were particularly vulnerable to the wartime restrictions in fuel and basic foodstuffs such as sugar and meat.[101]

Children with disabilities and those requiring vocational training were often sent to special institutions in other parts of the country. Throughout the war, the guardians continued to find training, employment and apprenticeships for their juvenile charges. Girls generally went into service, but it is recorded that at times they were too small, not strong

Figure 4.6 The workhouse and infirmary, Union Lane (now Normandy Road). © Andy Lawrence

enough or too 'saucy' in their ways and were returned to the workhouse until a new place could be found for them. The guardians supported the blind Leonard Marsh to study music at the Brighton Blind Asylum, paying £5 12s 0d for his exam expenses in September 1914; Canon Glossop, a member of the Board of Guardians, personally paid for his music lessons. It is not known what his thoughts were on hearing that Leonard's first job was as a concert party pianist.[102]

We have a child's view of the workhouse from Barbara Rapson, aged about seven and living in Blenheim Road in around 1917. She and her sister had regularly visited the County of Middlesex War Hospital at Napsbury to sing for the wounded soldiers when the lady who took them, Olga Dickson, suggested that they put on a concert for the inmates at the workhouse. Barbara Rapson described mute inmates who were unresponsive to the entertainment the trio put on, afterwards pleading with her mother not to be asked to repeat the experience.[103]

Rising costs of fuel and food and the scarcity of key commodities such as sugar made administration of the workhouse and the care of its inmates increasingly difficult. The buildings were dilapidated, expensive to maintain and in constant need of repair; this at a time when any capital expenditure or new building was more or less prohibited. All loans had to be sanctioned by the Local Government Board, which, in December 1914, authorised the building of a new boardroom and children's ward.

The building and completion of the boardroom went ahead, but it was not until August 1916 that action was taken to furnish the children's ward, by which time the shortage of bed space had become acute. It has to be noted, too, that the £1,275 loan to build the ward was less than half the amount borrowed by the guardians to create a very plush boardroom for its committee meetings.[104] However, the records show that patients suffering from tuberculosis or rheumatic complaints might still be sent to hospitals in Margate and Buxton, and expensive hospital treatments in London were regularly required for women contracting venereal diseases.

In September 1915 the clerk to the guardians was deputed to find places in industrial schools and national children's homes to relieve pressure because so many boys were being cared for at the workhouse.[105] In November the boys' ward was still overcrowded and some of the boys were sleeping, illegally, in the men's ward, a state of affairs outlawed by the 1913 Poor Law Institutions Order, which ruled that by 1915 all children should be in separate accommodation.[106] The guardians' plan had been to build a new children's home on land on Bernards Heath, but this was put on hold as a direct result of the war. This meant that they were struggling to comply with the 1913 regulations. The guardians were dependent for their income on the poor rate, which was fixed annually in advance. At the same time they were obliged to fund any St Albans inmates who had been moved on to specialist or psychiatric facilities, where costs continued to soar during the war years.[107]

Medical provision in the city

The Union infirmary provided medical care for the poorest in the community as well as the inmates of the workhouse, and was one of four hospitals in the city. All hospitals relied heavily on donations and became the poor relation in charitable terms during the war years, as the Red Cross and other military charities captured people's hearts.

The St Albans and Mid Herts Hospital and Dispensary, on the corner of Verulam Road and Church Crescent, was a voluntary hospital run by a management committee and funded by subscriptions and donations. The annual accounts for 1916 show that, while donations had increased, there had been a fall in regular subscriptions and gifts received from wealthy individuals and contributions from church collections, flag days and fêtes were not as large as in previous years.[108] By 1918 the hospital was in deficit and the overdraft cleared only by generous donations from wealthy benefactors. The hospital appealed for continued financial support as ordinary expenses had risen from £1,688 in 1914 to £2,773 in 1918.[109]

The Sisters Hospital in Union Lane treated infectious diseases such as diphtheria. Admissions in 1916/17 suggest that from 1915 there was a significant increase in cases of diphtheria. Barbara Rapson, referred to earlier, caught the disease and recalled being taken in the late evening by horse-drawn ambulance to the Sisters Hospital, where a needle was pushed into her spine. 'I screamed at the top of my voice and they said I was very naughty. I thought they were going to murder me and there was I rent [torn] from my mother.'[110]

The Hertfordshire County Asylum at Hill End cared for patients belonging to workhouse unions from across the county. A number of male staff members at Hill End enlisted and in 1915 the asylum's visiting committee decided that it would not be safe for any more staff to be released. When in 1917 the War Office tried to conscript more men, the committee stood firm.[111] Because of the difficulties caused by reduced staff levels and increased numbers of patients the committee asked the Board of Guardians in St Albans to retain as many of the aged and weak-minded as possible in its workhouse, rather than send them to the asylum. Many of the new patients at Hill End were men from the services, affected by the trauma of war. In its 1917/18 annual report the committee stated that many of these patients were dangerous and difficult to manage with depleted staff.[112]

The organisation and provision of community nursing, led by county councils and local nursing associations, had greatly increased before the war. As part of these developments the St Albans and District Nursing Association was established in May 1917, in the process acquiring St Peter's Nursing Home in Hatfield Road.[113] It appears that the income from nursing private patients at the home largely funded community nursing, along with donations and church collections. Accounts for the first year show an income of £2,545 and a deficit of £176 19s 2d. It was suggested at the first annual meeting that a fête be held to wipe out the deficit and a number of ladies volunteered to organise it.[114]

Influenza delivers a fatal blow

Throughout the war years there were outbreaks of tuberculosis, diphtheria, German measles and chickenpox, but it was not until late October 1918 that a full-scale epidemic affected St Albans. A report, headlined 'Influenza Rampant', stated that doctors were busy, schools

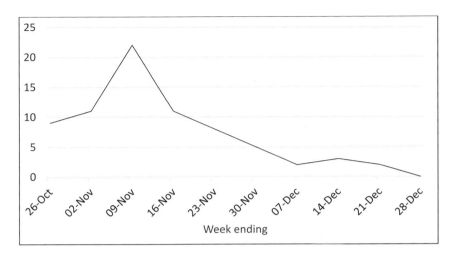

Figure 4.7 Peak in deaths recorded in early November 1918. Source: Medical Officer of Health Report for 1918

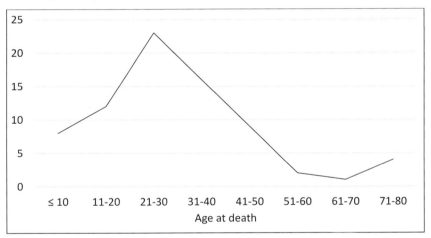

Figure 4.8 Most deaths from influenza occurred in the 21–30 age group. Source: Medical Officer of Health Report for 1918

closed and that there had been several deaths. Some 30 per cent of elementary school children and 18 of their teachers caught influenza at this time.[115] The following week's paper, under the headline 'The Insidious Flu – the epidemic at St Albans', told of whole families who had been struck down. Doctors were 'worked off their legs' as they struggled to complete their daily rounds. Flu had broken out among patients and staff at the County of Middlesex War Hospital at Napsbury, which at one point had 300 cases. The Union infirmary made beds available for 46 soldiers, while a further 70, all suffering from influenza, were nursed in the YMCA hut in St Peter's Street. On 9 November, when the long, drawn-out war was almost at an end, 20 people in St Albans were reported dead of influenza. The newly elected mayor, Alderman Arthur Faulkner, acknowledged the debt owed to the 'noble' St Albans and District Nursing Association, whose members had worked tirelessly, going from house to house to help those in need.[116]

In all, 75 civilian deaths were attributed to the epidemic in St Albans by the end of December 1918 and around 15 soldiers died of the illness in the city (Figures 4.7 and 4.8). In the end, death came to those on the home front in St Albans not from bomb-laden Zeppelins but from a wave of epidemic disease. Set against the millions who lost their lives at the front, 75 dead from flu is not a significant number, but nevertheless it must have been a bitter blow for the families in St Albans, who experienced this cruel twist of fate just as peace had finally arrived.

Conclusion

The inhabitants of St Albans, that city slumbering in the shadow of an ancient cathedral in 1914, roused themselves to achieve an extraordinary amount in four years – a period of intense activity and no doubt powerful emotions, from excitement and pride to fear and grief. They sewed countless comforts for the troops, saved hundreds of thousands of pounds for the war effort, played host to billeted soldiers and supported the troops, the wounded, the POWs and the Belgian refugees. In most respects they epitomised the often-talked-about 'second front' in the battle to win the First World War.

Notes

1. The first encounter and exchange of gunfire between British and German troops took place at Casteau in Belgium on 22 August 1914, <http://www.thehistorypress.co.uk> accessed 15 February 2016.

2. 'Notes on the war', *Herts Advertiser* (*HA*), 15 August 1914.

3. P. MacGill, *The amateur army* (London, 1915), p. 16.

4. 'More censorship!', *HA*, 29 August 1914.

5. 'Notice to friends of soldiers', *HA*, 19 September 1914.

6. 'Local man in the trenches', *HA*, 7 November 1914. Note: the shells were named after Jack Johnson, a famous American heavyweight boxer.

7. See, for example, 'Our roll of honour', *HA*, 12 September 1914.

8. 'Hertfordshire', *Bedfordshire Advertiser and Luton Times*, 18 September 1914.

9. Hertfordshire Archives and Local Studies (HALS), DP91/25/1, Christ Church Parish Account Book, 1897–1921, 3 March 1915; HALS, DP96A/11/2, St Saviour's parish magazine, February 1917; HALS, DP93/29/5, St Peter's parish magazine, December 1914.

10. A. King, *Memorials of the Great War in Britain: the symbolism and politics of remembrance* (London, 1998), pp. 49–50. War shrines were erected in the following locations: Albert Street, Bardwell Road, Boundary Road, Cannon Street, Clock Tower, Culver Road, Day's Yard (off Holywell Hill), Fishpool Street, Hart Road, High Street, Holywell Hill, Kimberley Road, Lower Dagnall Street, New England Street, New Kent Road, Orchard Street, Oster Street, Pageant Road, Prospect Road, Sandridge Road, Sopwell Lane, Spicer Street, Temperance Street, Union Lane, Upper Dagnall Street, Upper Heath Road, Verulam Road, Walton Street.

11. HALS, DP93C/29/2, St Paul's parish magazine, June 1916.

12. 'St Albans', *HA*, 18 August 1917. For information about the abbey parish street memorials see Chapter 8.

13. 'The loss of the Bulwark', *HA*, 5 December 1914.

14. 'Pte T. Bickerton. Another St Albans soldier missing', *HA*, 11 May 1918.

15. T.A. Bickerton, *The wartime experiences of an ordinary 'Tommy'* (n.p., 1964), pp. 20, 27.

16. Museum of St Albans, Leaflet entitled *City of St Albans Defence Of The Realm (Consolidation) Regulations 1914*. See HALS, DP/93/29/6, St Peter's parish magazine, October 1915, for reference to church services being altered.

17. J. Birch, 'The 1915 Hertford Air Raid' (2012), Our Hertford and Ware, part of Herts Memories network, <http://www.ourhertfordandware.org.uk> accessed 15 February 2016.

18. 'Alien enemies in St Albans', *HA*, 15 August 1914.

19. 'Unregistered aliens, St Albans publican arrested', *HA*, 26 September 1914.

20. 'The enemy in our midst, rounding up the aliens', *HA*, 24 October 1914.

21. 'Editor under arrest', *HA*, 26 September 1914.

22. 'The greatest crime – *RMS Lusitania* torpedoed with 2000 souls on board', *HA*, 15 May 1915.

23. 'The anti-German movement: trouble at a St Albans factory', *HA*, 15 May 1915.

24. 'Foreigners at a local works: deep well tube works men see the management', *HA*, 15 May 1915.

25. 'Letters: "anti-German movement"', *HA*, 22 May 1915.

26. Advertisement, *HA*, 1 December 1917.

27. 'Feeding German prisoners', *HA*, 7 December 1918.

28. R. Wigglesworth, 'UK to pay back all first world war debts', *Financial Times*, 3 December 2014, <http://www.ft.com> accessed 15 February 2016.

29. 'Government borrowing at home', RBS Remembers 1914–1918, <http://www.rbsremembers.com> accessed 15 February 2016.

30. 'War thrift', *HA*, 1 January 1916.

31. 'Government borrowing at home', RBS Remembers 1914–1918, <http://www.rbsremembers.com> accessed 15 February 2016.

32. Bank of England archive, M7/196, 1914–1921 (unpublished war history), p. 394, <http://www.bankofengland.co.uk> accessed 15 February 2016.

33. K.G. Burton, *A penknife to a mountain: the early years of the National Savings Committee* (London, 1999).

34. 'Report on War Savings Week', *HA*, 22 July 1916.

35. 'War savings in St Albans', *HA*, 27 July 1918.

36. 'The spirit of thrift', *HA*, 13 January 1917.

37. HALS, DP/96A/11/2, St Saviour's parish magazine, February 1917.

38. 'The spirit of thrift', *HA*, 13 January 1917.

39. Editorial about the war savings clock, *HA*, 24 February 1917.

40. 'National war bonds', RBS Remembers, 1914–1918, <http://www.rbsremembers. com> accessed 15 February 2016.

41. 'War loan', *HA*, 20 January 1917.

42. 'The great victory loan', *HA*, 24 February 1917.

43. The Royal Flying Corps merged with the Royal Naval Air Service to become the Royal Air Force (RAF) on 1 April 1918.

44. 'Gun Week, renamed St Albans Thanksgiving Week', *HA*, 7 December 1918.

45. 'Editorial', *HA*, 27 July 1918.

46. 'Notes on saving: No. 10 – How men can save in the home', *HA*, 19 October 1918.

47. F. Petty, *The Pudding Lady's recipe book with practical hints* (London, 1917), Preface.

48. C. Harris, '1914–1918: How charities helped to win WW1', 27 June 2014, <http:// www.thirdsector.co.uk> accessed 15 February 2016.

49. Ernest Gape was the military representative on the St Albans City Military Service Tribunal. See Chapter 2.

50. 'Helping the dependants', interview with Ernest Gape, *HA*, 3 January 1920.

51. J. Meyer, *Men of war: masculinity and the First World War in Britain* (Basingstoke, 2009). See blog by Dr Meyer, 'Disability and Masculinity in the First World War', posted 5 June 2014 on The History Press website – <http://www.thehistorypress. co.uk> accessed 15 February 2016.

52. 'City samaritans', *HA*, 19 August 1916.

53. 'Mrs Slade's working party', *HA*, 8 July 1916.

54. 'Hertfordshire regiments' prisoners of war', *HA*, 27 October 1917.

55. 'Belgians arrive at St Albans', *HA*, 19 September 1914.

56. HALS, SBR/894A, City Council Minute Book, 1912–16, letter to Local Government Board, 27 January 1915.

57. 'St Albans City Council meeting', *HA*, 13 February 1916.

58. 'Belgian relief fund', *HA*, 13 May 1916.

59. H.E.L. Mellersh, *Schoolboy into war* (London, 1978), pp. 99–100.

60. 'St Albans & the war: how women may help', *HA*, 29 August 1914. Miss Jacob did not live to see the end of the war. She died aged 82 in April 1918.

61. 'St Albans social problem', *HA*, 22 August 1914.

62. 'The maids and the troops. A spirited protest', *HA*, 29 August 1914.

63. 'The maids and the soldiers', *HA*, 5 September 1914.

64. 'Patriotic Club', *HA*, 5 June 1915.

65. 'Local war items', *HA*, 6 November 1915.

66. 'St Albans column: aid to young women and girls', *HA*, 2 March 1918.

67. HALS, HCC 21/9, Hertfordshire County Council Education Committee Minute Book, 1914–15, 22 June 1914, p. 155.

68. 'St Albans High School AGM Report', *HA*, 21 November 1914. St Albans School Archive, St Albans Grammar School Minute Book, 1910–16, letter to chairman of governors from headmaster, 25 July 1914.

69. HALS, HEd2/27/1, Garden Fields School Log Book, 1896–1931.

70. HALS, HEd2/28/1, Priory Park School Log Book, 1901–31.

71. St Albans School archive, School Minute Book, letter to chairman of governors from headmaster, 25 July 1914.

72. 'Teachers with the Colours', *HA*, 26 June 1915.

73. HALS, HEd2/27/1, Garden Fields School Log Book, 1896–1931.

74. Ibid.

75. HALS, HEd2/28/1, Priory Park School Log Book, 1901–31.

76. HALS, HEd2/27/1, Garden Fields School Log Book, 1896–1931.

77. 'School handwork', *HA*, 1 April 1916.

78. HALS, HCC 21D/8, HCC Finance and General Purposes Sub-Committee Minute Book, 24 September 1915.

79. N. Watson, *St Albans High School for Girls – an illustrated history* (London, 2002); St Albans High School for Girls archive, School Report 1919 and School Record Book.

80. HALS, HEd2/28/1 and HEd2/27/1: the log books show that almost half the pupils at Priory Park and a quarter at Garden Fields were not present for afternoon registration on 11 November 1918.

81. 'Our duty in war time: less of pleasure, luxury and amusement', *HA*, 27 March 1915. The government called a halt to race meetings that year, citing public sentiment.

82. All the following are references to *HA*: 'Herts naturalists', 5 June 1915; 'The county museum', 12 February 1916; 'Natural History Society visit to Kew Gardens', 8 July 1916.

83. St Albans & Hertfordshire Architectural & Archaeological Society (SAHAAS) Council Minute Book, 31 March 1917.

84. SAHAAS Minutes, 20 July 1916.

85. Letters, *HA*, 8, 15, 22 and 29 July and 12 August 1916.

86. B. Peatling and B. Smith (eds), *Always a scout: a glimpse into St Albans scouting since 1908* (Gateshead, 1984).

87. D. Parker, *Hertfordshire children in war and peace, 1914–1939* (Hatfield, 2007).

88. M. Paris, 'Film/Cinema (Great Britain)', 1914–1918-online. International Encyclopaedia of the First World War, <http://encyclopedia.1914–1918-online.net/article/filmcinema_great_britain> accessed 15 February 2016.

89. 'St Albans column: "St Albans Cinema"', *HA*, 22 July 1916.

90. 'St Albans column: "St Albans Cinema"', *HA*, 2 September 1916. Note: Lord Kitchener, Secretary of State for War, was drowned at sea on 5 June 1916.

91. Advertisement, *HA*, 12 January 1918.

92. Advertisement, *HA*, 10 June 1916. See Chapter 1 for price of cinema tickets.

93. Advertisement, *HA*, 10 March 1917.

94. 'The Lord's Prayer and the war', *HA*, 5 May 1915.

95. 'Cathedral intercession service and public meeting', *HA*, 5 June 1915.

96. H.R. Wilton Hall, *A Chronicle of the Cathedral Church 1914–1920*, St Albans Cathedral Muniment Room.

97. HALS, DP93/29/6, St Peter's parish magazine, March 1915.

98. HALS, DP93C/29/2, St Paul's parish magazine.

99. H.R. Wilton Hall (compiled D. Lapthorn), *Bernard's Heath and the Great War: extracts from the diary of H.R. Wilton Hall* (St Albans, 2009).

100. 'The Churches and the war: contemplating settlement', *HA*, 13 March 1915.

101. For details of food shortages and rationing see Chapter 6.

102. HALS, BG/STA/17, St Albans Board of Guardians Minute Book, 1913–15, September 1914.

103. D. Broom, *My St Albans memories: an oral history of life and times in St Albans* (St Albans, 2001), p. 88.

104. HALS, BG/STA/17, Board of Guardians Minute Book, 28 January 1915.

105. HALS, HSS/8/6/1, St Albans Union rough Minute Book, 1911–30, 19 September 1915.

106. J.S. Heywood, *Children in care: the development of the service for the deprived child* (London, 1959), p. 67.

107. HALS, BG/STA/19, St Albans Board of Guardians Minute Book, 1918–20. For example, notification of cost increases for patients held at Hill End Asylum: 7 October 1915, p. 32; 5 October 1916, p. 225; 4 October 1917, p. 407. In this period the cost per head per week went from 11s 8d to 16s 4d.

108. 'The hospital year: a fall in subscriptions', *HA*, 3 March 1917.

109. HALS, SBR/3572, St Albans and Mid Herts Hospital and Dispensary: Annual Statements from the Management Committee, 1914–19.

110. Broom, *My St Albans memories*, p. 86.

111. HALS, Acc 3959, B. Anderson, *Nearly a century: the history of Hill End Mental Hospital, St Albans, 1899–1995* (1998), p. 34.

112. Ibid.

113. 'Herts convalescent home', *HA*, 5 May 1917.

114. 'St Albans and District Nursing Association: first annual meeting', *HA*, 8 June 1918.

115. HALS, HCC HEd5/19/1, St Albans Local Education Sub-Committee Minutes, 23 October 1918.

116. 'Our day', *HA*, 16 November 1918.

CHAPTER 5

The challenge for business

In the 30 years leading up to the outbreak of war in 1914 the industrial base of St Albans had developed from one dependent on agricultural trade to a more robust mixed economy. Newcomers to the city, such as the boot and shoe manufacturers and printing companies using the latest equipment, operated from the same streets as the established straw hat makers, some of whom had been trading in St Albans for more than 70 years.[1] All were to face substantial challenges as the country's need for men and munitions had, for much of the war, primacy over all other considerations. Some local businesses, often through a mixture of luck and planning, had good wars. Most did not.

That the war was going to last years, not months, was announced in parliament by Lord Kitchener, secretary of state for war, in August 1914 and reported widely in the national press. At the same time he acknowledged that this would be a war of attrition in terms of men and machinery, fought on a wide front, not just in Europe.[2] The British had an empire not only to call on for resources but also to defend. Strategic locations, such as the Suez Canal and oilfields in Mesopotamia, had to be secured. As importantly, it would also be a war of attrition measured on a different scale, that of production. For the army the forecast demand for munitions was unprecedented. Replacing merchant ships lost to German U-boats would be vital. This would be a war fought not just on land and sea, however, but for the first time in the air. Britain had to develop its embryonic aircraft industry to produce competitive planes in large numbers. Added to the military imperative were the needs of the home front. The country had to grow as much of its own food as it could and manufacture and export goods to generate hard cash to pay the bills. All this activity required manpower.

The term 'manpower' was first coined during the war.[3] It was defined by one historian as 'the development of policies which would enable men and women to do the work of one and a quarter or even one and a half persons, and, while increasing everybody's productivity, to ensure that such work was directly beneficial to Britain's conduct of the war'.[4] It was a term, however, which was easier to define than to implement. Humbert Wolfe, director-general of labour relations at the Ministry of Labour during the war, wrote afterwards that it was the duty of the State to manage and balance the following four conflicting wartime needs:

1. A sufficient supply of men, of whatever military age be decreed, physically fit for fighting, must be provided to supply and replenish the Forces.
2. The larger the combatant forces the greater will be the number of men and women required at home to equip, clothe, and feed the Forces.
3. While the normal ranks for industry will be heavily drained for these two purposes, it will be imperative to provide the labour which will guarantee the provision of the necessities of the civilian population, i.e. food, heat, light, clothes, transport, etc.
4. Finally, as the war continues, the strain on the financial resources of the country, and particularly upon its international credit, will grow heavier, and it will therefore be necessary to provide labour to keep the export trades of the country working at the highest point compatible with the fulfilment of the first three calls.[5]

As an example of how difficult it was to balance these needs, it took until early 1918 for a general acceptance to emerge across government that building ships for the Navy and aeroplanes for the Royal Flying Corps had become more important than reinforcing the army.[6] Until that point the army's requirements had taken precedence. It was also in 1918 that Britain achieved 'total war', in which strategic military planning was fully integrated with industrial production. Over the intervening years the country took faltering steps towards this goal. The introduction of conscription in March 1916, with its dependence on the military service tribunal scheme, was key to this. For the first time, using the tribunals described in Chapter 2, it became at least possible to integrate national and local needs.

In considering how the war affected the business community in St Albans, this chapter focuses on the ramifications of the developing practice of manpower planning on the local industries that directly engaged nearly 26 per cent of those recorded in the 1911 census as being employed.[7] Central government departments, such as the Ministry of Munitions and from 1917 the Ministry of National Service, developed and promoted processes to overcome industry's understandable reluctance to release skilled men to the military. These policies included replacing a worker joining the army by someone with roughly similar skills and taking strategic businesses ('controlled establishments') under limited government control. By the end of the war there were over 6,000 of these in the country[8] and at least three in St Albans, of which one was the Grimston Tyre Co., run by the Earl of Verulam's son, Lord Grimston. While understanding the effect on the business community in St Albans of these two important processes has proved tantalisingly out of reach, a third, dilution, is discussed later in the chapter.

St Albans and munitions production

Probably the most significant industrial development of the war years was the growth of munitions production. Prior to August 1914 the army had a need for 'things that go bang' on a scale commensurate with its status as little more than the colonial police force described in Chapter 2. However, from the first few weeks of the war it was clear to military planners that existing rates of production would be insufficient to meet the requirements of military expansion laid down by Lord Kitchener. The creation of the Ministry of Munitions under David Lloyd George following the 'Shells Scandal' of May 1915[9] introduced mass production, with new factories built across the country, including, in Hertfordshire, at Watford and Letchworth. Such investments often brought economic benefits to these areas as the factories provided well-paid employment for a largely female workforce.

No factories were established in St Albans to produce armaments. On a superficial level the reason for this appears to be straightforward. It will be clear from the industrial profile of the city, described in Chapter 1, that there was no history of heavy engineering before the war. There were, however, several light engineering firms, at least one of which, W.H. Thorpe & Co., based in the city centre, turned to producing munitions components. Their output was probably on a very small scale.[10] As is shown below, the St Albans Gas Co. developed a new chemical business for armaments manufacture.

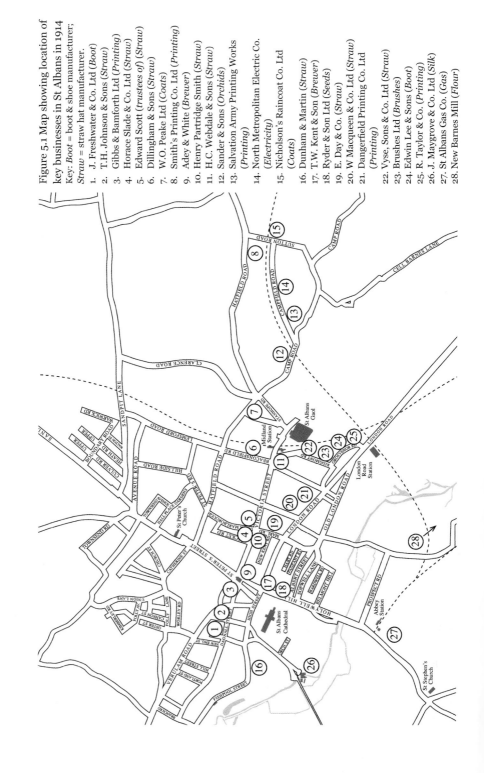

Figure 5.1 Map showing location of key businesses in St Albans in 1914
Key: *Boot* = boot & shoe manufacturer; *Straw* = straw hat manufacturer.

1. J. Freshwater & Co. Ltd (*Boot*)
2. T.H. Johnson & Sons (*Straw*)
3. Gibbs & Bamforth Ltd (*Printing*)
4. Horace Slade & Co. Ltd (*Straw*)
5. Edward Scott (*trustees of*) (*Straw*)
6. Dillingham & Sons (*Straw*)
7. W.O. Peake Ltd (*Coats*)
8. Smith's Printing Co. Ltd (*Printing*)
9. Adey & White (*Brewer*)
10. Henry Partridge Smith (*Straw*)
11. H.C. Webdale & Sons (*Straw*)
12. Sander & Sons (*Orchids*)
13. Salvation Army Printing Works (*Printing*)
14. North Metropolitan Electric Co. (*Electricity*)
15. Nicholson's Raincoat Co. Ltd (*Coats*)
16. Dunham & Martin (*Straw*)
17. T.W. Kent & Son (*Brewer*)
18. Ryder & Son Ltd (*Seeds*)
19. E. Day & Co. (*Straw*)
20. W Macqueen & Co. Ltd (*Straw*)
21. Dangerfield Printing Co. Ltd (*Printing*)
22. Vyse, Sons & Co. Ltd (*Straw*)
23. Brushes Ltd (*Brushes*)
24. Edwin Lee & Sons (*Boot*)
25. R. Taylor & Co. (*Printing*)
26. J. Maygrove & Co. Ltd (*Silk*)
27. St Albans Gas Co. (*Gas*)
28. New Barnes Mill (*Flour*)

However, a closer examination shows that the absence of any significant operation in St Albans was more a case of missed opportunities, both before and during the war, rather than a shortage of skills and facilities. A comparison with Luton, 12 miles to the north-west, is instructive. Over the previous 30 years Luton had developed a good track record in attracting new industry. Its chamber of commerce and the borough council's New Industries Committee were particularly active, combining to offer advantages such as cheap land, low rates and inexpensive electricity.[11] Luton continued to be an attractive location in the war years as well. From 1916 onwards an existing concern, George Kent Ltd, undertook to erect and equip buildings for filling fuses, all at the expense of the government. The operation grew quickly to employ around 600 people, about 90 per cent of whom were women.[12] In contrast, St Albans's two equivalent bodies appear to have taken a *laissez-faire* attitude to this form of promotion. Before the war, the chamber of commerce focused mostly on retail business[13] and no evidence has come to light that the city council's New Industries Committee ever met.[14] Rates in St Albans were high, and formed a bone of contention for business leaders in the Fleetville and Camp areas during discussions about the boundary extension in 1913.[15] Moreover, electricity from the North Metropolitan generating station in Campfield Road was expensive and the supply unreliable.[16]

St Albans remained an unattractive prospect when the Ministry of Munitions sought to build capacity in the area in 1916. A correspondent writing under the alias 'Local Manufacturer' in a letter published in the *Herts Advertiser* late in 1916 indicated that the officials from the ministry had considered St Albans as a location for new facilities. He went on to report that, although there was spare factory accommodation at the time, the cost of doing business in the city was prohibitive and the officials looked elsewhere.[17] Not everyone was disappointed. The editor of the influential *Herts Advertiser*, Harry Carrington,[18] took a provocative stance, worried that 'tall chimneys of numerous factories [would be] repugnant in the extreme and [suggested] that any scheme of commercial development must be carried out with due regard to the three-fold interests of St Albans – the antiquarian, the residential and the commercial'.[19] The needs of the military played no part in his consideration (Figure 5.1).

Even though St Albans failed to attract government investment, it would be wrong to assume that local businesses did not contribute goods to the war effort. There were, as Wolfe had noted in the second of his four 'needs' above, opportunities to supply the rapidly growing army with 'munitions' in

Figure 5.2 St Albans Gas Co. works, 1926. © Historic England. Licensor canmore.org.uk

the wider sense of the word. The city's clothing manufacturers individually won several military contracts during the war. For example, Nicholson's, the raincoat manufacturer of Sutton Road, produced army greatcoats.[20] W.O. Peake Ltd of Hatfield Road had a contract for khaki tunics.[21] Messrs Miller & Cooke of Verulam Road made socks and cardigans for soldiers.[22] Even one of the straw hat manufacturers produced overalls for munitions workers.[23] Away from the clothing trade, Brushes Ltd of Grosvenor Road had by March 1917 made 1.6 million brushes for horses and soldiers under military contracts from the beginning of the war.[24] This represented around 90 per cent of the company's output.[25]

For some businesses, wartime exigencies drove them into new relationships with the government. For the straw hat firm E. Day & Co. this was a boon, as will be shown later.[26] For others, such as the St Albans Gas Co., located at the bottom of Holywell Hill (Figure 5.2), the benefits of a government-imposed relationship where none had existed before were less certain. In August 1914 the company's directors must have anticipated difficulties in managing their established business of providing lighting and heating for the district. Some idea of the problems they encountered can be gleaned from data provided at the annual general meeting in 1919: 'The cost of coal on pre-war prices had gone up over 60 per cent, oil for enrichment by 300 per cent, wages 82 per cent, fire clay and other materials over 100 per cent.'[27] As these increases were not passed on to customers, the shareholders bore the brunt.

What the company's directors could not have forecast in August 1914 was the obligation imposed on them to develop a new line of business. With German supplies now out of bounds, the government looked to the domestic gas industry to adapt production to produce benzol and toluene (then 'toluol'), essential ingredients for munitions manufacture. In June 1915 the company's engineer reported:

> On instructions received from the [government's] High Explosives Committee, Toluol was to be extracted from the Gas. This was being done by washing the gas with tar, which necessitated the fixing of a tar separator at a cost of £152 10s. It was resolved that same should be erected.[28]

This investment was just one of several over the next three years intended to facilitate the production of these chemicals. However, it was an expensive process and costs rose. In June 1916 the directors agreed to spend £1,000 on a new 'oil-washing process'.[29] There is no evidence that the government provided any funding or that the work turned a profit. A personal letter addressed to the company's directors from the director-general of the Explosives Department at the Ministry of Munitions thanked them for their support. He noted in particular that the process is 'not profitable for gas companies' and 'for those the size of St Albans it is a loss'. It was vitally important work, however: 'those who are supervising the production of benzol and toluol are doing as much for their country as the men who are fighting at the Front'.[30] This letter must have provided a useful defence against any attacks on the probity of the investments.

For the gas company the benefits of this new relationship were equivocal. For other local companies munitions production was an important extension of existing business relationships with the government and were, on the face of it, beneficial to both parties. Thomas Mercer & Co. was one of these. Mercer's, based in Eywood Road close to the gas works, made ships' chronometers. It was a significant manufacturer in a small specialised industry characterised by inefficient production processes. As

shipping losses resulting from attacks by German U-boats on the British
merchant fleet mounted, the Admiralty desperately needed to raise
production. Frank Mercer, the son of the company founder, was summoned
back from military service in Egypt to help the Admiralty develop and
introduce new practices to the industry. As Mercer's own workforce, just
30 in 1914, rose to 58 by the end of the war, it can be inferred that output
grew significantly as well.[31] The company's importance to the Admiralty
brought other benefits. A challenge for all companies at this time was not
only recruiting skilled workers but also ensuring that they, mostly men,
remained in production, particularly when conscription was introduced in
March 1916. Thankfully for Mercer's the importance of the business to the
national interest solved any problems in this regard: the Admiralty largely
protected the company against this risk by 'badging' remaining eligible
men and later giving them 'protected occupation' status.[32] However,
whatever special relationship Mercer's had with the government lasted
only so long. When the war ended, business dried up overnight.[33]

Thus, the protection of the company's skilled workers, an asset for any
company, was a collateral benefit of the extended relationship between
Mercer's and the Admiralty. Other businesses in St Albans which could not
pass that national interest test faced significant challenges in holding on
to their own key workers. As outlined in Chapter 2, the members of the St
Albans City Military Service Tribunal adjudged whether, under the terms
of the Military Service Act (MSA), the national interest would be better
served keeping each man in production or sending him into the army.

The role of the tribunals
The short introduction to the tribunal system in Chapter 2 belies its
importance and complexity.[34] As has been shown, it was created with
little notice late in 1915 to give men attesting under the Derby Scheme the
right to apply to postpone enlistment. The introduction of conscription
in March 1916 under the MSA reinforced its role, as the tribunal now
had to consider whether to exempt men from compulsory enlistment.
Membership of the tribunal was extended from five to nine to cope with
the anticipated workload of new cases. What cannot have been clear to
these tribunal members, old and new, was what their primary objective
should be. To judge from Wolfe's 'needs', listed on page 130, the tribunal
had to strike a fine balance between four conflicting manpower objectives.
The guidance provided to the tribunals by the Local Government Board

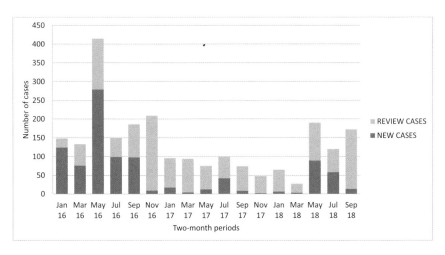

Figure 5.3 Chart showing number of cases heard by the St Albans City Military Service Tribunal, January 1916–October 1918.

(LGB) broadly reflected Wolfe's strictures. The tribunals had to apply the national interest test set out in section 2 (1) of the MSA: 'it was in the national interests that the [applicant] should, instead of being employed in military service, be engaged in other work in which he is habitually engaged' – that is, retained in civil employment. The LGB defined 'national interest' in broad terms that also echoed Wolfe's 'needs': 'It covers not only services which minister directly to the prosecution of the war but also services which are essential to the country at the present time, whether, for instance, in the maintenance of the food supply or of the export trade.'[35]

The rather general nature of this guidance perhaps reflected the government's uncertainty about its manpower policy. The goal was clear, of course. The policy had to coordinate the military and industrial demands of the country, but how to achieve this was a complex challenge. An attempt to develop such a policy under the auspices of Lord Lansdowne, minister without portfolio in Asquith's government, had failed in February 1916.[36] Moreover, with the military situation worsening, surely the requirements of the army overrode all other concerns? That is certainly what the War Office believed, but it is not what happened. The response of 2,000 or so tribunals across the country was startling. In March 1916 779,336 men (68 per cent) were successful in their applications for exemption. A total of 371,500 in total were compulsorily enlisted.[37] Decisions at the city tribunal reflected the national picture. Forty-nine applicants were granted exemptions in March, with only 22 rejected[38] (Figure 5.3).

This shortfall in expected recruitment, together with demands placed on the army as a result of the Easter Rising in Ireland, forced the government to react. The result was the Military Service Act (Session 2), which, in May 1916, extended conscription to married men aged between 18 and 41 inclusive. As shown in Figure 5.3, the rapid increase in new cases heard at the city tribunal in May and June was the result, and clearly the government's actions must have been having an effect on the business community in St Albans. An assessment of the challenge faced by one of the city's two large boot and shoe manufacturers at the hands of the tribunal brings to light just how difficult it became to conduct business in 1916 and beyond.

The experience of the boot and shoe manufacturers

Based in Grosvenor Road, Edwin Lee & Sons had been producing boots and shoes in St Albans from the early 1890s. The owner, Edwin Lee, was a former mayor of St Albans and an original appointee to the city tribunal in November 1915. His factory had been extended in 1906 and again in 1913, by which time the firm employed around 100 men and the same number of women. Using equipment driven by 'suction gas and electric motors', Lee's produced women's and children's boots and shoes for domestic consumption, but not military boots, which were then the preserve of the Northamptonshire manufacturers. It did, however, have a good export trade with markets in Europe and South Africa.[39]

Lee's first engagements with the city's tribunal as an applicant were on 23 and 24 June 1916, when he sought exemption for 20 of the firm's workers on the grounds that it was in the national interest that they remained working for him. Two of these applications were for his sons, Edwin Samuel and Alfred Joseph Lee, both of them managers in the company. Judging from the reports of the tribunal's previous hearings in the *Herts Advertiser*, Lee presented a stronger case than any other business leader to date. His experience as a member of the tribunal may explain this. The hearing on 23 June was the tribunal's thirtieth[40] and he had attended all but three of these. As a result he was able to draw on this experience to structure his case in a way that he hoped would appeal to his fellow members on the tribunal.

As reported in the newspaper, Lee's case for his sons reflected two of Wolfe's four 'needs', namely that due heed should be paid to the home and export markets. Lee made several key points. Firstly, with the government having 'taken control' of 300 other factories to manufacture boots, not just for the British army but also for those of France, Italy and Russia, production for the domestic market was under threat; Lee's existing capacity should be maintained to produce boots for women and children. Secondly, the firm had recently turned down export orders from France as they were already short of staff with 52 men having joined up; these were lost opportunities to fill up the country's coffers with desperately needed hard currency. For good measure he also declared that the firm paid £12,000 in wages every year into the local economy, representing important tax revenue for the Exchequer. The report of the hearing also described the financial struggles Lee's faced. With the firm already operating 20 per cent below capacity, its balance sheet was being affected by interest payments on idle machinery. Clearly, for a variety of reasons, some national, others personal, Lee desperately needed all the skilled men he could retain.[41]

He must have been content with the result of the hearings. Of the 20 employees, 17 were granted exemptions, all of whom were confirmed to be in certified occupations – that is, occupations which the government deemed to be in the national interest. Only two applications were rejected: Harold Todd of Pageant Road and Charles Chippett of Cavendish Road, two of six clickers for whom applications had been made.[42] However, though successful, it is clear from an analysis of the city tribunal's caseload that Lee had won just the first of many battles at the tribunal concerning these men. By October 1918 a further 75 applications had been made for them, mostly by the company. The remainder were by the military representative to the tribunal, Ernest Gape, keen to overturn existing exemptions. Business leaders and their employees wanted long periods with no change. They did not get this. The twin government manpower imperatives represented in the first two of Wolfe's 'needs' ensured that Lee's workers were always at risk at tribunal hearings.

This risk manifested itself in rule changes instituted by the government in responding to changes in military and industrial strategies. These changes could take the form of legislation, such as the two MSAs of 1916 that introduced conscription firstly for eligible single and widowed men and then for married men. Enacted as a direct result of the German spring offensive in 1918, the Military Service (No. 2) Act of that year extended the upper military age from 41 to 51 and established a tighter regulatory framework around exemptions. Officials also tweaked the certified occupations lists. These were important documents and all members of the tribunal and leaders of larger businesses in St Albans would have had a copy. Updated lists were issued periodically, reflecting changing manpower strategies. As a result, occupations which had been previously included might disappear in the new issue. The minimum age at which men working in certified occupations could be exempted was also liable to be adjusted, always, it must have seemed, upwards. More surreptitiously, officials also adjusted the rules and processes surrounding medical grading.[43]

Table 5.1 shows how these rule changes affected the clickers on Lee's staff. The city tribunal only very rarely granted absolute exemptions – perhaps four at most. The remainder had a time limit associated with

Table 5.1 Boot clickers' exemptions at the St Albans City Military Service Tribunal, 1916–18.

Date in force	Document	Terms
February 1916	Official List of Certified Occupations	Not exempt
March 1916	Military Service Act	All single men and widowers (without dependent children) over 18 and under 41 deemed to have enlisted
May 1916	Military Service Act (Session 2)	All men of 18 years of age and over but under 41 deemed to have enlisted
July 1916	Certified Occupations List R.94	All clickers exempt until 25 September 1916 but, from then, only married men of 25 years and over employed as clickers
November 1916	Certified Occupations List R.105	All married clickers exempt; unmarried clickers exempt only if 31 years of age or older
February 1917	Certified Occupations List R.117	Not exempt
May 1918	Military Service (No. 2) Act	Upper military age limit extended to 51
September 1918	Certified Occupations List R.136 (Revised)	All clickers deemed to be in a certified occupation if born before 1880 (Grade 1, physically fit men) or 1889 (Grade 2, for those less fit)

Notes: For an explanation of medical gradings see p. xix.
Source: TNA, MH 47/142/1–3, *Books, booklets and pamphlets*, 1916–18.

them, usually no more than six months. When that expired Lee's had to reapply for the renewal of the exemption. Moreover, Gape, the military service representative, could apply to have cases reviewed by the tribunal (these renewals and reviews are shown in Figure 5.3 as 'review cases'). Such applications would be based on any new rules described in Table 5.1 pertaining at the time of the hearing. The company needed its clickers and made a further 32 applications just for the four clickers who were exempted in June 1916 through until September 1918. Three of them managed to see out the war working for Lee's in St Albans, their low medical grading as Grade 3 men helping their cause.[44]

The interpretation of 'national interest' could change as well, and sometimes to the benefit of local industry. As Edwin Lee had forecast at that June 1916 hearing, the loss of capacity in the boot industry had serious repercussions. Who was left to make new boots for the domestic market? By late 1917 this was becoming a significant problem and the government took the decision to mandate production of so-called 'wartime boots' for women and children. These were to be made to standard specifications and distributed at controlled prices with agreed profit margins.[45] Lee's benefited from this development, stating in January 1918 that they were working on a government order to produce 5,500 pairs a month.[46] Such contracts gave the company a form of protection at the tribunal that it had not had before. The reintroduction of clickers to the certified occupations list later that year must have also brought a degree of confidence.

The tribunal and the printing businesses

Compared with the struggles of the boot and shoe manufacturers the printing companies, another of the city's large employers, faced even more problems. They represented a successful and growing sector in the city, with several firms moving to the area from the 1890s onwards. In addition to the five companies outlined in Table 5.2 there were also several jobbing printers in the city centre who operated on a much smaller scale. Successful they may have been before the war, but the four war years were to prove challenging for all of the companies and particularly for two of them. Justifying that their employees should be retained in the national interest proved to be a tough test. This section considers why this was the case.

One of the problems the printers faced was that the government, working through the LGB, certainly felt there was little of national interest in what the print companies had to offer. The February 1916 certified occupations

Table 5.2 Outline of the five largest printing companies in St Albans, spring 1914.

Name	No. of employees (est.)	Principal focus of business
Smith's Printing Co. Ltd	240	Magazines, long runs of pamphlets, catalogues, label work, letterpress and litho Horticultural work a speciality; catalogues and general advertisement and mail-order literature
Salvation Army Printing Works	200	Production of *The War Cry, The Bandsman* and other Salvation Army newspapers and journals. Some printing for YMCA and other Christian organisations
F. Dangerfield Printing Co. Ltd	160	Printing large posters for underground operators in London and omnibus companies
Richard Taylor & Co.	49	Ornithological printing
Gibbs & Bamforth Ltd	n.k.	Local newspaper publisher including the *Herts Advertiser* Book and journal printing (including the *Transactions of the St Albans & Hertfordshire Architectural & Archaeological Society*) Catalogue printing Cardboard box production

list included only those print workers working on newspapers.[47] This must have startled owners and managers of the local firms, as they began from March 1916 to get to grips with how the system worked. Some relief was provided when electrotypers and stereotypers (but only married men aged over 31) in the general trade were added to the July 1916 list.[48] In 1918 the list was greatly extended, but by then capacity in the St Albans trade had been severely cut.[49]

Two companies were particularly badly hit. F. Dangerfield Printing Co. Ltd, based on the corner of London Road and Alma Road, was one of them. The firm had continued to supply London transport companies with recruiting and promotional posters for all but the last year or so of the war.[50] By December 1916, however, matters had become serious. At a tribunal hearing Frederick Dangerfield, the owner, was depressed about the future. The newspaper report recorded him saying 'it was no longer a case of making a profit, but only to carry on until his two [sons] came back to enable them to carry on. If it was only as far as he himself was concerned, he would "chuck it" tomorrow.' His firm had lost 80 per cent of its male staff. Any opportunity he had to train women already on staff to take over from the men was prevented by at least one of the print unions.[51] The challenge facing companies such as Dangerfield's was to find a niche from which they could defend their male staff by showing that they were doing work in the national interest. Dangerfield's did make such a claim in September 1917, but it is not recorded what this type of work was.[52] By March 1918 the company employed just 47 staff, compared with 160 before the war. Post-war it appears to have recovered from these vicissitudes and was still operating from its base in Alma Road until taken over in 1940.[53]

Smith's Printing Co. Ltd, the largest print company in the city in terms of staff, suffered problems of a similar magnitude. There was one difference, however: Smith's disappeared from the city around 1919.[54] It is not clear to what extent its wartime experiences caused this; what is clear, however, is that Smith's, like Dangerfield's, failed to attract sufficient work of national importance. Ernest Gape, the military representative, made his position alarmingly obvious at a tribunal hearing in 1917. While he acknowledged that the company had 'parted with a tremendous lot of hands, [Smith's] was not in the national interest'.[55] By June 1918 the workforce had dropped from around 240 pre-war to fewer than 80. Machines were lying idle 'under blankets'.[56] This once-booming company sub-let part of its premises to Sir Howard Grubb's telescope company. Probably at the instigation of the Ministry of Munitions, Grubb's removed from Dublin to an empty part of the Smith's buildings in Hatfield Road to carry on wartime production of periscopes for submarines and sights for guns. Manufacturing in England was almost certainly deemed more secure than having the company's wares at risk from German torpedoes in an Irish Sea crossing.[57] Although the chronology is uncertain, Smith's Printing appears to have closed up its St Albans operations early in 1919 before selling its landmark premises to Grubb's in 1920.

It was not all gloom for the local printing companies. Gibbs & Bamforth Ltd appear to have had a better war, being protected by the diversity of its operations. The company did have its problems, however. Its small cardboard-box-making operation probably ceased trading late in 1916, when the last male employee was called up.[58] On the general printing side of the business it appears to have lost the contract to print over one million copies of the 1916 edition of Samuel Ryder's seed catalogue. It had previously held the 1915 contract[59] (see Figure 5.8). It also failed the tribunal's national interest test on several occasions in 1916/17.[60] However, it was the importance of the *Herts Advertiser* that offered some salvation, albeit later in the war.[61] By this time Gibbs & Bamforth claimed that the paper's circulation had reached record numbers, with many copies sent to local men 'in training camps or engaged in the sterner work in the trenches or upon the high seas [and they] depended on the *Herts Advertiser* for home news'.[62] When conscription was introduced protection was offered to companies publishing newspapers and the February 1916 List of Certified Occupations recorded 13 occupations associated with newspaper production including linotype operators, an important role in the process.[63] However, by July of that year only ten were listed, linotype operators being one of those dropped.[64] By 1917 Gibbs & Bamforth were down to their last two operators. At a tribunal hearing in July the company's managers warned that if either of these two men was compelled to join up production of the *Herts Advertiser* would stop. On this occasion Gape supported the printers and both men appear to have carried on working. He justified his position by stating that he had seen evidence that the government believed that local newspaper production was of national importance.[65] The newspaper continued to be printed for the rest of the war and the company was able to invest in a new press late in 1919.[66]

Business owners and the national interest

As will be clear from the previous sections, the members of the city tribunal had to make many difficult decisions. This was certainly the case when considering whether company managers and directors should be granted exemption. The complex decision framework was laid out in the April 1916 List of Certified Occupations, which stated:

> *Proprietors and Managers*: The directing head of every considerable business of real national importance should be given exemption from military service. If there is more than one directing head, the Local Tribunal should consider whether the business is of such size or complexity that more than one head is essential.[67]

Figure 5.4 George Day (seated), surrounded by his family. Back row left to right: sons Alfred, Arthur and George junior, and son-in-law Ernest Rose, 1916. © Pat Moore

The tribunal members had to consider not only whether it was in the national interest to keep the man in his role but also whether his was a 'considerable' business and also one of 'real national importance'. There was an added complication, one of perception. Directing heads were different from their employees. They had made substantial investments in their enterprises by way of cash, goodwill and stock. If compelled to enlist they risked losing control over the direction of these businesses to which they were committed, and in such difficult times. In light of this, why should not their cases be considered differently? Some of the tribunal members, such as Edwin Lee the boot manufacturer, would have empathised.

St Albans had a preponderance of family-owned businesses of 50 employees or more, the straw hat trade being predominant. Of the 11 local hat firms, six applied for exemption for a total of ten directing heads, all bar one of whom was a family member.[68] Three brothers, all managers working in E. Day & Co., made use of their right to apply (Figure 5.4). At the first hearing in May 1916 the tribunal told them that one had to enlist and left the decision to the brothers as to which one. They opted for the youngest, George (junior).[69] The application of the middle brother,

Arthur, was rejected on appeal in February 1917.[70] The remaining brother was Alfred and, although a physically fit man of military age, he managed to see out the war working for the business. As will be seen, the company had developed a new line of business producing military sun helmets (see Figure 5.7). The inference can be drawn from this that the tribunal, in protecting him, believed that Alfred was working for a considerable company of national importance and, as the remaining manager, his continuation in that role was in the national interest.[71]

Owing to the helmet business, the case of Alfred Day was a fairly clear-cut decision for the tribunal. More contentious was the case of Christopher Webdale, the managing partner of another family-owned straw hat manufacturer (Figure 5.5). He was married, just 28 years old and medically fit, so ideal for service at the front. The company had some 120 workers before the war, supplying a busy export trade.[72] By mid-1916 the firm had lost one-third of those employees, probably through their skilled men volunteering for the army. The city tribunal, as ever, did not look favourably on the straw hat manufacturers, judging that their businesses were not of national importance and that retaining their

Figure 5.5 The Webdale family, with Henry (seated) and his son Christopher standing with his arm on his father's chair, *c*.1910. © Timothy Cornfield

managers was not in the national interest. In June 1916 Henry Webdale, the 61-year-old owner of the company, applied on his son's behalf. Henry announced that he had retired from the business the year before (1915), leaving Christopher in sole control. He was not now able to pick up the reins again, as too much time had elapsed. Gape appears not to have believed this. Moreover, affronted that a man of Christopher's physique was making straw hats in St Albans rather than serving his country in the army, Gape fought father and son at eight tribunal hearings between the summer of 1916 and the following winter. In March 1917 Gape finally got his man. It is difficult to imagine the stress the process must have caused the Webdales and the effort taken by all parties just to draw one man from industry into the army. On several occasions the father had threatened to close the business if the case were lost. This was something that worried the tribunal members, as this action risked throwing dozens of employees out of work and onto the support of the country. Henry Webdale was certainly not the first directing head in St Albans to use this warning to force the tribunal's hand, but this time it was no idle threat.[73] Late in 1917 Webdale announced in the hat trade journal that, 'since his son had been taken for the Army, it was impossible for him to carry on and he was therefore reluctantly compelled to wind up the business'.[74] Christopher was killed in action in France in August 1918.[75]

The employment of women

One noticeable change during the war years was the increase in women workers. In the 1911 census for St Albans, of the 4,223 women recorded as being employed, nearly one-third (1,323) were working in manufacturing. A similar number were in domestic service of some description. Unsurprisingly, it was to women that the government looked to make up the shortfall in industrial capacity caused by the loss of men to the military.

This strategy made good sense, but there were plenty of obstacles in the way. One of these was the general attitude to the employment of women. Reports in the *Herts Advertiser* of tribunal hearings provide insight into the minds of local business leaders of the day, all of them men. Comments such as 'women could not do the wet cleaning because it was heavy work', made by the owner of a firm of dry cleaners, appear to contain some logic.[76] Others, such as the application by Rowland Cutmore for his last male barber,[77] provided an opportunity for levity for the tribunal members, a brief respite from the toil of their deliberations:

> Mr Gape (*military representative*) said that haircutting and shaving was not necessarily a man's job. Look at the ladies doing this work in London! Mr Beal (*tribunal member*): I am afraid it would be a shock to St Albans (Laughter). Councillor Townson (*tribunal member*): it would be a great attraction. Mr Cutmore (*applicant*) said St Albans was different. How many of the gentlemen would come to his establishment if he had ladies shaving them? Members: We would all come! (Laughter).[78]

While Cutmore was perhaps understandably keen to keep his gentleman's hairdresser a male preserve, some of the comments heard at the tribunal appear tainted with sexism. Harold Boon was the chief accountant at the Salvation Army Printing Works in Campfield Road. His employers appealed on the grounds of national interest to retain him in their business printing *The War Cry* and other newspapers and journals. Boon's work could not be done by women as, according to

> Mr Robinson (*applicant's legal representative*): It is work which requires brains. The Mayor (*tribunal member*): Ladies have brains to-day, Mr Robinson. Mr Robinson: Yes, but these brains need training. Mr Fairbairn (*manager of the company*): four ladies could not do the work that the chief cashier was now doing.

The argument was of little use, as Boon was given just one month's exemption and finally called up later in October 1916.[79]

Perhaps the most interesting view of the employment of women comes from German-born Frederick Sander, who was naturalised in 1889.[80] He was a renowned orchid grower with extensive nurseries off Camp Road and in Bruges in Belgium. By 1916 Sander was having a mixed war. On the one hand, he had lost access to his nursery in Bruges following the German invasion. On the other, he was picking up business in South America and the USA from German competitors hit by the Royal Navy blockade.[81] Echoing the fourth of Wolfe's 'needs', Sander used these export opportunities in his application to the tribunal in May 1916 to have five of his male employees exempted. After all, he claimed, his business was in the national interest, his exports generating essential hard currency for the Exchequer. Sander had already lost 23 men to the services and needed these five to keep the business going. Asked by tribunal members why he was not recruiting women to replace them, he replied that he could not put any women in charge of one of his 40 glasshouses. While this bland statement reported in the *Herts Advertiser* provides no more than the merest hint of his attitude, his surviving letters are revealingly explicit.[82] Sander wrote in one of them: 'No, girls are no good. Out of sixteen we have here, only one is tolerable. They have killed and are killing thousands of plants. You cannot teach them.'[83] Perhaps the women's inability to handle heavy equipment in the glasshouses was the cause of his frustration.

While it is unclear why Sander reported such bad experiences, it would be wrong to suggest that his opinions and those of other businessmen in St Albans were typical of the time. After all, the 1911 census indicates that over 1,300 local women were already working in manufacturing, albeit with no evidence that any of them were in 'white collar' roles. Further progress was being made in some areas by 1916. In March of that year women were recorded for the first time working for the St Albans Gas Co., being 'enlisted in all departments where they are suitable, the service of those [men] leaving hav[ing] been replaced with female labour'.[84] In November the two large boot and shoe manufacturers, Lee's and Freshwater's, jointly placed a prominent advertisement in the *Herts Advertiser* calling for women to apply for a raft of new jobs with 'many new operations being taught'[85] (Figure 5.6). A similar notice was placed by the owners of the flour mill at New Barnes the following week, with the strapline 'An opportunity occurs for a few strong women to earn good wages in these mills. Full wages will be paid whilst learning the work.'[86] The surprise is that it seems to have taken local employers 24 months to realise that, with the war forecast to last years and manpower shortages already evident in those first months of the war, recruiting and training women should be treated as a matter of expedience.

Judging from the wording in their advertisement, it is probable that the 'Call to Women Workers' made by the boot makers was an attempt to implement dilution. This was a government-inspired initiative to place unskilled or semi-skilled workers in normally skilled jobs, training them in just one small part of the extended process. In doing so, the skilled men could be drawn into the military with little or no consequence for the manpower needs of the country. The process by which dilution could be effected was defined at the time as: 'Through the subdivision of skilled tasks into their simplest processes, through the introduction of automatic

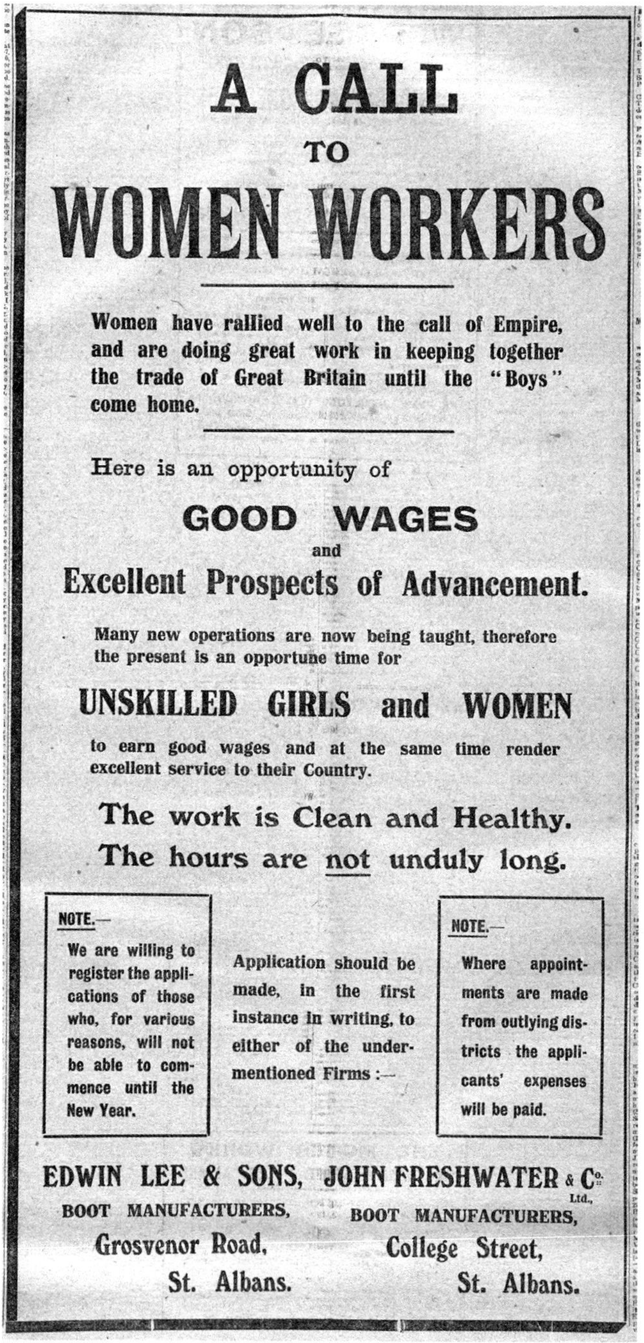

Figure 5.6 Job advert placed by Edwin Lee & Sons and John Freshwater & Co Ltd, *Herts Advertiser*, November 1916. © Hertfordshire Archives and Local Studies

machines which required little skill to operate and through the constant process of training and "upgrading" of dilutees.'[87]

Owing to the nature of the surviving sources, identifying examples of dilution in the city's industries is a difficult task. However, what is available generally indicates that there were many problems with it. A year after first reporting that they were employing women to replace men lost to the army, the St Albans Gas Co. recorded limited and frustrating results. For unspecified reasons, perhaps lack of training, these new female workers were unable to fully replace the men. The directors noted that:

> Whether in the office, in the district attending to the consumers, or on the Gas Works, [the women] are most loyal and endeavour to do their best ... the greatest inconvenience is, however, experienced in the loss of men on the distribution. Many applications are received for new customers and fixing, cooking and heating stoves [*sic*], which [it] is not possible to comply with.[88]

The case of Smith's Printing in Hatfield Road is more clear-cut and an interesting example of what at least was intended by the policy of dilution. As has been shown, Smith's was a business that had problems justifying to the city tribunal that its continuing operation was of national importance. On the face of it, it had a head-start on other businesses in the city, as even in 1914 around half its workforce of 240 were women.[89] However, it faced a significant hurdle were it to promote these semi- and unskilled women to replace skilled men. Smith's Printing operated in a heavily unionised sector. A fractious relationship between the company and the main union, the St Albans Typographical Society (TS), continued throughout the war years, with the question of dilution being a particular flashpoint between the two sides. As the managers of the business readily accepted, training women workers to replace skilled men, although far from ideal, made sense. However, the managers and the union were not of the same mind. Matters came to a head with applications by the company to keep Herbert Swain (a printer's cutter) and Arthur Ralph and Arthur Sharp (both machine minders) working for them instead of being forced to join up. This was a desperate fight for Smith's. The managers applied initially for the exemptions and then for renewals for these three men on a total of 30 occasions between September 1916 and May 1918; this represented about 40 per cent of all Smith's applications.[90] If the decision went against them at the city tribunal, the managers appealed to the Hertfordshire County Appeal Tribunal (CAT). The reason for this fierce fight was the attitude of the TS. The union would not permit women to replace these men. As Ernest Townson, one of the managers,[91] said: 'if I put on girls to do this skilled work the Union would take away all my men'.[92] While the company itself, the tribunal members and Gape, the military representative, all accepted that dilution would release three men for the army, the intransigent policy of the union prevented this from happening. The TS's definition of 'national interest' was different from the employers' and the tribunal members.

While there were problems in the printing trade, a form of dilution worked to the benefit of the city's largest straw hat manufacturer. Based in a modern factory off Marlborough Road, E. Day & Co employed over 300 workers in 1914, of whom about 210 were women. The company had, according to its publicity, developed a 'world-wide trade in men's straw hats'.[93] On the face of it, Day's, like the city's other straw hat manufacturers, was destined to struggle in the war. Supply-chain dislocation was one problem, particularly in the early months of the war. For example, straw plait coming from the Far East faced shipping problems, and dyes, a German specialism, were now blockaded.[94] Voluntary and then compulsory recruitment hit the company hard. The number of hat blockers, the skilled artisans in the manufacturing process, had dropped from 31 pre-war to just seven in May 1916.[95] There was a total of 53 male employees of military age in 1914, and by February 1917 just four eligible men remained.[96] As with Smith's Printing, appearances were deceptive. Day's had a very good war for the simple reason that the company developed a new product line. This was the manufacture of military sun helmets for use by soldiers fighting in the fierce heat of Gallipoli, Palestine and points east.

Day's picked up its first helmet contract from the War Office in the early summer of 1915. By the end of the war it had made around 750,000 helmets in total, initially from straw and then from the more traditional cork.[97] What was novel about Day's production was the process:

> The practice in London for the last thirty years had been for the materials – the linen, cork and khaki drill – to be given to the workmen who delivered the completed helmet ... all the processes were undertaken by the same workman. Prior to the war ... there never had been any females employed in that industry.[98]

Day's restructured production by carrying out the

> Scientific organisation of the factory into teams of men and
> women, each team completing a helmet and each man and
> woman in a team doing his or her allotted share of the work of
> manufacture; mass production as distinguished from production
> by an individual; the introduction and use of machinery and
> the elimination of all physical strain or hard manual labour.
> Unlike the London factories, where the helmet was given out to
> the worker who built it by hand, at [Day's] each helmet passed
> through a dozen hands.[99]

So, the company had taken a process based on piece work done solely
by men and turned it into a semi-mechanised process largely staffed by
women (Figure 5.7). The success of this innovation can be traced in the
reports of hearings of Day's and its competitors at the city tribunal. While
all the producers struggled to justify the manufacture of straw hats as

Figure 5.7 Military sun helmet production at E. Day & Co., 1918. © Imperial War Museums
(Q28672)

Figure 5.8 Front cover of Ryder's seed catalogue, 1916. © RHS, Lindley Library (LIB0002165)

being of national importance, losing large chunks of their workforce as a result, Day's helmet department received a degree of protection. The case of Thomas Jones of Cape Road was a good example. He was foreman in the department and initially exempted by the tribunal from conscription for 12 months before being granted a Certificate of Protection by the Ministry of Munitions in the middle of 1917.[100] This was a rare, perhaps unique, award in the straw hat trade in St Albans. Day's success can also be seen in the growth in the female workforce. As previously stated, the firm started the war with around 200 female employees. By 1918 over 700 women were working at the factory, with probably no more than a handful of men involved.[101] Diluting the process through mechanisation and the introduction of women workers was the key to the company's success. After all, there was no need to rely on any (perceived) caprice of the city tribunal to protect male workers from conscription. Day's competitors must have looked on with envy.

Taxes and restrictions

Government expenditure grew 13-fold between 1913/14 and its peak in 1917/18. To pay for the war it employed all three of the traditional methods of raising funds: borrowing, printing money and increasing rates of taxation. For example, the standard rate of income tax rose from 6 per cent to 12 per cent in the November 1914 war budget, reaching 30 per cent in 1918/19. The numbers of people paying the tax jumped from 1.1 million to 3.5 million by the end of the war as the level of exemptions dropped.[102]

It was the budget of September 1915 that brought home to business leaders in St Albans just what lay in store.[103] The new excess profits duty was the first time companies, rather than just their shareholders, had been taxed. While the variety of new and increased taxes was shocking, it was the threat of substantial rises in postal rates that caused anxiety in St Albans. In a city with several mail-order companies, the prospective rise in postal rates was a serious blow. A lengthy report in the *Herts Advertiser* investigated how the new rates would affect three businesses in particular: printers Gibbs & Bamforth and Smith's Printing, and Ryder's, the distributor of penny packets of seeds. An interview with Samuel Ryder provided the most illuminating part of the report. He described in detail the company's dependence on the postal system for both marketing and distribution. For example, they posted 1.25 million catalogues a year (Figure 5.8). Ryder estimated that the increased postal rate on catalogue despatch would be at least £7,500 on top of the existing cost of £5,000. The new rates would add a further £6,000 to his order fulfilment costs[104] and he would have to raise the price of his packets from 1d to 3d just to cover these new costs. Under pressure from the mail-order industry the government partially backed down.

While increases in taxation affected all businesses in St Albans the beer trade, consisting of two breweries and many publicans, faced innumerable restrictions.[105] The duty on a standard barrel of beer jumped from 7s 9d to 23s in the first wartime budget in November 1914, climbing to 50s in 1918.[106] Less expected were government orders in 1915 to brewers to reduce production to 70 per cent of pre-war levels and the introduction of controls on the price of a pint. The need to manage the consumption of raw materials in part explains these measures, but there were also hints of a moral panic surrounding beer drinking in wartime.[107] David Lloyd George, a leading temperance advocate and also then chancellor of the exchequer, claimed in a speech in March 1915 that: 'We are fighting Germany, Austria and Drink; and as far as I can see the greatest of these three deadly foes is Drink.'[108] This oft-quoted soundbite reflected what others thought. While the outcome of the war remained uncertain, the consumption of alcohol should be restricted. It was the threat to the local community of having so many soldiers billeted in the city that worried some. The temperance movement, increasingly supine since its late-Victorian heyday, mobilised and paid for a missioner to visit local army camps to convince soldiers to take the teetotal pledge. The campaign met with success, and claimed that around 1,000 soldiers had made the commitment by March 1915.[109] The establishment of counter-attractions such as the Patriotic Club and YMCA tents, where soldiers could gather without the presence of alcohol, reflected this desire as well.[110]

Even with the activities of the temperance agitators, public houses should have been thriving with so many soldiers based in and around the town for the duration of the war. There is, though, little evidence to support this contention. One publican, Stanley Alcock of the Red Lion hotel in the High Street, was made bankrupt in 1916 and blamed the officers billeted on him for not spending enough money. He noted contemptuously that they were 'ginger beer and water drinkers'.[111] Others reported their struggles when they applied to the tribunal for exemption. The reply of William Leatherdale, the licensee at the Lower

Red Lion in Fishpool Street, to a suggestion by the tribunal that he sell his business before enlisting was typical: 'Who'd have a public house now?'[112] It is not difficult to understand this despair. Opening hours in St Albans had been curtailed by the local magistrates as early as August 1914 and drinking customs such as treating and the long-pull had been banned across the country.[113] Even when customers could legally buy a drink they found both the price and strength of their pint controlled by central government: a pint had doubled in cost to 4d by 1916 and brewers had been obligated to produce low-alcohol beer from late 1917 onwards, something disdainfully called by a Watford brewer 'the present compulsory diluted liquid, erroneously called beer'.[114] New licensing laws and regulations introduced to control consumption were complex, as the lengthy reports of cases brought against two publicans for illegally selling beer to soldiers showed.[115] By the end of the war shortages of beer and spirits due to the lack of raw materials meant that pubs closed even when they could have been open. The Duke of Marlborough on Holywell Hill was shut two days a week because of this.[116] Last but not least, there is some evidence of a change in attitude to alcohol consumption in St Albans during the war. In 1913, 45 people were found guilty at the city petty sessions of offences involving drink, such as drunk and disorderly.[117] By 1918 the number was just four.[118] There was good cause for the temperance advocates to be pleased.

Sharing the publicans' uncertainties were the owners of the city's two breweries. In 1918 Harold Adey, director of Adey & White in Chequer Street, reported that his sales had dropped by 40 per cent since 1914. Shortages of ingredients, manpower and coal were the cause.[119] Larger brewers suffered similar declines, Whitbread recording a 54 per cent drop in production at its Chiswell Street brewery in London.[120] However, it would be wrong to conclude that this was an indicator of wartime depression in the beer trade. Overall, many breweries across the country, particularly the larger ones, traded profitably, supported by full employment and, later in the war, lower unit costs.[121] It was generally the smaller brewers who suffered.[122] This might explain the decision in 1918 of the Kent family, owners of the other brewery in St Albans, to merge the business with Adey & White. The death of the head of the family, Thomas Kent, in April 1917, followed swiftly by those of two of his sons within days of each other at the beginning of August, both killed in action, may also have led the remaining family members to take this course.[123]

Conclusion

Much has been written about the stress faced by both soldiers on the front line and by their families at home waiting to hear from them. Though of a different magnitude, it is clear that the business community had a stressful time too. The loss of skilled workers, significant tax rises, restrictions on trade – all new elements of the economy – had to be managed. Some businesses, such as Smith's Printing Co., fared badly, unable to find the right opportunities to protect their finances. Others appear to have traded successfully. E. Day & Co. was one of these, finding a niche in the hat trade that could justifiably be said to be in the national interest.

As the government pushed and prodded the country's industry towards 'total war', the city tribunal clearly played an important role in trying to interpret rapidly changing manpower policies against the backdrop of the local economy. The tribunal also had to oversee manpower in the production and distribution of food in St Albans, something that went right to the stomachs of the people. The next chapter considers, among other topics, how the city's butchers, bakers and grocers were treated by the tribunal, especially in the tough winter of 1917/18.

Notes

1. See Chapter 1 for a fuller discussion of the structure of business in St Albans.
2. P. Simkins, *Kitchener's army: the raising of the new armies, 1914–1916* (Barnsley, 2007), p. 39.
3. K. Grieves, *The politics of manpower, 1914–1918* (Manchester, 1988), p. 2.
4. Ibid.
5. H. Wolfe, *Labour supply and regulation* (London, 1923), pp. 1–2.
6. Grieves, *Politics of manpower*, p. 192.
7. The estimate of 26 per cent is based on the analysis of the 1911 census for the city by Mike North, a member of the Home Front Project Group.
8. H. Wolfe, *Labour supply and regulation* (London, 1923), p. 157.
9. See H. Strachan, *The First World War*, vol. 1 (Oxford, 2001), pp. 1067–9, for more information on the 'scandal'.
10. See 'The city tribunal', *Herts Advertiser* (*HA*), 24 June 1916. Deep Well Boring Ltd on the Sandridge Road was involved in munitions production but was based outside the city boundaries.
11. J. Dyer et al., *The story of Luton* (Luton, 1964), pp. 170–1.
12. Ministry of Munitions, *The history of the Ministry of Munitions*, the National Factories, VIII, Pt 2 (London, 1922), pp. 170–1.
13. HALS, SBR/3384, City Council Correspondence File etc., *St Albans Chamber of Commerce Annual Report*, 1918. The report does list a Manufacturers' Exporters' and Importers' Section, but this was established only in July 1917. See 'St Albans traders', *HA*, 28 July 1917.

14. For evidence of the committee's existence see 'Chamber of Commerce annual report for 1913', *HA*, 2 May 1913.

15. See Chapter 1.

16. N.C. Friswell, *Northmet: a history of the North Metropolitan Electric Power Supply Company* (Horsham, 2000), p. 121.

17. 'Correspondence: "St Albans & munitions"', *HA*, 6 January 1917.

18. Carrington had taken over from the previous editor, Frederick Usher, in June 1916.

19. 'The government and the farmers', *HA*, 27 January 1917.

20. 'The city tribunal', *HA*, 8 July 1916.

21. 'Herts appeal tribunal', *HA*, 3 August 1918.

22. 'Getting together – genial atmosphere at St Albans workers' gathering', *Hertfordshire News and County Advertiser*, 24 December 1919.

23. 'Overalls for munitions workers', *HA*, 30 October 1915.

24. *Pictorial Record: St Albans* (London, 1915), p. 16.

25. 'Only man who dresses Bass', *HA*, 17 March 1917.

26. See pp. 152–3.

27. 'St Albans Gas Company', *HA*, 29 March 1919.

28. HALS, PUG 13/1/6, St Albans Gas Co. Directors' and Shareholders' Minute Book, 1914–21, June 1915 quarterly report, 16 June 1915.

29. Ibid., 21 June 1916.

30. 'St Albans Gas Co.', *HA*, 23 March 1918.

31. T. Mercer, *Mercer chronometers, history, maintenance and repair* (Ashbourne, 2003), p. 54. Of the 58 staff members 22 were women, but it is not known how, if at all, they replaced skilled men already lost to the army.

32. 'The city tribunal', *HA*, 11 March 1916. The National Archives (TNA), MH 47/142/2, *Schedule of Protected Occupations*, 7 July 1917, p. 16.

33. Mercer, *Mercer chronometers*, p. 54.

34. See pp. 43–50.

35. TNA, MH 47/142/1, *Circular relating to the Constitution, Functions and Procedure of Local Tribunals*, 1916, p. 5.

36. Grieves, *Politics of manpower*, p. 56.

37. Simkins, *Kitchener's army*, p. 157.

38. Data extracted from HALS, SBR/865, St Albans City Tribunal Minute Book, 1915–18.

39. The description of Lee's business is based on the *Pictorial Record: St Albans*, pp. 16–17.

40. The city tribunal had first met on 10 January 1916.

41. 'The city tribunal', *HA*, 1 July 1916. The discussion of the hearing for the 20 men was based on this report.

42. Ibid. The applications of Chippett and Todd were perhaps rejected as they were the only two of the six clickers who had attested under the Derby Scheme, so showing a willingness to serve; the others were conscripts. Clickers played a key role in the boot-making process, cutting the uppers for the boot from leather.

43. See J. McDermott, *British military service tribunals, 1916–18: 'a much abused body of men'* (Manchester, 2011), pp. 187–91, for a discussion of the problematic role of the army medical boards in grading.

44. See the note on medical gradings, p. xix.

45. A. Fox, *A history of the National Union of Boot and Shoe Operatives, 1874–1957* (Oxford, 1958), p. 372.

46. 'St Albans city tribunal', *HA*, 26 January 1918.

47. TNA, MH 47/142/1, *Group and Class Systems, Notes on Administration, Appendix 6, Official List of Certified Occupations (10 February 1916)*, pp. 97–8.

48. TNA, MH 47/142/1, *Group and Class Systems, Notes on Administration, 7 July 1916 (R.94)*, p. 12.

49. TNA, MH 47/142/3, *List of Certified Occupations, 26 September 1918 (R.136 revised)*, pp. 15–16.

50. See the collection of posters on the London Transport Museum website <www.ltmcollection.org/posters/index.html> accessed 1 January 2016.

51. 'The city tribunal: two out of three to go', *HA*, 23 December 1916. For the issue with the unions see pp. 151–2.

52. 'County tribunal', *HA*, 8 September 1917.

53. M. Fookes, *Made in St Albans* (St Albans, 1997), p. 16.

54. In 1920 Smith's Printing had both ceased to own its premises in Hatfield Road or occupy them. See HALS, SBR/interim catalogue, City Rate Book, October 1920.

55. 'Herts appeals', *HA*, 14 July 1917.

56. 'St Albans city tribunal', *HA*, 18 May 1918.

57. Personal communication, Jonathan Mein and Mike Neighbour, 11 January 2016. See also G.M. Sisson, 'Mirror images', *Vistas in Astronomy*, 35 (1992), p. 346; TNA, MUN 4/5307, Liquidation of contracts, 1919–20; MUN 4/5311, Liquidation of contracts, 1918–19.

58. 'County tribunal', *HA*, 2 December 1916.

59. Judging from the printer's details in these editions, local competitor Richard Taylor & Co. had the contract for the 1916 and 1919 editions.

60. For example, 'St Albans tribunal', *HA*, 18 November 1916. The company had as many as 16 compositors before the war but just three in 1916; some of these may have volunteered rather than have been conscripted.

61. The company also published the *Luton News & Bedfordshire Chronicle* (from March 1916 renamed the *Luton News & Bedfordshire Advertiser*).

62. 'Important newspaper development', *HA*, 22 November 1919. See 'Adieu', *HA*, 24 January 1947 where the editor, Harry Carrington, claimed that the circulation was around 9,000 in 1916.

63. TNA, MH 47/142/1, *Group and Class Systems, Notes on Administration, Appendix 6, Official List of Certified Occupations (10 February 1916)*, p. 98.

64. TNA, MH 47/142/1, *List of Certified Occupations, 7 July 1916 (R.94)*, p. 12.

65. 'Military service', *HA*, 28 July 1917. In the TNA, MH 47/142/3, *List of Certified Occupations*, 26 September 1918 (R.136 Revised), discretion was given to the Director of National Service for the region or the National Service Representative (i.e. Gape for the city tribunal) to agree to exemptions for newspaper editorial and publishing staff, presumably where this was in the national interest.

66. 'Important newspaper development', *HA*, 22 November 1919.

67. TNA, MH 47/141/1, *Comparison of Previous List of Certified Exemptions with list of 4 April, 1916, showing the material alterations apart from age limits (R.94)*.

68. Now retired from general management, George Day, the owner of the company, was a member of the city tribunal. He stood down when applications relating to the company were heard.

69. 'City tribunal', *HA*, 5 August 1916.

70. 'County tribunal', *HA*, 24 February 1917.

71. 'St Albans Army appeals', *HA*, 11 May 1918.

72. 'The city tribunal', *HA*, 1 July 1916.

73. See 'Herts appeal tribunal', *HA*, 6 October 1917, where Gape commented about such threats that 'they never do shut'.

74. *Hatters' Gazette*, November 1917, p. 397.

75. Anon, *St Albans roll of honour* (St Albans, n.d.), p. 26.

76. 'The city tribunal', *HA*, 3 June 1916. The applicant was M. Smith & Co.

77. Cutmore's hairdressers was at this time located in Market Place.

78. 'The city tribunal', *HA*, 3 June 1916. Titles in italics added for exposition. The tribunal granted two months' conditional exemption for the employee Sidney Newbury, for whom Cutmore was applying.

79. 'The city tribunal', *HA*, 1 July 1916. Boon received one month's exemption, extended by a further three months in September 1916.

80. TNA, HO 144/304/B4882, Nationality and naturalisation papers for Friedrich Sander, 1889.

81. 'The city tribunal', *HA*, 13 May 1916.

82. Ibid. Sander achieved moderate success at the hearing with the tribunal granting exemptions for two of the five men. However, even these were rescinded by January 1918.

83. A. Swinson, *Frederick Sander, the Orchid King* (London, 1970), p. 226.

84. HALS, PUG 13/1/6, St Albans Gas Co. Directors' and Shareholders' Minute Book, 1914–21, March 1916 shareholders' meeting.

85. 'A call to women workers', *HA*, 18 November 1916.

86. 'New Barnes Mill', *HA*, 25 November 1916.

87. TNA, MUN 5/72/324/1, Minutes of Dilution Section, Department of Labour, confidential memo of the DA section of the Labour Department.

88. HALS, PUG 13/1/6, St Albans Gas Co. Directors' and Shareholders' Minute Book, 1914–21, March 1917.

89. 'St Albans city tribunal: a trio of printers' men', *HA*, 30 June 1917.

90. These figures have been extracted from the project group's database of St Albans City Military Service Tribunal cases.

91. Councillor Townson was also a member of the city tribunal but stood down to make cases relating to Smith's Printing Co.

92. 'The TS and women printers', *HA*, 14 July 1917. See HALS, Acc 5148, St Albans Typographical Society Minute Book, entry for 13 April 1916. This confirms that the local union was implementing a national directive.

93. *Pictorial Record: St Albans* (London, 1915), p. 21. The estimated number of female employees is based on the project group's analysis of the 1911 census.

94. 'The straw hat trade in the St Albans and Luton district', *Hatters' Gazette*, 1915, pp. 93–4.

95. 'The county tribunal', *HA*, 27 May 1916.

96. 'The city tribunal', *HA*, 10 February 1917.

97. 'E. Day (St Albans) Ltd', *St Albans as a Visitors' Resort ... The Official Handbook*, etc. (Cheltenham, 1919), pp. 42–3. See also '100,000 army helmets', *HA*, 28 August 1915.

98. 'Legal – helmet making by females', *Hatters' Gazette*, 1920, p. 411.

99. 'Legal – females and helmet making', *Hatters' Gazette*, 1920, p. 555.

100. 'City tribunal's busy sitting', *HA*, 14 July 1917.

101. 'St Albans exemptions', *HA*, 9 February 1918.

102. S. Broadberry and P. Howlett, 'The United Kingdom in World War I, business as usual?', in S. Broadberry and M. Harrison (eds), *The economics of World War I* (Cambridge, 2005), pp. 215–17. See also Chapter 4 for further discussion of taxation.

103. G.R. Searle, *A new England? Peace and war, 1886–1914* (Oxford, 2004), p. 811.

104. 'Budget effects on local enterprise', *HA*, 25 September 1915.

105. The 1911 census for the city recorded over 180 workers working in the beer trade.

106. T.R. Gourvish and R.G. Wilson, *The British brewing industry, 1830–1980* (Cambridge, 1994), pp. 318–19.

107. Ibid.

108. P. Jennings, *The local: a history of the English pub* (Stroud, 2007), p. 185.

109. HALS, DP93/29/5, St Peter's parish magazines, 1915–24, April 1915.

110. See Chapter 4.

111. 'Entertaining officers', *HA*, 26 August 1916.

112. 'St Albans help for the army', *HA*, 20 May 1916.

113. HALS, PS21/10/7, St Albans City Petty Sessions, Alehouse Licensing Minutes, entry for 10 February 1916. Treating was the act of buying rounds for others; the long pull serving more than the correct measure.

114. HALS, Acc 3883, Benskin's Directors Private Minute Book, 1902–68, report of proceedings at the AGM held on Wednesday 18 December 1918. Benskin's owned 25 public houses in St Albans at the time.

115. 'Distinction between a "pass" and a "permit"', *HA*, 21 August 1915.

116. 'Licensed victualler to go', *HA*, 23 February 1918.

117. 'Fleetville licence', *HA*, 7 February 1914.

118. 'St Albans licensing', *HA*, 6 February 1919.

119. 'The city tribunal', *HA*, 22 June 1918.

120. Gourvish and Wilson, *The British brewing industry*, p. 331.

121. Unfortunately, financial figures for the city's brewers have not survived to throw light on the local situation.

122. Gourvish and Wilson, *The British brewing industry*, p. 331.

123. *St Albans roll of honour.* Lionel Kent died on 31 July 1917, his brother Harold just four days later.

CHAPTER 6

Feeding the city

This chapter will explore some of the ways in which the men and women of St Albans coped with the shortages, price rises and ever-expanding bureaucracy that surrounded the feeding of themselves and their families during the First World War. Producers, shopkeepers and consumers all had their own particular difficulties to face. As the impact of the war was felt in every farmhouse, shop and kitchen, questions of fairness were brought to the fore in a way that demanded attention from those charged with keeping the nation and the city fed.

I n David Lloyd George's memoir of the war years he highlighted the role that maintaining the food supply had played in the Allied victory.[1] Although there were shortages throughout the war and prices rose at a frightening rate, the war effort at home and on the fighting front was maintained; people may have been hungry and longed for a more varied diet, but starvation was avoided. In Germany, where problems around food were much more severe, famine was a very real spectre from the early days of the war and in the opinion of many played a major role in the collapse of the will to fight among the German population.

Yet, when war broke out in August 1914, nobody could feel confident that this would be the case. In 1914 Britain imported over 60 per cent of its total food supply, but, crucially, that figure disproportionately represented the types of food which made up the working-class diet: chilled meat from Australia, for example, tended to be the cheaper cuts, while 80 per cent of the lard and 75 per cent of the cheese consumed in British homes came from overseas.[2] By 1914 only one loaf in five was made from home-grown wheat,[3] and the nation was almost totally dependent on overseas producers for its sugar, much of which was particularly vulnerable to any continental war; two-thirds of sugar used in Britain was produced by the sugar beet farmers of Germany and Austria.[4]

A sign of things to come in that first week of the war was the reluctance of Britain's merchant fleet to leave port for fear of enemy attack, compounded by the reluctance of insurers to cover the risk. This only increased pressure on retailers' pre-existing stocks; queues, price rises and fear of food riots saw the government post two divisions of the British Expeditionary Force on standby to deal with any widespread civil unrest. A government commitment to underwrite 80 per cent of any losses to shipping reassured fleet owners, if not crews.[5]

A further strain on food supplies was the rush of the military to secure as much of the available food as it could to feed the expanding volunteer army. An island nation surrounded by fish-rich seas should have been in a good position, but again the requisitioning by the navy of almost 80 per cent of the fishing fleet created further difficulties.[6]

While in the memory of Lloyd George a food catastrophe during the war was averted, nevertheless the people of Britain found themselves having to deal with shortages and rising prices on a daily basis. Successive governments had placed their economic faith in a policy of *laissez-faire*, but in time of war it failed to protect many of those on whom the war effort relied. While a number of initiatives were introduced which reflected that understanding, it would take some time before it was agreed that in certain areas the markets could not always be left to decide.

Little wonder, then, that at a time of already heightened anxiety there were cases of consumer protest and direct action against those thought to be making a profit from people's fears.[7] In August 1914 a Hitchin butcher who raised his prices by 25 per cent found his shop and home attacked by a crowd reported to be 1,000-strong; good order was restored only when he agreed to return prices to their pre-price-rise level.[8]

There were no accounts in the *Herts Advertiser* of such direct action in St Albans, but local traders were on the receiving end of a lot of criticism for being too quick to raise prices; they, in turn, placed the blame for any shortages squarely on the shoulders of customers. A local baker defended himself, saying, 'it is the people themselves who are making all this trouble. If they would go along quietly everything would be all right.' The manager of one grocery store reported that 'those who usually spent about a sovereign had given orders up to £5 and £10', and one gentleman had taken away in his motor car 'a dozen tins of tongue, two dozen tins of milk, two dozen tins of corned beef, half a side of bacon, two hams, a hundredweight of flour, and other provisions'.[9]

Behind these actions lay a fear that people could no longer rely upon the certainties of just a few weeks earlier. Those with access to ready money or indeed motor cars were able to respond in a way that was denied those from poorer households, and this brought with it further anxieties around morale and public order.

The realities of a nation at war highlighted how communities came together in times of need, but also made plain the deep inequalities which existed within them; this was particularly so in relation to food. The commercial realities of supply and demand meant those from poorer families were at a serious disadvantage when it came to keeping food on the table. Food prices rose by 61 per cent over the first two years of the war, at a time when average weekly wages failed to keep pace.[10]

While the government would set up a range of committees and initiatives to oversee issues relating to food, it was always vulnerable to those who argued that the measures introduced failed to protect the poorer members of society. In the autumn of 1914, in response to demands for a ceiling on prices, the government published a list of suggested maximum prices; the maximum price very quickly became the normal price, fuelling inflation even more (Figure 6.1). With food supplies at the mercy of the German fleet, and conditional upon the success of the global harvest, the demands of the military and the good conduct of retailers, calls for a fairer distribution of food grew louder.

In November 1917 Gravesend introduced the first local rationing scheme and was followed soon after by Birmingham.[11] In January 1918, 81 residents of the Camp district, to the east of St Albans, signed a petition calling for the rationing of a range of products, including meat and margarine, and the St Albans Trades and Labour Council called on the newly established St Albans Local Food Control Committee to introduce their own local rationing scheme.[12] The committee responded that there was little point in the 'scattering of thousands of food cards upon the city, with little or no probability of food being forthcoming in exchange for the cards', and instead urged the government to undertake a properly organised distribution and rationing policy.[13]

A national rationing scheme was finally introduced in early 1918. Shopkeepers and consumers were required to register in order to sell or purchase a prescribed allowance of sugar, butter, margarine or lard, and meat. The impact of rationing in allaying those fears of unfairness helped to steady the ship, although problems of distribution continued. Introduced only in the last year of the war, rationing was extended into peacetime as the disruption of a nation at war with its neighbours settled and normality was restored.

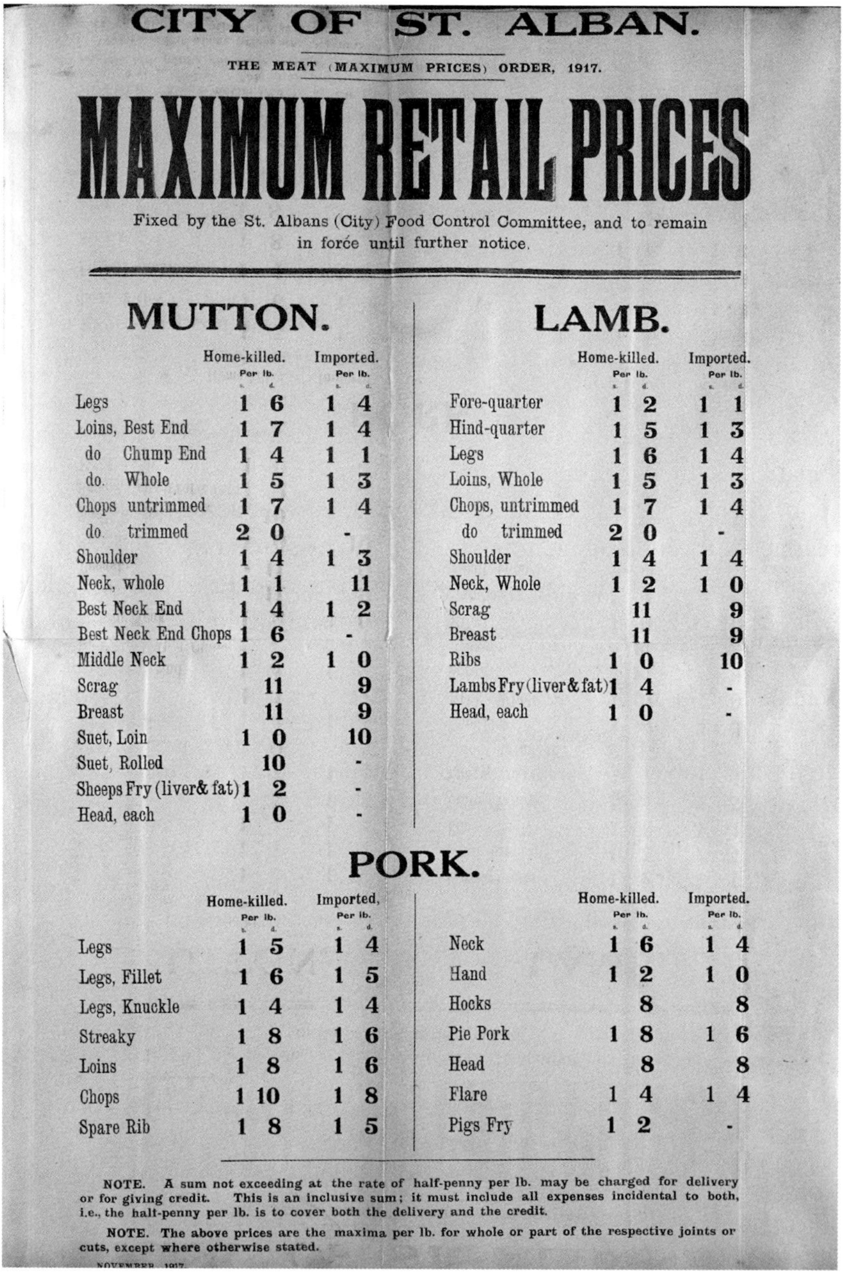

CITY OF ST. ALBAN.

THE MEAT (MAXIMUM PRICES) ORDER, 1917.

MAXIMUM RETAIL PRICES

Fixed by the St. Albans (City) Food Control Committee, and to remain in force until further notice.

MUTTON.

	Home-killed. Per lb.	Imported. Per lb.
Legs	1 6	1 4
Loins, Best End	1 7	1 4
do Chump End	1 4	1 1
do. Whole	1 5	1 3
Chops untrimmed	1 7	1 4
do. trimmed	2 0	-
Shoulder	1 4	1 3
Neck, whole	1 1	11
Best Neck End	1 4	1 2
Best Neck End Chops	1 6	-
Middle Neck	1 2	1 0
Scrag	11	9
Breast	11	9
Suet, Loin	1 0	10
Suet, Rolled	10	-
Sheeps Fry (liver& fat)	1 2	-
Head, each	1 0	-

LAMB.

	Home-killed. Per lb.	Imported. Per lb.
Fore-quarter	1 2	1 1
Hind-quarter	1 5	1 3
Legs	1 6	1 4
Loins, Whole	1 5	1 3
Chops, untrimmed	1 7	1 4
do trimmed	2 0	-
Shoulder	1 4	1 4
Neck, Whole	1 2	1 0
Scrag	11	9
Breast	11	9
Ribs	1 0	10
Lambs Fry (liver & fat)	1 4	-
Head, each	1 0	-

PORK.

	Home-killed. Per lb.	Imported. Per lb.		Home-killed. Per lb.	Imported. Per lb.
Legs	1 5	1 4	Neck	1 6	1 4
Legs, Fillet	1 6	1 5	Hand	1 2	1 0
Legs, Knuckle	1 4	1 4	Hocks	8	8
Streaky	1 8	1 6	Pie Pork	1 8	1 6
Loins	1 8	1 6	Head	8	8
Chops	1 10	1 8	Flare	1 4	1 4
Spare Rib	1 8	1 5	Pigs Fry	1 2	-

NOTE. A sum not exceeding at the rate of half-penny per lb. may be charged for delivery or for giving credit. This is an inclusive sum; it must include all expenses incidental to both, i.e., the half-penny per lb. is to cover both the delivery and the credit.

NOTE. The above prices are the maxima per lb. for whole or part of the respective joints or cuts, except where otherwise stated.

NOVEMBER 1917.

Figure 6.1 Maximum prices poster, 1917. © Hertfordshire Archives and Local Studies (LFCC, SBR/863)

The story of food during the First World War reflected the decisions of individuals, businesses and local and national government, and is grounded in concerns around personal, commercial and civic survival. The rest of this chapter will explore that story in light of the particular experience of the people of St Albans, showing how the war affected that most basic of needs: keeping hunger at bay.

The food problem

For much of our understanding of what happened during the war we have to turn to the pages of the local press. The *Herts Advertiser* offers an insight into the concerns of the authorities and the messages they wanted to convey to the general public, as well as a glimpse into the difficulties experienced by the city and the strategies deployed to meet them.

In those first wartime editions the approach adopted was one of reassuring the local population that, while the situation was unusual, there was no need to panic. The newspaper carried a mixture of stories about food which promoted a message of business as usual, but were written with a new sense of community co-operation and a weather eye on those who sought to exploit the situation to their own advantage. Amid stories of price rises and shortages the comment was made that 'dustbins were being cleaned and kitted out as storage bins for flour at a few – it is to be hoped a very few – St Albans homes'.[14]

That tone of disapproval marked what was an obvious policy throughout the war of shaming people into behaving well. A fortnight into the war the editor wrote:

> The 'scare' of a week ago has practically disappeared and the reckless demand for large stocks of various articles of popular consumption is almost a thing of the past ... altogether, the general position as it affects the working class home is very much easier than it was during the whole of last week.[15]

Those inverted commas around the word 'scare' were deliberately aimed at shifting the run on food away from a problem of supply and onto the shoulders of the irresponsible, particularly those wealthier members of the St Albans community who were creating artificial shortages and price rises which were hitting those with less disposable income to spend on food. Of course, for the concerned mother of small children and perhaps other family dependants, the buying of additional supplies may have seemed less like panic buying and more like prudence in the face of the unknown. It is hard, however, to see anything other than panic behind the actions of an unidentified consumer who stockpiled a large number of tins of tripe, which eventually made their way to the office of the town clerk following an amnesty on hoarding. The *Herts Advertiser* speculated on their 'ripe and venerable appearance', and suggested that, rather than being passed on to local charities, they might be better offered to the curator of the local museum; their eventual fate remains unknown![16]

The idea that 'the food problem' boiled down to the selfish behaviour of consumers, rather than problems of supply, became harder to sustain as time went by. Prices of basic foods such as flour and sugar were quick to rise: in the first week of the war the price of granulated sugar increased by 1¾d to 4d a pound, and by the following May the price of a 4lb loaf had more than doubled from 3½d to 8d.[17]

With few other measures at their disposal to regulate the food supply, the pages of the *Herts Advertiser* reflected a national policy which exhorted the general public to avoid waste. The women of St Albans in particular were identified as key in this respect and were on the receiving end of a lot of advice on how to keep their households fed. A syndicated piece that appeared regularly, 'A Column for Ladies – Pen Pictures by Penelope', urged women to consider more imaginative meals. One article suggested ten different ways to serve herring, although 'boiled' and 'boiled with cabbage' suggests a certain straining after new ideas.[18] Penelope told her readers to use the fat around meat as suet, swap margarine for butter, and replace tea with a cocoa-substitute as it was a 'nourishing and less nervous drink' – a convenient discovery given the difficulties of getting tea into the country.[19]

In December 1915 St Albans City Council's Thrift Committee advertised for speakers for a series of lectures on cookery aimed at the wives of workers and cooks employed at the larger houses, 'the outcome of which, it is hoped ... may be a decided wave of economy in the kitchens of the city'.[20]

A visit to the St Albans cinema in the summer of 1918 might have included the treat of a short Ministry of Information film *The Secret*.[21] This told the story of a marriage under threat as a husband is tempted by the amazing dumplings being offered by the lady next door. Luckily, the marriage is saved when his wife spies on their neighbour and learns the secret of her success – grated potato to replace the suet.

We can only speculate on what women who had been budgeting and preparing meals for years felt about all this advice and finger pointing, but such articles and initiatives demonstrated an awareness of food as an aspect central to the war effort and one which touched every home, although, as many were quick to point out, some homes more than others. In December 1917 a soldier's wife complained:

> We are always pestered with people knocking on the door telling us to economise. We do not ask for pity but what we do ask is that the Mayoress ... should go round the better class and get them to empty their pockets of surplus coppers and give all the children from 2½ to 8 [years old] whose fathers are defending our shores a jolly good time this Christmas.[22]

Christmas was a time of year resonant with food, and that first Christmas of the war the *Herts Advertiser* announced that the festive season would be celebrated as usual, with butchers 'intending to kill about the usual quantity of stock' (Figure 6.2).[23] However, there was a warning that beef, veal, pork and turkey were likely to be very expensive, with a knock-on effect on the cheaper cuts of meat. Food was available, but at a price.

Figure 6.2 Pigs at the St Albans Christmas stock market, December 1914. Source: *Watford Illustrated Review*, 19 December 1914, p. 3. © Hertfordshire Archives and Local Studies

One further casualty of the season was a decline in the custom of donations of gifts of meat for the poor, with 'a Christmas trade a good deal below the norm ... anticipated in that particular direction'.[24] Whether this was the result of squeezed purses or a switch to other charitable giving to support refugees, the wounded and those away fighting was unclear. The good people of St Albans found themselves faced with many appeals for money, food and other donations, which, at a time of rising prices and shortages, represented quite a challenge. In November 1914 local schools organised the collection of chocolate to be sent to the troops. It all proved too much for one young lad, who arrived with a one-inch-square piece – all that remained of a bar wrapped in very crinkled paper which had clearly been much tampered with.[25]

With shortages mounting and prices rising it is not surprising that there should have been grumblings about unfairness, with people keeping a keen eye on just who was getting what. In December 1915 a proposal was made that, in a break with custom, the workhouse might start serving residents meat sourced from overseas. It came to nothing, but the *Herts Advertiser* commented that, while having no desire to deny the poor access to prime English meat, it was rather strange that the paupers should be better fed than many who contributed to the cost of their care.[26]

For some the war was an opportunity for commercial profit, as they exploited the gaps left by food shortages. Bird's Custard was promoted as a way 'to save the meat bill'. Served with boiled puddings, it was 'as nourishing as meat and costs much less'.[27] In December 1917 the *Herts Advertiser* carried an advertisement for 'Freeman's Real Turtle Extract', which proclaimed itself as 'the most delicious and nutritious soup'.[28] Priced at 3d a tablet, it set to 'a stiff jelly' and was ideal 'for those who find the meat and bread allowance insufficient to maintain their usual strength. A plate of turtle soup enables you to eat less because you require less'; delicious indeed!

The commercial self-interest behind such advertisements was not lost on those who relied on the producers and retailers of food to keep body and soul together. The idea that some were doing well out of the war led to complaints of profiteering and exploitation of people at their most vulnerable. Farmers and shopkeepers in particular were seen as those who were having 'a good war' as prices rose, but for these groups the war brought its own problems as they sought to raise levels of production and keep the nation fed.

The challenge for farmers

One of the immediate problems faced by farmers on the outbreak of war was the loss of those skilled labourers who had volunteered to join up. Farm workers were some of the poorest paid members of society and were traditionally a rich source of recruits for the armed forces. Precise figures are hard to uncover, but it was estimated that by 1916 Hertfordshire farms had seen a 28 per cent reduction in the number of labourers of all types employed.[29]

Uncertainties about the future saw many companies lay off workers in those first weeks of the war, and farmers were encouraged to apply to their local labour exchange to find additional hands.[30] The *Herts Advertiser* reported that young men and women in London had offered to come and help with the harvest.[31] Given later statements by farmers about their unwillingness to employ women it is hard to see the arrival of people from the factories and the cities causing anything but raised eyebrows in Hertfordshire's farmhouses.

Farmers themselves called on schools to delay the start of the autumn term to allow boys to help in the fields.[32] In St Albans a practice of allowing 13-year-olds to be released from school was adopted, and managers of local schools were asked to extend school holidays during harvest, borrowing the days from holidays in less busy times of the farming year.[33] Boy scouts, beyond school-leaving age but too young to enlist, were also deployed to help out.[34]

Following the introduction of conscription many farmers applied to the St Albans City Military Service Tribunal on behalf of their remaining workers on grounds of work of national importance; their success rate varied, as the balance between the need to produce food and the need to fill the gaps in the military shifted. Councillor Francis Giffen applied on behalf of his son, also named Francis, who was managing Townsend Farm, arguing that he himself was too old, as well as too busy, to run the farm.[35] Giffen junior's case was not helped by the fact that he was also running a sandpit business at London Colney and had until recently been a partner in the family's electrical business as well as part-owner of a Watford cinema.[36] In the eyes of the tribunal, this marked him out as somebody who could not truly be called a farmer. Giffen may well have considered himself a farmer alongside his other roles, but as a physically fit man he was vulnerable and failed to convince the tribunal.

Farmers were able at peak times of activity to call upon the services of soldiers stationed in local camps and prisoners of war; the latter first arrived in Hertfordshire in late summer 1917.[37] In April 1918 a camp was opened in St Michael's parish, and by May there were around 50 men in place, housed in the vicarage; in June 1919 there were still 46 men employed on local farms.[38] There were initial concerns around the use of these men, particularly when it was suggested that the prisoners should be housed on the farms rather than guarded in camps: a saving in terms of time and energy, but the cause of some anxiety among local residents about their personal safety.[39]

Farmers may have had concerns around employing male prisoners of war or former factory workers, but their most vocal area of complaint was about being told to take on more women. When reading comments about women's abilities – or lack of them – it should be remembered that these might be exaggerated in the hope of strengthening an argument before the tribunal for a favoured employee. An application on behalf of John Mead, ploughman and gravel pit manager on Lord Verulam's Sopwell Home Farm, stressed his importance as one of only two ploughmen working 160 acres. There were six women employed on the farm, but while they did what was asked of them they were 'not capable of handling the young horses they were breaking in'. Mead received an exemption conditional upon remaining as a ploughman, although the military services representative on the local tribunal, Ernest Gape, was not happy that Mead had been 'dug out of a gravel pit temporarily' as part of the application.[40]

Dairy farmers in particular complained that women were not suited to the work. An application on behalf of Percy Cox, cowman at St Germain's Farm, St Michael's, hinged on the farmer's need for four cowmen to handle his large herd of dairy cows. Asked why he employed no women, he replied that it 'wasn't suitable for women to go into a cowshed at five o'clock in the morning', an argument which received short shrift from the tribunal.[41]

Farm work was demanding, involving long days, varying weather conditions and the management of animals and machinery; it was skilled work, and cowsheds, stables and hayfields could be dangerous places. In June 1916 a meeting at the Patriotic Club heard from Betty Glossop, daughter of Canon Glossop, about her time as a member of the Women's Land Army. She painted a very positive picture of the experience, saying she 'had never felt better in my life', describing an 11-hour working day which began at 6.30am and included ploughing, muck-spreading, weeding, carting and taking care of the horses.[42]

For the first two years of the war the government continued to follow a *laissez-faire* policy on farming that could be summed up as 'the best farming is that which pays the farmer best'.[43] Policy changed with the formation of Lloyd George's government in December 1916 and the passing in the following summer of the Corn Production Act, which devolved powers to county committees to compel the ploughing-up of pasture with the incentive of a guaranteed price on wheat.[44]

Estimates for the amount of land which might potentially be affected in the St Albans area were 5,000–8,000 acres, and of this a little over 3,000 acres was thought suitable for the growing of wheat, barley and potatoes.[45] A team of inspectors visited every farm, both to monitor standards and to determine which land should be ploughed. It was not always as straightforward a process as was implied, as simply ploughing up grassland did not ensure a good crop. In August 1917 Lord Verulam was served with a notice to plough a part of Potters Crouch Farm, St Michael's, totalling 44 acres, ready for the 1918 harvest. The crop failed; his application for compensation on the grounds that, as he had warned, the land had not been suitable was rejected.[46]

Farmers could not always see the logic in switching from one crop that was needed to another. John Brown of Hedges Farm, St Stephen's, argued that he had a large dairy herd grazing on a field selected for ploughing and it would be more useful to raise yields on proven arable fields than to jeopardise milk production.[47]

Some, however, saw possibilities in the call to plough up land. In January 1918 William Moores, tenant of Oaklands Farm, received notice to prepare two fields for ploughing and sowing with wheat. He replied that the fields in question were not part of his farm, but he was quite happy to plough up a different field, known as Fleetville Meadow, as 'this meadow is the one I have not been able to use for the last four years as the people of Fleetville have made it a regular playground, and if this is ploughed up it will be a benefit to the county'.[48] Just what the people of Fleetville were doing on the land is unclear, but clearly this was one situation where a farmer was able to make use of the authority of the committee to bring about improvements which suited his own purpose.

Estimates of how much additional wheat was produced as a result of these interventions are difficult to make, but by the end of July 1918 almost 15,000 acres of grassland had been turned over to wheat, barley and potatoes across Hertfordshire as a whole.[49] However, the importance of the campaign is that it reflected the very central role that bread played in the daily diet of so many people and its significance in government concerns around food supply.

Bread production and distribution

Bread prices rose steeply; by April 1916 consumers were paying 9½d for a 4lb loaf, almost three times the pre-war price, although it was never rationed.[50] As late as October 1918 a report to the War Cabinet argued that to do so would be risky as 'it would be impossible to ration bread equitably as between class and class'.[51] Bread formed a major component of the working-class diet and any restrictions might have a knock-on effect on production levels. However, various measures were introduced, both to make the wheat go further and to discourage waste.

From March 1917 onwards, in an effort to reduce consumption, bakers were forbidden to sell bread that was less than 12 hours old.[52] In April 1917 a Flour Mills Order was introduced that imposed government control on mills, an essential part of the chain from field to table.[53] Specific instructions were laid down on how bread should be manufactured and flour graded, with various ratios of wheat flour to other substances such as rice, barley, semolina, rye or beans. Quality could be variable, as noted by one contributor to the *Herts Advertiser*: 'Can small loaves be re-pulped like paper? I ask because in very truth I purchased one which an axe would glint. It was as hard as marble, uncuttable and almost unchippable. I took it back and wondered what would be done with it in these waste-not days.'[54]

In March 1918 millers were authorised to add potatoes to the mix and a representative from the Ministry of Food visited St Albans to demonstrate to local bakers and millers how this might be achieved.[55] As a first step, potatoes, ground to a flour-like consistency, would be added at a ratio of 15 lbs to every 280 lb sack of flour; however, it was expected that this would be raised as people adjusted to the new flour. It was estimated that even at the 15 lb level it might result in a saving within St Albans of 750 quartern (4 lb) loaves every week, although it proved difficult to find a wholesaler prepared to take on the order owing, it was felt, to 'the cumbersome formalities for obtaining payment' when there was a good market for potatoes elsewhere.[56] Wartime bread had a poor reputation among customers, but the need to extract as much from the wheat as possible meant that it was more nutritious than much of the white bread favoured before the war.[57]

Milk supply and quality

The very direct relationship between producer and consumer meant that milk was particularly vulnerable to concerns about quality and safety, especially given its association with the feeding of babies and children. This was not a problem which arose just because of the war – dairy hygiene was an issue long before 1914 – but there were real concerns that public confidence in the food chain was crucial at a time when anxieties around food might tip over into civil unrest. The watering down of milk was a recurring complaint among suspicious consumers. In September 1915 the city council passed a resolution that vendors of milk whose product was shown to be compliant with standards of quality and fat content might publicise this fact. Clearly this was meant as a way of raising standards as a whole and reassuring the public that the council was in control of the situation.[58]

However, the dilution of milk, while annoying to customers, was not the worst problem to come out of the dairy. The city's veterinary inspector passed as acceptable milk that had been diluted by up to 90 per cent, and in 1916 he told the council that 'clean milk was far more important as regards health than milk with a little water added'.[59] He was sympathetic to the problems of those who kept dairies, as they were struggling to maintain standards of cleanliness when faced with a labour shortage, praising the more 'up to date' dairy managers who had taken on board his suggestion to use a half-covered pail to reduce levels of hair, dirt and other substances within the milk. Yet clearly there had been and would continue to be problems of hygiene, although not all problems were the result of sloppy milking practices.

In November 1914 Charles Addington of The Creamery, Chequer Street, was summonsed to answer a charge of selling milk to which 'a certain preservative' had been added. The certain preservative in question was formaldehyde, and the particular danger it posed was that it made it impossible for the public health inspector to detect any underlying problems with the milk. The supplier of the milk was Jacob Reynolds of Heath Farm Dairy, and his dairy manager testified that, while the milk in question came from their cows, with so much demand for milk from the billeted troops there was no need for them to add preservatives as they could barely keep pace with demand as it was. Reynolds was cleared of any wrongdoing, but Addington was found guilty and fined £5.[60]

Yet even more serious than the use of formaldehyde was the problem of tuberculosis bacteria. At the start of the war the Tuberculosis Order (1913) was suspended by the government, but the city council agreed that

Figure 6.3 A tribunal-inspired Christmas card sent to Heath Dairies the year conscription was introduced. The legend reads: From all the ills that man could mention, may all at the Heath get 'total exemption'. Christmas wishes from F.H.K. Mardell, 1916 © Chris Reynolds, Genealogy in Hertfordshire

they would continue to require samples to be taken for public analysis.[61] In early 1915 the inspector reported that, of ten samples taken from one herd, nine had shown evidence of tuberculosis. When asked by Alderman Arthur Faulkner whether 'a dark-coloured sediment in the bottom of a glass of milk would mean that it was tuberculous?' the inspector answered that 'if there is a slimy deposit in the bottom of milk, that in all probability is a mixture of puss [sic] ... from the inflamed udders of an infected cow'.[62]

The price of milk rose steadily. In August 1914 a quart cost 4d and this had risen to 6d by December 1916; a year later the vendors agreed a price with the food control committee equivalent to 7½d a quart.[63] A contributory factor was the rising price of animal feed, not helped by the regulations that stipulated greater use of the wholegrain in flour for human consumption. Jacob Reynolds defended price rises on the grounds that the cost of a dairy cow in 1916 had doubled on its 1913 price, with similar rises in the price of feed and a 30 per cent rise in the price of labour.[64]

Some farmers, faced with rising costs and a good market for meat, sent their dairy herds to be slaughtered, which in turn affected the amount of milk available. In April 1916 the inspector reported that the number of cowsheds in the city had fallen from 14 to ten, with the average number of cows in milk down to 150 from 165 the previous year;[65] by December 1917 four farmers were known to have switched out of milk production entirely.[66] In the opinion of one milk vendor, James Maunder of Paxton Road, 'as the Government had the power to take a man and put him in the trenches, they should have the same power to compel a farmer to produce milk for the people'.[67] Maunder was struggling to get enough milk to supply his customers. As a small business he was unable to compete with the prices being paid by larger concerns, particularly London wholesalers. By 1917 he was facing a daily shortage of 50 quarts of milk from local sources, a situation made worse by the refusal of his usual supplier, Arnolds of Finsbury Park, to sell him his regular order of 'rail' milk.[68] By the end of the war Maunder was relying totally on local producers of milk to maintain his business.[69]

The largest milk delivery company in St Albans was Jacob Reynolds's Heath Farm Dairy, which by November 1918 was handling 4,327 gallons of milk a week, of which 1,305 gallons were coming direct from local producers.[70] Seven of Reynolds's men had volunteered for the military prior to the introduction of conscription and his application to the tribunal on behalf of three further men in June 1916 was unsuccessful, causing him real difficulties (Figure 6.3).[71]

By June 1918 it was acknowledged that shortages of milk and the problems of getting it to customers were serious. Those in the trade appearing before the tribunal were given further extensions and released from any requirement to join the Volunteer Training Corps, 'as they were busily engaged early and late and the tribunal regarded the distribution of milk as a most important department of food supply'.[72]

One particular area of concern was the impact of rising milk prices on the younger generation. In October 1916 the city council called a 'Milk Conference', which heard evidence from farmers, retailers and concerned residents.[73] Questions were raised as to why St Albans prices were higher than those of surrounding areas; at Luton, it was reported, a co-operative of suppliers was keeping the price at 5d a quart, compared to 6d in St Albans. Representatives from the Quaker-run adult school called on the dairymen to consider the impact of price rises on children, and wondered whether the time had come to take control of prices away from the producers and suppliers; a depot in town, run by the council, would ensure a fairer price.

Producers and suppliers defended themselves vigorously and no price reduction was achieved or depot set up. However, the following week it was announced that William Slimmon, of Marshal's Wick Farm [sic], to the north-east of the city, had offered to set aside eight quarts of new milk per day to be sold at 4d per quart to deserving participants nominated by the school, with the proceeds going to St Albans and Mid Herts Hospital.[74] Slimmon was one of those mentioned in 1917 as having given up his dairy, and no information has come to light on whether his example was followed by any other farmer. By January 1918 the food control committee was forced to call on adults to reduce their own consumption of milk to free up more for children.[75]

Shortages of labour and government directives did pose real problems for farmers. However, there was little sympathy for their position from the general public, and this extended to the problems faced by shopkeepers, who were at that pivotal point in the food supply chain where shortages and higher prices came up against the shopping lists of customers.

The war and the shopkeepers

In 1914 *Kelly's Directory* listed 23 butchers' shops in St Albans. There were the local men working out of just one shop, such as Edward Hawkins Smith of London Road and Edward George of Catherine Street. Then there were those who had built up a small chain of shops: Harry Patience, trading under the name of Joseph Wheelhouse, was doing well with premises in Hatfield Road, the High Street and Holywell Hill, while George Steabben had shops in Market Place, Hatfield Road and, further afield, Fore Street in Hatfield. Three large national chains were represented in St Albans: the London Central Meat Company, with two shops, and the Empire Meat Company and W. & R. Fletcher Ltd with one apiece.

The war brought challenges to these different types of business. The large chains in particular had to deal with the problems of losing employees to the call for volunteers; the London Central Meat Company claimed in 1916 that 325 of their workforce had joined up and that they had closed many branches, including their Hatfield Road shop in St Albans.[76] For the government departments charged with securing supplies to keep the ever-expanding military machine fed, it made sense to deal with larger companies, with their country-wide outlets and contacts. These lucrative contracts in themselves caused some ill-feeling among those smaller businesses who missed out, but the introduction of conscription in 1916 brought those feelings of unfairness to the fore.

The larger chains, faced with the potential loss of so many of their staff, negotiated an agreement with the government that any man not passed fit for general service should be granted a conditional exemption. Most of the butchers who operated in St Albans did so as one-man businesses, often relying on family labour, and for these the recruitment factor became a much more critical issue as conscription became a reality; suddenly they faced the very real possibility of losing their livelihood, if not their life. Military service tribunals found themselves in the awkward position of having to refuse applications from local men whose enforced recruitment would see the closure of their business while knowing that others, of similar levels of fitness, were benefiting from their employers' favourable arrangements with the government. In February 1917 the mayor, James Flint, expressed his annoyance very forcibly in a meeting of the city tribunal and received support from the rest of the members present; Fred Keech, the labour representative, went so far as to suggest the tribunal 'go on strike against such action by the War Office', although his colleagues drew back from quite so radical a suggestion.[77] In March 1917 the favourable treatment of employees of the larger chains was removed.

With the food question such a prominent part of people's daily lives, the weighing up of national need against local and personal interest was a particularly tricky balancing act for the tribunal. The Local Government

Board called upon tribunals to consider men working in the same trade as a collective, which for the retailers involved was a major shift in how they perceived themselves – from rivals to colleagues.[78] In St Albans the military service representative, Ernest Gape, argued that, rather than presenting themselves as individuals, the butchers of the town should be considered as a group, the question being: how many butchers did it take to keep a city fed?

In March 1917 five butchers found themselves having to answer this question before the Hertfordshire County Appeal Tribunal.[79] The men were allowed to confer as a group and arrived at a compromise. Frank Hearn, a father of six, who worked at Thomas Potton's shop in George Street, had volunteered to go, and the remaining butchers had agreed to take on the killing of Potton's beasts and to make up Hearn's money to his wife. The offer was rejected. The five remaining butchers then further agreed to support the work of an additional man, to be chosen by the tribunal; Horace Oakley of Lattimore Road, the youngest of the group, was the man chosen to join the Colours.[80]

In June 1918 Gape appealed to the county tribunal to look once more at the men who made up the butchers' group. Walter Everett, referred to as an 'A' man (fully fit for army service), was required to join up, in spite of his claim that he was the sole support of his widowed mother alongside whom he ran the business; his fate was sealed by the evidence from Harry Patience, chair of the chamber of commerce butchers' group, that any men in this category might be spared. Thomas Morris undertook to support Everett's cooked food trade so that he might have a business to return to after the war.[81]

Hearn survived the war and returned home in April 1919, although whether to the same trade is unclear, as his employer, Potton, died shortly afterwards in August 1919.[82] Oakley was still to be found at his shop in Lattimore Road in 1922.[83] Of Everett we have unearthed no trace, so we can only speculate on whether he was able to pick up the pieces of his life once the war came to an end.

What those who went to fight felt about those of their group who did not is a story that is hard to uncover, but there must have been mixed feelings when the war ended. Edward Hawkins Smith, whose application against conscription was unsuccessful, survived the war and returned to his London Road shop in early 1919.[84] In recognition of his need to re-establish his business at a time of rationing he was allowed a licence from the food control committee to sell meat for one month (later renewed for a further month) to those not registered at his shop, and he quickly built up a customer base of 300–400.[85] However, when one compares that to the 1,549 registered with Harry Patience's Hatfield Road branch or the 2,600 customers of Alfred Wheaton's two shops in Verulam and Etna Roads, it would seem that Smith had his work cut out in rebuilding his business.[86]

A government report after the war claimed that support for the businesses of those who went to fight by those who stayed behind was not widespread, and that for small towns it was an idea which was 'impossible' to implement.[87] However, there does seem to have been an attempt in St Albans to negotiate a shift from rivals to partners, although in the absence of personal testimonies we cannot say just how much this enforced co-operation worked out on the ground.

What of other shopkeepers? For the grocers and bakers it was not a simple process. It is quite hard to pin down the number of grocers in St Albans both at the outbreak of war and beyond. *Kelly's Directory* (1914–15) listed 52 grocers, including the large chain of International Stores, which had a branch in Market Place. However, it was a trade where very small one-man or -woman businesses were common and, poorer in purse, these may not have wished to pay for a line in the directory when they already had a local customer base who knew where they were. In 1917 83 retailers registered to sell sugar, and that may give a stronger idea of the number of people involved in the trade.[88] In 1918 the solicitor representing Ernest Carter, an employee of grocers Thomas Oakley & Son, claimed that there were a large number of people 'who were doing a sort of front parlour trade', and it would seem that there was less sense of grocers, many of whom were women, as a discrete occupational group.[89]

There were 27 bakers' premises listed in *Kelly's Directory* (1914–15). With bread such a priority, when conscription was introduced bakers were given an exemption conditional upon continuing in the trade. However, as losses in the military became more serious Ernest Gape mounted a strong application for those earlier conditional exemptions to be re-examined. In May 1917 John H. Lee of Market Place failed in an application on behalf of his baker, 28-year-old Herbert Coe, who was classified as an A1 (fully fit for army service) man. It was this classification which marked Coe out for conscription and, at the hearing, Lee asked why they could not do as they had with the butchers and 'bring them all up together'.[90] Just one month later Gape called for a withdrawal of the exemptions of a further seven bakers.[91] The hearing of all seven men was adjourned for medical examinations and, at their next appearance, the decision was made to take the two A1 men, George Clarke and Arthur Merridale, the remaining five men to be given a further six months' exemption.[92] Remington Marsh, of Victoria Street, who had applied on behalf of three of his employees, told the tribunal that the bakers of the city had met and decided on a plan of co-operation. No specific details were given on how this might operate, beyond an agreement that the larger businesses would support the smaller, but it would seem that there was no nomination of specific men to join the army. By December 1917 the situation had shifted: an audit of men employed, numbers of customers, oven capacity and districts covered convinced the tribunal that there was no great overlap and that the city needed all the bakers that it had.[93]

Bakers were vital to the war effort, but the question remained of just where a man might be of most value. In March 1918 George Bowden, the MP for North East Derbyshire, who had a home in St Albans, raised in the House of Commons the case of a St Albans man, a master baker, who had been taken away from his business, which was now

> left in the hands of his young wife, an extremely delicate woman, and totally unfit to attempt to begin to manage a business. The last I heard of that case a few months ago was when I saw that poor woman having to strive, literally night and day, alone, to cope with the filling in of the various forms required by the Ministry of Food. At that very time the husband, I hear, was cutting the grass round the officers' mess where he was stationed at Aldershot.[94]

The man was unnamed, but the circumstances suggest that this may have been a reference to 38-year-old Gordon Forbes-Mangan, who first appeared before the tribunal in July 1916.[95] After a series of temporary exemptions an appeal to the county tribunal was rejected in June 1917.[96] His problem lay in convincing the tribunal that he was a *bona fide* baker. He had bought the business of Tyler & Co. in December 1915 and up until that time he had been working as a 'scientific accountant' in Barnstaple, Devon. He employed others to do the actual baking and, it was argued, his wife could quite easily run the business. He counter-argued that she was recovering from a serious operation and was not fit to take on the running of a business that served 700 customers. Forbes-Mangan survived the war but where he served and whether he spent his time cutting grass, as referenced above, remains unknown.[97] Mrs Forbes-Mangan herself appeared before the tribunal in later months to present a series of successful applications on behalf of her foreman bread baker, John Childs.[98]

Digging for victory

Many people sought to reduce their dependence on others for their food by growing their own, and the promotion of vegetable growing and the taking up of allotments became one of the government's major campaigns. The digging over of wasteland and parkland became a sign of patriotic commitment to the war effort, with King George V's example in replacing the flowers in his Buckingham Palace garden with vegetables celebrated as a sign of what might be done.[99] In St Albans a scheme was introduced whereby those who had a surplus of fruit and vegetables might take them along to William Young's offices in St Peter's Street for sale to passers-by (Figure 6.4).[100]

During the winter of 1915/16 the Board of Agriculture and Fisheries wrote to all local councils proposing strategies for 'the production of as much food as possible from allotments'.[101] However, St Albans councillors were cautious. The one recommendation they did endorse was to initiate a competition for the most successful grower, but it had to be largely self-funding and its administration fell to park superintendent David William Simmons. This required him to monitor plots on a monthly basis and allocate points based on different criteria.[102] When only three sites were operational this was achievable, but the rapid expansion in the number of plots, along with the need to collect the rents attached, would have meant an increasingly heavy workload on top of his normal duties.

Always conscious of the potential for allotments to be malodorous and unsightly additions to the landscape, wealthy residents had complained to Lord Verulam as early as 1910 about his allowing some to be established close to a major route into the city, and attitudes changed only slowly. In 1915, when the council set up allotments at Cunningham Hill, appearance was still paramount.[103] They insisted that 'all sheds must be aligned' and that no manure should be stored, although the latter condition was relaxed six months later.[104] Asked by Whitehall to relax the restrictions on keeping pigs, it was decided to do so only if directly asked by a resident.

In 1916 the council placed a newspaper advertisement offering new plots, but withdrew it when only 150 applications were received. With

FOOD ECONOMY

Sale of Surplus Vegetables and Fruit to prevent Waste.

At the request of the LOCAL FOOD ECONOMY COMMITTEE

MR. WILLIAM YOUNG

has kindly consented to SELL BY AUCTION,

At his Gateway, No. 4, St. Peter's Street
At NINE o'clock on

Wednesday & Thursday Mornings

ANY

Surplus Vegetables and Fruit

ALLOTMENT HOLDERS and others having Gardens are invited to send

Any Class of Vegetables & Fruit

(except Potatoes, which under the Defence of the Realm Restrictions cannot be dealt in), to Mr. Young's Gateway, before 9 o'clock on Wednesday and Thursday mornings.

No commission will be charged on the sales, and the gross receipts will be paid over to the owners the same day.

Consignments may consist of one kind or an assortment of vegetables.

Each package of Produce must have a tie-on label affixed, bearing the grower's Name and Address and the description of the contents.

J. FLINT,

Sept., 1917.   *Mayor.*

W. CARTMEL AND SONS, PRINTERS, VICTORIA STREET, ST. ALBANS.

Figure 6.4 The sale of surplus fruit and vegetables was part of the economy drive, as here in September 1917. © Hertfordshire Archives and Local Studies (LFCC, SBR/863)

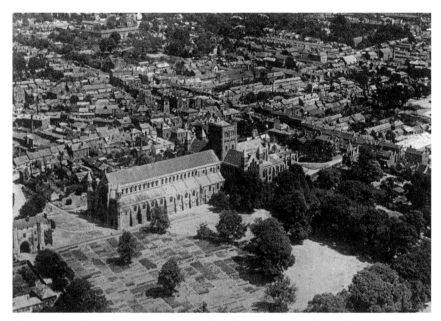

Figure 6.5 Aerial photograph showing wartime allotments in the Abbey Orchard, c.1920.
© St Albans Museums (PX8418_150133)

the problems around food shortages increasing, the Defence of the Realm (Acquisition of Land) Act in 1916 provided the legal framework for local authorities to seize land for use as allotments. There was a dramatic change in how the council thought about allotments and between January and May 1917 the number brought into service rose to 500, making an estimated number of 1,000 plots in use.[105] Some were extensions to existing sites, but most were on pop-up 'war plots', many of which may never have been formally recorded. Some temporary sites were managed by the council, but many were independent. Not only farmland but also miscellaneous paddocks or neglected patches of unrated ground that might one day make building sites were turned over and cultivated. With a little nudging the Midland Railway agreed in 1917 to create allotments, which it chose to administer itself, alongside the line in Lancaster Road.[106]

Land was made available at Old London Road, Kingsbury, Bleak House, Victoria playing field, the gasworks and along Beresford, Clarence, Hatfield, Jennings, Wellington and Wormleighton (later Gainsborough) Roads. There were 21 temporary allotments set up in Clarence Park, as well as sites on the Abbey Orchard, in St Michael's village and on various school grounds (Figure 6.5). Pupils and teachers at Hatfield Road Boys'

School got involved, turning over land within the school grounds, as well as plots on the Ninefields, north of Brampton Road.[107]

Cultivation was rarely easy. Making old pasture or rough neglected patches productive required hard work and soil improvement. At Cunningham Hill stones and flints were so plentiful that some plots were considered unworkable from the outset;[108] the golf course was saved, as the land offered was thought totally worthless as garden ground, although members did have to sacrifice two holes early in 1918 when required by the County War Agricultural Committee to plough up ten acres and sow corn for that year's harvest.[109]

The council adopted a number of strategies to support those new to gardening. In March 1917 Simmons gave the first in a series of lectures on growing vegetables and established a model plot in Clarence Park where skills, cultivation schedules and methods could be observed.[110] From January 1918 onwards he wrote a weekly column in the *Herts Advertiser* that carried practical advice on such areas as improving soil quality, as well as suggestions for crops to grow.[111]

Throughout the war the main crop was potatoes. There were potato fields in Fleetville and a potato club to manage them. The pupils at Birklands School in London Road and the local girl guides were growing potatoes, as was the manager of the sewage works. It was a crop that could be harvested in time for the same ground to be used again before the season ended. In April 1917 the council found itself taking delivery of 17 tons 5 cwt of seed potatoes for local allotment holders, most of whom would be planting at least half of their space with them.[112]

Alongside potatoes, the allotment gardener was expected to favour all those reliable standbys which were easy to grow and store. Broad beans, onions, root vegetables and cabbage could all be relied on to come good, while leeks, lettuce and rhubarb were available to most people. Simmons advocated cultivating a blackberry over a shed and extending the season by creating a hot bed and planting early. These were effective techniques if people could master them and had the time to put them into practice.

Whether all this advice was heeded and resulted in greater productivity is hard to ascertain. Simmons's tireless work in the cause of promoting allotments, raising standards and supervising the plots in Clarence Park and beyond was credited with having been instrumental in producing almost 3,000 tons of fresh food from the start of the war to May 1918. Much of this would have been produced on allotments, but also in people's gardens, and he deliberately addressed both in his advice columns. He alone produced two tons of carrots and beetroot in the borders at Clarence Park and the Friends' Burial Ground for the benefit of local hospitals.[113]

In October 1917 Simmons wrote to the town council requesting a new bicycle, as his current one was worn out from inspecting the growing number of plots,[114] and the following March his wages were increased to £2 10s a week, with a war bonus of 5s 6d.[115] Shortly afterwards, in May 1918, he received his call-up papers. In spite of support from the city council he received only a two-month deferment from the county tribunal, who commented that, having delivered so many lectures and articles on ways to increase production, he could now be spared for the military.[116] To enable his wife and family to remain in the house which came with his position as Park Superintendent the city council allowed her to take on the responsibility of collecting allotment rents.[117] In the end Simmons served for only a few months and was back in his post by January 1919,[118] although he left within the month for pastures new, employed as a seed hall manager for Samuel Ryder. It was noted in the council minutes that he had been offered a job with pay and conditions that the council were not prepared to match.[119]

A model idea for feeding the hungry

Allotments no doubt kept many a family from going hungry, but they did require large inputs of time and energy, which for many was a luxury they could not afford. One initiative introduced by the Ministry of Food in early 1917, designed to help those who were working long hours, was a scheme for a network of local kitchens and restaurants. The intention was that these would 'secure economy in food and in use of fuel', reduce waste and 'place within the reach of the working classes wholesome food instead of makeshift meals'.[120] Ownership and operation of the Model National Kitchens was entrusted to local authorities, and the first appeared in London in May 1917;[121] the St Albans premises did not open until almost 18 months later, in October 1918.[122]

Religious and charitable organisations in St Albans, as elsewhere, had a history of setting up soup kitchens to get poorer people through the winter, and individuals, too, responded to need: in February 1918, for example, Mrs Bates of Wellington Road, in the Camp district, managed to secure a supply of bones to set up a soup kitchen in her own home.[123] However, identification of such initiatives as these with poverty did mean that there

was a concern that the national kitchens would not be used by those who
might be in need but did not want to advertise it to the world. The St Albans
example would suggest that in fact the restaurant and take-away service
it offered were welcomed by many, although numbers after the initial
enthusiasm are hard to pin down and revenue failed to cover costs.

Prior to the opening of the St Albans national kitchen at the Corn
Exchange in Market Place, a committee was set up in April 1918 chaired
by Councillor William Fisk. It consisted entirely of men, which prompted
a letter of complaint to the *Herts Advertiser* from the local branch of
the National Union of Women's Suffrage Societies, calling for 'a certain
number of efficient women' to be added to the membership. Women were
employed to supervise the day-to-day running of the kitchen, but were not
given executive responsibility or the opportunity to serve on the committee
until November 1918. The council took out a ten-year loan from the Local
Government Board, borrowing £778 to cover the installation costs, with
the council providing the premises free of rent and rates.

Customers had the option of eating in the restaurant or taking the food
away. The *Herts Advertiser* reported that 'the proposal is to provide a
thousand portions per day and to cater for about 60 persons per day in the
well-equipped and exceedingly comfortable restaurant', where the menu
that first day included barley soup, roast beef and milk pudding.[124] A pint
of soup cost 3d and proved to be one of the most popular take-away items
on the menu, together with fried fish and hot potatoes. On the opening
day, 8 October 1918, there were long queues and not all prospective
customers obtained lunch. Plans for afternoon tea were shelved and, when
the kitchen re-opened for evening service, 400 suppers were taken away
or consumed on the premises.

The restaurant and take-away would seem to have served a need in St
Albans. With food shortages and rationing continuing after the war the
presence of the kitchen was seen as helpful, but by the end of 1920 trade
was falling off and the kitchen made a loss of £25 in the quarter leading up
to Christmas that year. It was felt that the general slump in the economy
was to blame, and in July 1921 the decision was taken to close it down.

Food control and rationing

For the first two years of the war the voices in government that argued
in favour of limited central control were for the most part those which
directed policy. However, by late 1916 it was becoming clear that a policy of

suggestion which relied on a message of waste as a moral issue and appeals to patriotic rather than self-interest was unlikely to deliver the necessary restraint or tackle the ongoing problems of equitable distribution of food across the country.

The establishment in December 1916 of a Ministry of Food was an indication of a desire to be seen to be doing something in the face of growing criticism of government indifference to the problems faced by the general population. Things did not change overnight, but spring 1917 onwards saw the setting up across the country of local food control committees which provided a framework for co-ordinated administration at the local level;[125] the first meeting of the St Albans food control committee took place on Monday 13 August.[126]

There was still resistance to anything other than voluntary initiatives. The *Herts Advertiser* was wary of rationing; it would be costly to run and was a blunt instrument that did not take into account the different circumstances of individuals. Rather, it suggested, those who were better off in the town should 'adopt a diet consisting of largely commodities that are beyond the reach of poorer people ... thus setting free foods that are cheaper'.[127] Women were again urged to do their bit. The dean of St Albans called upon to them to 'stop the waste', as they had it in their hands to 'save us from compulsory rationing, more registration cards, and vast expense. They are on their honour to do it.'[128]

While some people were engaged in sequential queuing, going from shop to shop to find sugar or sausages, others were able to enjoy six-course dinners at the Ritz hotel in London, which showed no sign of that voluntary restraint promoted by the government; an extreme example but one which was used to show up the failures of government to protect all its people.[129] In February 1918 one 74-year-old St Albans resident wrote to the *Herts Advertiser* asking whether something might be done to 'save the old people from waiting in the meat queue'.[130] The writer pointed out that it was 'very hard for women over 70 years of age to have to wait from one and a half to two hours'.[131] Hard indeed, but one can imagine that any sign of preferential treatment for any group or either sex would have been as hard to bear for others in that same queue.

The letter was addressed to the food control committee, whose membership of 12, the maximum allowed by the Ministry of Food, consisted of six members of the city council and six others representing women, labour, the chamber of commerce, and local branches of the Oddfellows and

Foresters societies.[132] The presence of only one woman on the committee, Edith Garrett, was a particular bone of contention. In February 1918 a meeting of the council, described as 'reminiscent of old times when citizens took a real live interest in the doings of their local legislators', received deputations from both the St Albans branch of the National Union of Women Workers and the St Albans Trades and Labour Council.[133] The women's group, led by Lady Grimston and Lady Thomson, argued that the committee would be required to implement some unpopular policies and, without confidence in the experience and abilities of the members, these policies, which particularly affected women, were more likely to fail. They called for at least two more women to join the committee, either by voluntary resignations of existing male members or by enlarging the membership. The council agreed to ask for an expansion of membership and in March 1918 four additional members, three of them women, were added to the committee.[134]

Appointed in that first instance for one year, the committee remained in operation until the end of June 1920. Reporting to the Ministry of Food, the committee acted as a conduit for the dissemination of the increasing numbers of directives around pricing and rationing; in addition, it had to implement what was described as 'a series of local revolutions in food supply'.[135] Local committees were given a degree of autonomy to make the various schemes work on the ground, although they were expected to keep the Ministry of Food informed of their decisions.[136]

In the months leading up to the introduction of rationing, the committee organised the registration of all food retailers, an audit of existing stocks and the distribution of sugar cards to every household. To achieve this it consulted butchers, bakers and milk vendors to discuss the thorny issue of setting a city-wide maximum price. To achieve the latter they consulted with other local committees at Watford and Harpenden, as well as drawing on the model list issued from the London office.[137]

The committee were not averse to active intervention when it was deemed necessary to defuse potentially angry situations. Three days before Christmas 1917 word spread that Maypole Dairy, in Market Place, had taken delivery of a fresh supply of margarine and by 9am a 'numerous and rapidly increasing queue' had appeared, waiting for the doors to open. Armed with new powers on seizure of stock, members of the committee arrived on the scene and took possession of the delivery, distributing it to other shops in the area. They were back again on the Monday morning, Christmas Eve, taking away half of the remaining margarine stock.[138]

Figure 6.6 Ration books issued to Elizabeth Bailey. © St Albans Museums (2009.5748; 2009.5716 x 3; 2009.5721)

It was this problem of distribution and the threat of unrest that finally saw the War Cabinet sanction the introduction of compulsory rationing. By June 1918 weekly personal allowances had been set at 8 oz of sugar, 5 oz of butter and margarine, 4 oz of jam, 2 oz of tea and 8 oz of bacon. Meat was rationed by price, with a weekly allowance of four coupons, each with a set value.[139] Customers were required to register with a single shop for each rationed item, so in practice that might mean one or several shops per household (Figure 6.6).

One particular bone of contention was offal. Butchers reported back to the committee that customers were refusing to use their coupons to buy offal, which they did not view as 'real meat'.[140] The committee, fearing it would otherwise go to waste, took the decision to allow the unrestricted sale of offal and faggots; the latter were made from the lowest quality offal and sold at only 1d or 2d each. Advised of this, the Ministry of Food overruled the committee, which nevertheless continued to press for change in the regulations.[141] The situation was eased somewhat by increasing the amount of offal available per coupon and removing faggots and black pudding from the scheme.[142]

The 'offal problem' serves to illustrate how those involved in food control were required to respond to a situation that was changing day by day. At just one meeting in April 1918 the committee processed a long list of those engaged in 'heavy work' and thus entitled to supplementary rations, heard applications from butchers wishing to change their meat supplier, considered requests for additional sugar for domestic jam making, organised the registration of butchers for the sale of bacon and dealt with an application for additional sugar from E. Day & Co. for meals supplied to their workers. This meeting started at 7pm and was not untypical of the sort of agenda that the members considered.[143] They could find themselves addressing issues ranging from an application for an allowance of tea for the mothers attending the infant welfare centre or a request for sugar to make lemonade at the Bank Holiday fête to lengthy discussions with butchers or milk vendors on prices and distribution.[144] They were required to hand down judgement on areas such as how many eggs a single household might preserve (the answer was a maximum of 100), what weight a meat pie should be if sold off ration (6 oz), or the price of a replacement ration book (3d).[145]

Sugar was a particular area of concern. In November 1917, after examining the applications to register for sugar from householders, institutions, caterers and manufacturers, it was calculated that St Albans

needed 28 tons 8 cwt and 10 lbs per month to meet demand.[146] There were
51 applications alone under the category of caterers, including tearooms,
hotels, restaurants and private clubs, and each had to be considered
carefully. Some, such as Bugler's on Market Place and the Patriotic
Club, were given the full amount requested, but these were unusual. The
committee presumably called on local knowledge when they agreed to allow
Mrs Williams of the Dolphin Tea Rooms, Holywell Hill, her full request for
72 lbs, while her St Peter's Street competitor, Annie Wright of the Windmill
Tea Rooms, received only 48 lbs of the 80 lbs requested; she was more
fortunate than Lucy Burlingham of St Peter's Street, whose claim was
turned down entirely as her establishment was 'too small to entertain'.[147]

Rationing helped to distribute what was available more fairly, but it
did not solve all the problems of shortages: setting a price was one thing,
but having the stock to sell was another. In February 1918 the committee
reported that meat was proving the most difficult area to deal with. The
government had set the level of supply at 50 per cent of the October 1917
amount; in St Albans this meant that around 23,000 lbs in dead weight
was allowed per week, but that first week in February just under half of
that was available in the market and the supply of foreign meat was very
unreliable and small when it did arrive.[148] In May 1918 there was a happy
accident when an additional 3,000 lbs of meat from the Ministry of Food
was delivered alongside that which had been requested. The committee
rather sportingly reported this; the Food Controller allowed the 'over-
supplied' meat to be retained and sold without coupons 'rather than run
the risk of it becoming unsaleable if returned to London'.[149] This one-off
windfall would have been welcomed by butchers, but again it was those
customers with money in their pockets who would have most benefited.

Conclusion

A chapter of this length can offer only a glimpse into the problems faced and
strategies deployed by the people of one market town during the First World
War as they tried to keep food on the table. Those who sat on committees
and tribunals intervened in the lives of their fellow citizens in a way that
was new to all concerned: be it farmers being told what to grow and where
to grow it, commercial rivals required to support each other or individuals
coping with restrictions on what they might or might not eat, bureaucracy
became a reality of everyday life. Those required to administer that reality
worked hard to do so during the war and beyond. Those at the sharp end

coped as best they could. Some businesses prospered, others did not; some people went hungry, others did not. Life on the home front went on.

Notes

1. D. Lloyd George, *War memoirs* (London, 1933–6), vol. 3, p. 1269 cited in L.M. Barnett, *British food policy during the First World War* (London, 1985), p. 1. David Lloyd George served as chancellor of the exchequer (1908–May 1915), minister of munitions (May 1915–July 1916), secretary of state for war (July 1916–December 1916) and prime minister (December 1916–October 1922), K.O. Morgan, 'George, David Lloyd, first Earl Lloyd-George of Dwyfor (1863–1945)', *Oxford Dictionary of National Biography*, Oxford University Press, 2004; online edn, May 2011 <http://www.oxforddnb.com/view/article/34570>, accessed 16 January 2016.

2. Barnett, *British food policy*, p. 3.

3. A. Armstrong, *Farmworkers: a social and economic history, 1770–1980* (London, 1988), p. 156.

4. A.G.V. Simmonds, *Britain and World War One* (London, 2012), p. 195.

5. Ibid., pp. 38–9.

6. Ibid., p. 203.

7. Ibid., p. 37.

8. 'Food riot at Hitchin', *Letchworth Citizen*, 7 August 1914.

9. 'The price of food', *Herts Advertiser* (*HA*), 8 August 1914.

10. Simmonds, *Britain and World War One*, p. 175; I.F.W. Beckett, *Home Front, 1914–1918. How Britain survived the Great War* (Richmond, 2006), p. 110. For more on wage rates see Chapter 1.

11. Simmonds, *Britain and World War One*, p. 214.

12. The food control committee was set up in August 1917 in recognition of the growing need to co-ordinate a local response to the problems of distribution and shortages of food. It acted as point of contact for national government, disseminating information and directives, and was tasked with the management of any rationing schemes should these become necessary.

13. HALS, SBR/863, St Albans Local Food Control Committee Minute Book (LFCC), 1917–20, 5 February 1918.

14. 'Local war items', *HA*, 8 August 1914.

15. 'The food problem', *HA*, 15 August 1914.

16. 'Stray notes', *HA*, 15 June 1918.

17. 'The price of food', *HA*, 8 August 1914; 'Bread goes up again', *HA*, 22 May 1915.

18. 'How to cook herrings', *HA*, 3 October 1914.

19. 'Domestic economy. Cheap foods', *HA*, 2 January 1915.

20. 'National thrift', *HA*, 4 December 1915.

21. Imperial War Museums, IWM 549–1, *The Secret* (1918) <http://www.iwm.org.uk/collections/item/object/1060023081> accessed 1 February 2016.

22. 'A soldier's wife's complaint', *HA*, 8 December 1917.

23. 'Christmas trade', *HA*, 19 December 1914.

24. Ibid.

25. 'Chocolate day', *HA*, 21 November 1914.

26. 'No foreign meat for paupers', *HA*, 4 December 1915.

27. 'T.W. Kent & Sons', *HA*, 9 December 1916.

28. 'Freeman's Real Turtle Extract', *HA*, 8 December 1917.

29. The National Archives (TNA), BPP IX.1 [Cmd24] Board of Agriculture and Fisheries. Wages and conditions of employment in agriculture. Vol. I. General report (1919) p. 39.

30. 'English crops and livestock', *The Times*, 28 September 1914.

31. 'Harvest employment', *HA*, 15 August 1914.

32. P. Dewey, *British agriculture in the First World War* (London, 2014), pp. 47–8.

33. 'St Albans rural schools', *HA*, 11 March 1916.

34. F. Brittain, *Milestones of 105 years of Hertfordshire scouting* (Borehamwood, 2013).

35. 'St Albans city tribunal', *HA*, 17 November 1917. See M. Neighbour, *St Albans' own East End, volume I: outsiders* (Hoddesdon, 2012) for more on Giffen's involvement in the expansion of St Albans.

36. 'Giffen Bros, electrical engineers and contractors', *Pictorial Record: St Albans* (London, 1915), p. 19.

37. HALS, AEC/1, Hertfordshire War Agricultural Committee Minute Book, 1916–19, 30 July 1917.

38. TNA, FO 383/508, 'Letter from Swiss legation', 1 July 1919.

39. HALS, AEC/1, 25 March 1918, 13 May 1918.

40. 'County appeal tribunal', *HA*, 24 June 1916.

41. 'St Albans tribunal', *HA*, 8 April 1916.

42. 'Miss Betty Glossop on the land', *HA*, 17 June 1916. See Chapter 3 for Betty Glossop's work as a VAD nurse.

43. R.E. Prothero, Lord Ernle, *English farming past and present* (London, 1961, 1st edn London, 1912), p. 393.

44. Dewey, *British agriculture*, p. 93.

45. 'Food and farming', *HA*, 17 November 1917.

46. HALS, AEC/20/41, Hertfordshire War Agricultural Committee, correspondence files Mid-Herts Division.

47. HALS, AEC/20/58. Hertfordshire War Agricultural Committee, correspondence files Mid-Herts Division.

48. HALS, AEC/20/1. The meadow referred to was formerly known as Home Meadow and was bounded by Beaumont Avenue, Farm Lane (now Farm Road), the junction of Hatfield Road/Beaumont Avenue and roughly the line of the present Beechwood Avenue. We are grateful to Mike Neighbour of Fleetville Diaries for this information.

49. HALS, AEC/1, 29 July 1918.

50. 'Price of bread', *HA*, 1 April 1916.

51. TNA, CAB 23/8/480, 1 October 1918.

52. Bread Order (1917), BPP XXVI Food Controller's Orders 1917–18.

53. Barnett, *British food policy*, p. 109.

54. 'Stray notes', *HA*, 19 January 1918.

55. HALS, SBR/863, LFCC, 5 February 1918.

56. Ibid., 22 May 1918.

57. Dewey, *British agriculture*, p. 226.

58. 'The milk supply', *HA*, 25 September 1915.

59. 'The city milk supply', *HA*, 13 November 1915, 'The milk supply', *HA*, 8 April 1916.

60. 'Preservatives in milk', *HA*, 21 November 1914.

61. 'St Albans city council', *HA*, 24 July 1915.

62. 'Our milk supply', *HA*, 6 February 1915.

63. HALS, SBR/863, LFCC, 17 December 1917.

64. 'The cost of living', *HA*, 7 October 1916.

65. 'The city's health', *HA*, 29 April 1916.

66. HALS, SBR/863, LFCC, 17 December 1917. The four farmers were Mrs Brown and Messrs Crawford, Slaughter and Slimmon.

67. Ibid.

68. Ibid.

69. HALS, SBR/863, LFCC, 10 December 1918.

70. Ibid., 10 November 1918.

71. 'Hertfordshire appeal tribunal', *HA*, 10 June 1916.

72. 'St Albans tribunal', *HA*, 13 July 1918.

73. 'Milk conference', *HA*, 4 November 1916.

74. 'Correspondence. "The milk conference"', *HA*, 11 November 1916.

75. 'Food production', *HA*, 5 January 1918.

76. 'Manager of a butcher's shop', *HA*, 4 March 1916.

77. 'City tribunal', *HA*, 17 February 1917.

78. J. McDermott, *British military service tribunals, 1916–1918: 'a very much abused body of men'* (Manchester, 2011), p. 132.

79. 'St Albans master butchers', *HA*, 17 March 1917.

80. In June 1917 a sum of £50 was deposited in Oakley's bank account, due to him under the agreement reached with his fellow butchers. Whether this was the only such payment is unclear. 'St Albans city tribunal', *HA*, 30 June 1917.

81. 'St Albans butchers', *HA*, 29 June 1918.

82. Frank Hearn's service record can be accessed in full at <http://www.findmypast.co.uk>

83. *Kelly's Trade Directory for Hertfordshire* (London, 1922).

84. 'County tribunal', *HA*, 27 January 1917.

85. HALS, SBR/863, LFCC, 30 June 1919.

86. 'St Albans army appeals', *HA*, 13 July 1918 (Patience), 'St Albans tribunal', *HA*, 27 July 1918 (Wheaton).

87. Report of the Central Tribunal appointed under the Military Services Act, 1916, p.11 cited in McDermott, *British military service tribunals*, p. 143.

88. HALS, SBR/863, LFCC, 17 September 1917.

89. 'Herts county tribunal', *HA*, 26 January 1918.

90. 'County army appeals', *HA*, 12 May 1917.

91. 'St Albans tribunal', *HA*, 16 June 1917.

92. 'St Albans city tribunal', *HA*, 30 June 1917.

93. 'St Albans exemptions', *HA*, 9 February 1918.
94. 'National Service', House of Commons debate, 19 March 1918 <http:// hansard.millbanksystems.com/commons/1918/mar/19/national-service#S5CV0104P0_19180319_HOC_353> accessed 16 February 2016.
95. 'The city tribunal', *HA*, 8 July 1916.
96. 'County appeal tribunal', *HA*, 2 June 1917.
97. St Albans City Absent Voters' List (1918), <http://www.stalbanshistory.org> accessed 13 February 2016.
98. 'St Albans city tribunal', *HA*, 23 August 1917, 8 December 1917, 9 March 1918.
99. Simmonds, *Britain and World War One*, p. 206.
100. HALS, SBR/863, LFCC, 3 September 1917.
101. HALS, SBR/883, Miscellaneous Committees Minute Book (MCMB), 1915–19, 29 January 1916.
102. Ibid., 9 February 1916.
103. Ibid., 22 September 1915.
104. Ibid., 11 March 1916.
105. Ibid., 26 July 1918. Placing an accurate figure on the number of plots in use is difficult. In the summer of 1918 Alderman Horace Slade reported that there were 2,532 plots being worked. To suggest that a further 1,500 plots had been brought into production between May 1917 and July 1918 would tend to support the theory that the definition of an allotment was open to interpretation.
106. HALS, SBR/883, MCMB, 28 April 1917.
107. Neighbour, *St Albans' own East End*, pp. 249–50.
108. HALS, SBR/883, MCMB, 27 October 1917.
109. Ibid., 11 March 1918, HALS, AEC/22/129.
110. Ibid., 10 March 1917.
111. 'Allotment hints. What to do next week', *HA*, 5 January 1918.
112. HALS, SBR/883, MCMB, 28 April 1917.
113. 'St Albans city tribunal', *HA*, 18 May 1918.
114. HALS, SBR/883, MCMB, 27 October 1917.
115. Ibid., 11 March 1918.
116. 'Herts army appeals', *HA*, 1 June 1918.
117. HALS, SBR/883, MCMB, 21 June 1918.
118. Ibid., 21 January 1919.
119. Ibid., 11 February 1919.
120. 'National kitchens', *The Times*, 5 February 1918.
121. Barnett, *British food policy*, p. 151.
122. HALS, SBR/883, MCMB.
123. HALS, SBR/863, LFCC, 7 February 1918.
124. 'St Albans national kitchen', *HA*, 5 October 1918.
125. Barnett, *British food policy*, p. 115
126. HALS, SBR/863, LFCC, 13 August 1917.
127. 'The rationing campaign', *HA*, 7 April 1917.
128. 'County council reflections, *HA*, 12 May 1917.

129. 'How they starve at the Ritz', *Daily Herald*, 24 November 1917.

130. 'An appeal to the Food Control Committee', *HA*, 9 February 1918.

131. HALS, SBR/863, LFCC, 13 August 1917.

132. The Oddfellows and Ancient Order of Foresters were Friendly Societies. Members paid a weekly subscription into a common fund which could be called upon to cover medical and funeral costs.

133. 'Local food control', *HA*, 9 February 1918.

134. HALS, SBR/863, LFCC, 15 March 1918.

135. Ibid., 24 December 1918.

136. Barnett, *British food policy*, p. 148.

137. HALS, SBR/863, LFCC, 1 November 1917.

138. 'The margarine queue', *HA*, 29 December 1917.

139. Barnett, *British food policy*, p. 148.

140. HALS, SBR/863, LFCC, 5 March 1918.

141. Ibid., 15 March 1918.

142. Ibid., 28 March 1918.

143. Ibid., 10 April 1918.

144. Ibid., 29 July 1918.

145. Ibid., 2 May 1918, 26 September 1918.

146. Ibid., 17 November 1917.

147. Ibid., 4 November 1917.

148. Ibid., 5 February 1918.

149. Ibid., 2 May 1918.

CHAPTER 7

The role of local government

The aldermen, councillors, officers and staff of St Albans City Council carried a heavy burden of responsibility throughout the First World War. Almost overnight the population of the city increased by around a third with the arrival of the military. This added substantially to the workload of the council, which was responsible for law and order, the maintenance of the town's infrastructure and public health. There were new regulations to enforce and, of course, all this had to be managed with a depleted workforce, as many council workers volunteered or were called up. During the course of the war priorities shifted from accommodating the army to managing a city struggling to cope with shortages of labour, materials and food.

Three men served as mayor of the city – at that time a position with executive and judicial powers – from 1914 to 1918.[1] The first was Alderman Horace Slade, who ran the family straw hat making business and had to deal with the city's transformation into a garrison town.[2] The strain must have been enormous and the 63-year-old Slade was unable to complete his term of office owing to ill health. The mayoral term ran from November at that time and councillor Bertie Charles Edwards, due to take office after Slade, assumed his responsibilities a month or so earlier.[3]

Edwards, a Liberal who represented the North Ward, was Australian by birth and worked as a company director in London for the Australian Merchants' Company, a business founded by his father.[4] The following November (1915) Alderman James Flint became mayor, a post he was re-elected to every year for the remainder of the war. All other councillors remained in post – barring infirmity or death – as local council elections were suspended by the introduction of the Election and Registration Act in 1915.[5]

Flint was something of a self-made man. He was born in Holmbury St Mary near Dorking in 1857 and moved to St Albans in 1889, where he was

Figure 7.1 James Flint, mayor of St Albans, 1915–18. © St Albans Museums (2006_6950)

licensee of the Pineapple public house in Catherine Street for 11 years.[6] Having worked as a builder's foreman and clerk of works on a large number of construction projects in London and Hertfordshire, he later became a property developer in his own right, building and letting houses in Etna Road and Grange Street (Figure 7.1). A pen-sketch gives an idea of this remarkable man, who took charge in the city's time of greatest need: 'Of stocky build, he carries weight in a dual sense. He is a square man, the heavy bearded jaws suggesting strength and determination, the piercing eye and the powerful forehead shrewdness and a cautious impartial judgement.'[7]

The energy, experience and ability of all three wartime mayors was crucial to the efficient running of the city, particularly in the case of Flint, who carried the responsibilities of office for three years.

The business backgrounds of the councillors closely reflected the trading profile of the town. They represented retail, the professions, construction and manufacturing. Some ran family firms, although there were at least two who managed other people's businesses. From coal merchants to retailers and significant, wealthy businessmen such as Samuel Ryder, the council had a range of skills to draw on and a deep knowledge of the business landscape of St Albans.[8] Two key officers working for the council were the medical officer of health Dr Henry E. May, whose practice was in the city, and the town clerk Edward Percy Debenham, a solicitor who combined his council responsibilities with professional practice in the family law firm.[9]

When war broke out the council was only just adapting to the increased responsibilities brought about by the extension of the city boundaries in 1913. Now it had to play a major role in preparing the city for war. Government powers increased considerably through the Defence of the Realm Act (DORA) 1914, and both central and local government became more intimately involved in organising the lives of citizens. The full council met quarterly, but during the war years both new and established council committees met more frequently and had devolved executive powers. The workload was so great that the majority of councillors were attending two or three sub-committee meetings a week in the early months of the war.[10]

Defending the city

On 31 July 1914 the Home Office issued St Albans head constable George Whitbread with detailed orders in the event of war. The police were instructed to help with the billeting of troops, the requisition of horses and vehicles and the protection of vulnerable points on railways and other means of transport, as well as being charged with keeping an eye out for undesirable aliens. By 2 August 1914 the police and boy scouts were guarding all bridges against possible attack, including the railway bridge across London Road. The police were instructed by the Home Office to carry firearms if it was thought advisable.[11]

Numbers in the force were reduced the moment war was declared, as four constables joined their respective territorial regiments. With the army in immediate need of competent drill instructors, constables Benn and North were seconded to the army.[12] Six new recruits were appointed to replace these men. Whitbread had the authority to register 100 special constables and at this time he enrolled 50 in the police special reserve, paying them 5s a day when they were on duty. From the date of mobilisation all police leave was cancelled and officers had to work long and irregular hours, a situation acknowledged in the local press: 'Be it said to their credit, that from the heads of departments down to the junior constable, this additional work has been cheerfully rendered – a fact which only increases the debt of gratitude due to them from the public.'[13]

The Admiralty, via the Home Office, was responsible for organising defence against aerial attack. Whitbread received instructions to reduce street lighting to make it more difficult for enemy pilots to navigate their way across the country.[14] When a British biplane appeared over St Albans in November 1914 it was such a rare sight that it caused great excitement.[15] The Home Office issued air raid precautions in June 1915, advising people to keep a supply of water and sand on upper floors, to shut windows and doors to prevent the admission of noxious gases and to make themselves aware of the nearest fire alarm post. The public were told to stay indoors during an air raid warning to avoid being hit by falling missiles or causing obstructions to emergency vehicles. Portable chemical fire extinguishers required a written guarantee that they complied with the specifications of the Board of Trade or some approved fire prevention scheme and the public was advised of the dangers of handling ordnance: 'No bomb of any description should be handled unless it has shown itself to be of incendiary type. In this case it may be possible to remove it without undue risk. In all other cases a bomb should be left alone and the police informed.'[16] A driver and two firemen were on duty at the fire brigade station every night from 9pm to 1am, each man being paid 3s per night.[17] By September 1915 the council ordered the St Albans Gas Co. to switch off all street lighting by 9.30pm, plunging the city into almost total darkness that autumn and winter.[18] In an appeal to the public, Mayor Edwards said:

> In view of the recent Zeppelin raids in the vicinity of London, it is a matter of the utmost importance that all lights in St Albans should be reduced to the lowest possible point or effectually shaded or obscured so that no bright light is visible outside. Traders and residents throughout the entire city are, therefore, urged to adapt such means as will ensure compliance with this necessary precaution.[19]

The lighting orders were advertised in the local press and the council and police, with the help of boy scouts, organised the distribution of printed notices to all households, places of worship, businesses and public buildings. The Saturday market was forced to close early because of the lighting restrictions.[20] Concern increased when on 13 October a Zeppelin passed over the centre of the city and hovered over St Stephen's Hill for about three minutes before turning towards London, without dropping any bombs.[21] The council supported the increased regulations, even though they made life difficult for everybody. To help people get about in the dark the council applied white paint to kerbs at crossroads and on other hazardous objects that people might stumble into on the darkened streets. The police were opposed to the measures, but were overruled by the council on the basis that the darkness had saved St Albans from aerial attacks and it would not do anything to increase the risk. The council also anticipated that shops would close earlier, therefore reducing the number of people on the roads and footpaths during the winter.[22] It was thought that church bells ringing after sunset might help Zeppelin pilots work out where the city was, so the bells fell silent on winter nights.[23]

There were areas that were too important to be under either council or police control, as both discovered when they tried to reduce the lights at the Midland railway station. The Lights (England & Wales) Order, 22 July 1916, did not apply to necessary working lights on railways (including lights in stations and in goods yards and marshalling yards). Stationmasters were notified from their own headquarters of impending air raids and acted according to instructions. The railway officials decided what light was necessary for the working of railways.[24]

Factory hooters were an everyday part of life in St Albans and one in particular came into its own in the war years. E. Day & Co.'s siren was utilised to give air raid warnings – three short blasts, followed by one long blast, repeated four times at intervals of 15 seconds. The all-clear sounded with one blast followed at an interval of 15 seconds by one long blast. Notification of air raid warnings applied to a large area, up to Norfolk, so did not necessarily mean an attack was imminent in the city.[25] Little notice was taken of the siren or the posters explaining what to do, and Mayor Flint reported that he and the police had tried to disperse a crowd of about 350 people gathered in Market Place following an air raid warning in 1917.[26] Unfortunately, residents in the north and west of the city could not hear Day's siren, so it was relocated to the top of the town hall.[27] The town clerk wrote to other factory owners asking them to reduce the noise level of their hooters to avoid any confusion with the air raid siren. In addition, the postmaster-general asked people not to use the telephone immediately after an air raid, leaving the exchange free to handle calls to the emergency services.[28]

There were concerns about the potential cost to property of air raids, and the council took out corporation properties aircraft insurance.

However, when the Hertfordshire Medical Volunteers, part of the Royal Army Medical Corps, enquired about liability insurance in the event of injury to its officers and men while on air-raid duty, the council declined to take responsibility. It instead approached the government committee on the prevention of distress, which referred them to the military, which in turn passed the problem on to the War Office.[29]

Maintaining law and order

By December 1915 12 men from a city police force of 35 had enlisted and there were concerns about the effect this might have on the protection of the city.[30] Men who were ineligible for the army owing to their age were encouraged to enrol as special constables and were used wherever possible. Whitbread complimented the specials on the work they were doing, saying 'They have been of the greatest assistance, and I cannot speak too highly of the work they have done.'[31]

As well as regular duties, the police had to enforce new regulations, including lighting restrictions applied to the city under DORA from August 1914. At first the police took a somewhat lenient view as residents and business owners adapted to the new regulations. However, lighting infringements continued and, from October 1915, people breaking the law in this way were taken to court and fined. An army surgeon living in Clarence Road complied with the lighting order only after a long discussion and was duly fined 20s. Shopkeeper Archibald Page was told by a constable to remove all the lights in his shop window and pull the blinds down fully. When the officer returned some time later he found that only some of the lights had been removed and the blinds were not fully down. When the case came to court the shop owner was fined 20s and complained that he might as well shut the shop altogether.[32]

Those driving or riding motor vehicles found themselves faced with new traffic regulations. A motorcyclist refused to stop when requested to by the police checking licences. He slowed down but then accelerated away, later claiming that he thought one of the military police had said 'all right'. The magistrates dismissed the case with 4s costs, and Flint cautioned the defendant to be more careful in future.[33] Lighting restrictions relating to motor vehicles applied to both civilian and military traffic and made driving at night quite dangerous. It appears that the military may not have been following the rules, as the town clerk queried the bright lights they were using, with the result that they had to make adjustments to their vehicles.[34] Lighting-up time in 1916 was half an hour after sunset, rather than an hour, presumably to help prevent accidents. Headlights were banned on all vehicles and sidelights were to be used. Those driving after dark in rural areas could, however, use their lights on full.[35]

It was an offence to receive any army property under any circumstances and two police constables of good reputation, with 14 years' service between them, paid heavily for accepting two small parcels of bacon from a soldier as a gesture of goodwill. Both were fined 40s and dismissed from the force. Chairman of the magistrates' bench, Mayor Flint, who heard the case, expressed his sadness at their position, but a moment's thoughtlessness had cost them dearly.[36]

Under the Police (Emergency Provisions) Act 1915 the right to retire on a pension was suspended until the war ended. PC Groom was just one of those who had to stay on in the force even though he had completed 26 years' service.[37] However, in January 1916 head constable Whitbread, aged 47, did leave the force, tendering his resignation on health grounds. The Watch Committee, which had responsibility for policing in the city, arranged that Whitbread would retire on two-thirds pension, but this was not the end of the matter. Shortly afterwards the Home Office intervened, and control and discipline of St Albans police passed to the county constabulary. The city force was the only one in the country to be transferred to another authority during the war.[38] Hertfordshire's chief constable, Major A.L. Law, took command from June 1916. St Albans City Council continued to pay salaries, wages, pensions and expenses plus £200 a year to the county treasurer for a superintendent of St Albans division and headquarters administration. Representatives of the local Watch Committee joined the county committee.[39] There is no doubt that Whitbread's resignation and the ceding of control of the city force to the county were linked, but the facts leading up to the crisis have proved difficult to establish.

Dealing with the army

After simply handing over buildings in the first weeks of the war, the council now had to look at how it was going to organise and meet the extra expenses created by the army's presence in the city. This was a new experience for all and a process of trial and error began. Assistant city surveyor John Negus kept an account of all the costs involved which the council expected the War Office to refund. He and the medical officer of health Dr May started long and complicated negotiations over the use of city buildings, services and facilities with the officer in charge, Major Cauldwell-Smith, who reported to the General Officer Commanding Third Army and the War Office.

In October 1914 the council charged the military £425 for the period to 31 October for structural work, scavenging (street cleansing), emptying cesspools and other services. A standard charge of 11s 2d per man per week was agreed on a fixed basis of 6,500 men.[40] The General Officer challenged this, as he considered collecting house refuse and emptying cesspools as part of the normal city costs which should be paid out of the rates. The council referred the matter to the Local Government Board (LGB) for advice, and after discussions the council accepted this argument.[41] There were also negotiations over rents for public buildings, recreational areas such as Clarence Park and the public baths in Victoria Street. The old police station in Chequer Street was taken over from 10 August 1914 at a rent of £5 a month, agreed in November 1914.[42] However, in December the government land agent of the Third Army decided it was only worth 10s to 12s 6d per week. The army agreed to pay 12s, which was accepted, but the council ensured that there was a clause in the contract binding the army to make good any damage to the property when they vacated it.[43]

Negus had to consider several factors when setting a rental value for the use of Clarence Park. A large number of troops were billeted there, so roads had to be built and water provided; from 29 March to 17 May 1915 45,000 gallons of water were used.[44] After the war the turf would have to be replaced and any damage made good. The army offered a weekly rent of £4, plus gas and water costs, rather than the £5 rent set by the council.[45] Charges were set for the army's use of other amenities, including Victoria Playing Fields (off Verulam Road), used for company drill and inspection.[46]

The 1916 Local Government (Emergency Provisions) Act obliged the council to provide storage for soldiers' furniture and effects and the basement area of Pageant House in Victoria Street was set aside for this purpose, with yet another committee formed to set charges and administer the service.[47] The police had to enforce a list of items banned by the council from being stored at Pageant House, including gunpowder, Lucifer matches, cartridges, fireworks, preserves, oils and other articles liable to leakage.[48] In 1918 live cartridges were found in a household dustbin and the public was warned of the dangers to themselves and council refuse collectors of discarding ammunition in this way.[49]

A major worry and cost was the damage to the roads and street lamps caused by military vehicles. The army was charged £5 for a lamppost damaged in Grimston Road by an army car. The council claimed 25s for a motor speed sign damaged by a soldier; the soldier's pay was only 13s 1½d a week, so the army asked for this to be taken into consideration. The council approached the War Office over the problem of damaged road signs and street lamps, arguing that it was unfair that the courts expected them to enforce the payment of a fine by an individual soldier, although responsible for the damage, rather than the army itself.[50]

In March 1917 a survey of military and civilian traffic showed that one-third of the tonnage passing through the Peahen crossroads was military, an indication of just how its presence in the city affected daily life.[51] The army took priority in all matters and in November 1916 it requested a list of the names and ages of those with conditional exemptions who could help build roads in France: by October 1917 three men, two of them aged over 40, had been conscripted for this purpose, although one was discharged and returned to his council position that month.[52]

There were two other problems relating to road usage that the council had to contend with. The firing ranges at Gorhambury and Chalk Hill, Chiswell Green, were in almost daily use and it was the council's job to send an employee out to put up a board and red flag next to the clock tower to alert travellers to road closures when the firing ranges were being used.[53] It also had to tackle the military about early morning drill, parades and marches, starting as early as 6am in residential streets. Residents had complained about the tramp of so many boots and a commanding officer agreed to minimise the noise as much as possible (Figure 7.2).[54]

Sanitary arrangements

Of particular concern to the medical officer of health and assistant city surveyor were the potential dangers to health following the large influx of men billeted in private homes and public buildings throughout the city in August 1914. With no time to raise such matters at council, the medical officer of health Dr May, with the mayor's support, took immediate measures to meet the needs of the army and protect the health of the city. The waterworks company provided an additional 100,000 to 150,000 gallons of water per day. Many of the soldiers were accommodated in tents, so, to avoid the contamination of ground water, no latrine trenches were dug in the city or rural district without Dr May's approval. He even

Figure 7.2 A policeman holds back the traffic as soldiers march through town.
© Hertfordshire Archives and Local Studies (NE980/AA/14a)

provided a water trough at the entrance to the Grange Estate for the increased number of horses.[55] Many of the public buildings, schools and houses commandeered as billets did not have sufficient toilets, so pails filled with earth were provided and emptied daily by 8pm. Toilet paper was freely supplied to the army to minimise as far as possible the risk of the drains becoming blocked with coarse or unsuitable paper.[56]

May's rapid response to the situation in August 1914 suggests that he must have prepared an emergency public health plan in advance. His task would have been easier if the Fleetville area had already been connected to mains sewage – a key reason for the city boundary extension in 1913. However, the major part of this work was shelved until after the war, although a smaller-scale project to extend the sewers to the Bernards Heath area, and the Wiles & Lewis tallow works in particular, did go ahead.[57] The work was carried out in August 1914 with an LGB loan of £10,000 at 3.5 per cent interest on the basis that the work would provide employment for those who had been laid off owing to the closure of export markets following the outbreak of war.[58] The council managed to borrow a further £3,400 to complete work in hand at the sewage works in Park Street. In the meantime, the sewage system remained overloaded and many households continued to rely on council-employed 'night-soil men' to empty cesspools.[59]

The failure to extend the sewer system was a cause of continuing resentment that erupted into a major political row in March 1916. Smith's Printing Company in Fleetville complained to the LGB that even though the city boundaries had been extended the council would empty the cesspools only if paid to do so. The firm had paid higher rates for two years since becoming part of the extended city, having previously been part of St Albans Rural District, where the rates were lower, but for this increase in rates Smith's believed it received no extra services, adding that it had to pay the higher rates at a time when it was facing other financial pressures brought on by the war. In June 1916 Fleetville companies, including Smith's, St Albans Rubber Company, Grimston Tyres Ltd, Nicholson's Raincoat Company Ltd and Engineering and Arc Lamps Ltd, escalated the issue, sending a petition to the LGB. The council's response was to state that without expansion at the sewage works the sewers could not be extended, further countering with the argument that labour and other costs had risen considerably because of the war and that these costs fell primarily on the citizens of the old city.[60] The council also stated that it had never been intended to vary rates according to which houses were or were not connected to the sewers.[61]

In an effort to alleviate the problem the 'activated sludge experiment' was tried out in late 1917, although shortages of steel held up the progress of the project for a month or so.[62] It attracted interest from those who dealt in such matters at home and abroad,[63] and in August 1918 35 members of the Metropolitan District of Sewage Works Managers Association were given a guided tour and a detailed explanation of how the system worked, followed by a tea party on site.[64] Land at the sewage works in Park Street was used to grow food during the war: six-dozen fruit trees were planted and two acres of seed potatoes were set. Oats grown to feed council-owned horses were a useful additional crop, as prices had risen sharply.[65]

St Albans was short of public toilets for women, a problem that became acute in 1914 with the influx of so many wives, daughters and girlfriends visiting the men in khaki. One ratepayer highlighted the 'crying need of the hour' in a letter to the press, stating that 'Something must be done, sir, and done now, to stay what is becoming a public scandal and a stigma on our City.'[66] There were two possible options for new conveniences: the old police station in Chequer Street or the construction of underground toilets at the town hall. Temporary ladies' conveniences were opened in fire station yard, Victoria Street, on 25 December 1914: a useful Christmas present for all ladies visiting the city. The conversion of the old police station having been rejected by the LGB on the grounds that it was too close to other buildings,[67] work went ahead in February 1915 to build the underground toilets at the town hall at an estimated cost of £1,200.[68]

Protecting health

As well as his work on sewage and public toilets, Dr May also had to work with the military on the health of the newly arrived troops, as any outbreaks of illness could affect the local population. By November 1914, apart from one case of chickenpox, there had been no infectious disease or any illness due to insanitary conditions.[69] May and the military agreed that in the event of any outbreaks he would be notified and those troops suffering from smallpox, scarlet fever or diphtheria would be moved to local isolation hospitals. The Sisters Hospital made its disinfecting equipment available for the military to use on the kit of those infected with lice and other diseases; by November 1914 1,000 blankets and kits had been treated.[70] In his 1915 annual report Dr May gave details on the location and causes of military deaths in the city. Of the 19 recorded, the largest number (nine), not surprisingly, occurred in Bricket House, the Red Cross Hospital. The remainder occurred in the St Albans and Mid Herts Hospital (four), Sisters Hospital (two), private homes (two) and the Royal Army Medical Corps hospital[71] and Union Infirmary (one apiece). Causes of death ranged from common illnesses of the day such as pneumonia, scarlet fever and blood poisoning to deaths due to accidents involving trains, motorcycles, hand grenades and weed killer.

Venereal disease (VD) was a major problem for the army as it incapacitated large numbers of troops and necessitated specialist treatment at hospitals such as Shafford Military Hospital near St Albans, on the Redbourn road. This consisted of huts originally constructed to house troops on land at Childwickbury owned by racehorse owner Jack Barnato Joel.[72] The council put up warning posters about VD on all public buildings and notice boards and asked employers to follow suit.[73] The county council paid for regular front-page notices in the local press warning of the risks and offering free treatment in London hospitals carried out in strict confidence.[74]

In spite of the increased population, the city's health remained good. Infant mortality in St Albans was 50 per cent lower than the national average, and the death rate compared favourably with elsewhere.[75] Dr

May's annual medical reports during the war included illnesses affecting the city's population that were quite common at the time, such as diphtheria, scarlet fever and German measles.

The council was keen to preserve its independence from the county council on health issues. It did not support a Hertfordshire County Nursing Association scheme to provide nursing care for measles cases, and May was asked to report on establishing an alternative scheme.[76] He took his role very seriously and was attentive to the smallest detail to maintain a healthy city. He believed in prevention, so he educated people through the local press with articles on subjects such as the 'fly peril'.[77] May was responsible for the sanitary condition of all council-owned buildings and the clean state of the city in general. He appointed an assistant sanitary inspector, who checked all backyards, gardens and anywhere manure was stored, spraying the heaps of dung with a special paraffin sprayer every week.[78] When there was a diphtheria outbreak the county council was at odds with May and did not support his plan to supply children with individual boxes of pens and pencils in schools to avoid cross-infection.[79] May also criticised the LGB in his 1918 report for failing to insist that local doctors refer all cases of measles to him to enable an accurate estimate of outbreaks to be recorded.

Antenatal care and the scientific study of mother and child from conception and early years were only just developing at the beginning of the twentieth century. In 1914 the county council appointed eight nurses to act as health visitors to the county. Margaret Ransom, then serving with the Territorial Force Nursing Association in Liverpool, was appointed the first health visitor for St Albans.[80] The LGB advised that there should be some suitable supervision of a child's life from the earliest age until the time they started school, and in 1914 the county council appointed Dr Helen Swatman to cover maternity and child welfare in the city. In his 1915 report May announced plans to open a maternity centre for St Albans. Having set up a committee of five councillors and three women the plan was abandoned, the county council having announced plans to open a maternity hospital.[81] However, a centre for infants and children was opened in St Albans at the Friends' Meeting House in Lattimore Road and by 1918 some 555 children had been seen, although the space available was such that only the weighing of babies and some infant consultations were possible.[82]

The war years' statistics show that the city's health remained good. The death rate per 1,000 of the population in 1913 was 11.11 and it rose significantly in 1918 to 15.45 only following the influenza outbreak. Discounting the 75 deaths from influenza, the figure was 12.27. In the first years of the war there was no major change in the birth rate but from 1917 to 1919 there was a drop. In 1914 the figure was 20.84 but in 1917 it dropped to 13.22, rising slightly in 1918 to 14.36. However, while numbers fell, the proportion of illegitimate births rose. This may have been partly due to the number of troops training in the area but it is also possible that some couples did not have time to get married before the father was called up. Fifteen babies were born to unmarried mothers in 1914; in 1915, the first full year of the war, the number rose to 25 and in 1918 to 43.[83]

Pay and war bonuses

The administrative burdens of managing in wartime put a financial strain on council resources. Nevertheless, from the start of the war, it continued to pay a proportion of wages and salaries to support the families of men on active service. Each case was considered on its merits, as there was no single council-wide policy on how this should be applied. For example, the stepmother of chief clerk A. Pearce received 7s 6d a week with 4s 9d a week invested, which he could take when he returned to his old job.[84] G. Hill, a horse driver, married with three dependent children, earned on average £1 3s 6d per week. His wife was given 12s per week and 3s 3d was retained until Hill resumed his employment.[85] The money set aside for employees was invested in the Post Office Savings Bank. The council also provided for families in other ways: free medical attendance and medicine were provided for dependants of serving men. Ernest Gape, secretary of the Soldiers' and Sailors' Families' Association, distributed pamphlets to any families needing this help.[86]

Five members of the surveyor's department had joined up by the beginning of September 1914, including the city surveyor, John Ashurst, who served as a transport officer attached to the Mounted Brigade of Field Ambulance (Territorials). The army released him temporarily in August 1916 for 14 days to attend to urgent city projects that he had started before the war.[87] Ashurst was promised his job would still be there for him on his return, and in the meantime he received full pay less his army pay.[88] Such arrangements were formalised in 1916, with the Local Government (Emergency Provisions) Act requiring all authorities to pay the balance between employees' military pay and allowances and their former civilian pay.[89]

Following the introduction of conscription in 1916 the council applied to the St Albans City Military Service Tribunal on a number of occasions. In February 1917 12 exempted council officials and employees were recalled to the tribunal. Three exemptions were removed, but the others were upheld.[90] Such was the drive to conscript all available men in the summer of 1918 that Dr May, who was carrying out such a vitally important role in St Albans, received notice that he would be graded and possibly called up. The Urban Authority & General Purposes committee was unanimous that he should be exempted if called, as his work was essential for the efficient maintenance of the city's public health.[91]

The army needed men, but so did agriculture, and food was a national priority. In April 1917 the council agreed to loan any man with agricultural knowledge to local farmers to help with preparing and sowing the land for harvest. Constables James Bowyer and Francis Russell were seconded to help on Kingsbury and Little Cell Barnes farms.[92]

The council faced not only shortages of labour but also demands for higher wages from those still employed. Competition from businesses engaged on war work, as well as the rising cost of living, gave workers the confidence to call for increased pay. The issue was complicated by the fact that each department negotiated its own wage increases, which created a domino effect as employees of one department learned of increases elsewhere. In May 1915 the council workmen asked for a pay rise to help make ends meet. A special committee recommended that war bonuses should be paid, enabling the council to adjust wages if necessary once the war ended.[93] A year later, workmen in the parks department put in a claim for another pay rise to match wages being earned by building labourers in the city. An additional war bonus of 1s a week was granted. In October 1916 similar demands came from the highways department for rises to match drivers in other councils. Horse and cart drivers received an extra 1s, making a total of 27s a week pay, which included a 3s war bonus. The inspector of nuisances was also told to get sou'westers and waterproof jackets for the house refuse collectors to wear in bad weather.[94]

The police, too, were starting to compare their wages with those of officers in other forces. A new pay scale based upon years of service was agreed in May 1915. The approximate cost per police officer would be £190 per annum, half of which would come from the Exchequer contribution received from the county council. In December 1916 the council was petitioned by St Albans police officers, who provided evidence of higher pay rates in 28 other forces. A war bonus of 3s per week was paid to address the issue and meet the increased cost of living.[95] These additional costs had to be found from cuts elsewhere, and over £90 was saved on police uniforms alone.[96] By May 1917 city policemen were paid the same as the county police and the war bonus was increased to 4s per a week, with an additional 6d per week for each child residing at home and not in paid employment.[97]

The Home Office now saw police pay as a national rather than a local issue. It planned to hold a conference to secure some uniformity of action on police pay, war bonuses and allowances, to which the Watch Committee was invited to send representatives.[98] There was some sympathy for the position of the police officers and, not waiting for the outcome of the conference, Mayor Flint authorised an advance of £3 in October 1917 pending the adoption of the new scale, which was finally agreed in November.[99]

Filling the gaps in the police force left by those leaving for military duties was difficult, yet, as with other professions and businesses, the idea of women as replacements was met with some scepticism. Towards the end of the war there was a move to recruit women police officers for the first time in St Albans, but this came to nothing despite other, similar-sized towns such as Oxford having introduced them.[100] The proposal had the support of many organisations and individuals, including the medical officer of health

Figure 7.3 Men of the police special reserve in St Albans, in front of Hatfield Road Boys' School, c.1918–19. © Hertfordshire Archives and Local Studies (Off Acc 688)

Dr May and Lady Grimston, and 625 people signed a petition calling for women police in the city. However, the council, and indeed the Watch Committee itself, were split over this issue.[101] The county police force also opposed the proposal, claiming that there was not sufficient suitable work available, while the chief constable Major Law expressed the views that women were not amenable to discipline and were likely to get pregnant before they had served sufficient time to repay the cost of their training, and that there were no suitable toilets in police stations.[102]

The force did, of course, have the services of the special constables (all male) to call on, and the *Herts Advertiser* supported a campaign to reward them in some way in 1917. Suggestions included awarding a long service badge (Figure 7.3). One correspondent, whose penname was 'Appreciative', thought something practical, such as 'leggings and some satisfactory weatherproof covering, especially now the dark and dirty nights are upon us, instead of compelling them to wear their own everyday attire', would be of more value.[103] St Albans followed the county example and awarded badges to 120 men who had completed three years' service at a special parade. They were also given boots and 30s apiece.[104]

In May 1917 St Albans council finally addressed the issue of pay across the entire workforce by carrying out a survey providing a breakdown of wages and bonuses. As a result, the pay of some individuals was reviewed and increased.[105] The only person who appears not to have received a pay rise in four years was Dr May, who had worked so tirelessly to safeguard the health of the city. He received a well-earned pay rise in July 1919, when he applied to the council directly.[106]

Contracted-out services

The council out-sourced some of its work to firms such as John Cable Ltd, which held three council contracts:

- The collection of household refuse and its delivery to the waste destructor, the furnace at the North Metropolitan Electric Power Supply Company (Figure 7.4);
- The supply of a driver and horses to pull the city fire engine, providing a response to fire brigade emergencies 24 hours a day; and
- The provision of a horse and driver to transport bedding, items requiring disinfection and patients suffering from scarlet fever or diphtheria to the Sisters Hospital from anywhere in St Albans.[107]

Figure 7.4 St Albans electricity works, shown on the right, with two smoking chimneys (1921). © Historic England. Licensor canmore.org.uk

The first contract was agreed in April 1913 and the second and third in February and May 1914 respectively. The proprietor, John Cable, had been trading in St Albans for 35 years and employed 80 men.[108] The war was to prove financially disastrous for him. The council was sympathetic to the effect the war had on the financial viability of contracts negotiated before the demands of wartime. Following an appeal by Cable, a sub-committee was set up to consider his company's position.[109] The finance committee accepted that the costs associated with the refuse contract had risen considerably, as in some areas where troops were billeted rubbish had to be collected daily rather than weekly. Though not keen to revise the contract, the council did agree 'as an act of grace' to give Cable an additional sum of £200, due to be paid on 30 April 1915, subject to the satisfactory completion of his duties.[110] However, in January 1915 he told the council that he would have to increase the cost of hiring each horse, cart and man to 10s a day. An exchange of letters between the council, Cable and his solicitor followed and in April 1915 it was suggested by Cable's solicitor that perhaps the Board of Trade should be drawn in to arbitrate on the matter, but this did not happen. The council agreed to pay £35 a month above the contract rate while costs such as fodder remained high. The extra £200 would be paid again if the work was completed satisfactorily. However, in March 1916 Cable asked the council to release him from the contract, offering a payment of £200 as compensation for breaking the contract, or for the council to increase what he was paid and at the same time take over some responsibility for providing labour and fodder. The highways committee took over the refuse collection but this was not the end of Cable's problems.[111]

In February 1915, when a call came in about a fire at the Blue Lion public house in Portland Street, nobody at Cable's answered the call from the fire brigade to send the horses to pull the fire engine, and a fireman had to cycle to the St Peter's Street office to stir the company into action. Cable then changed the notification system for fires, which breached the contract. The Fire Brigade Sub-Committee expressed its concern, but Cable kept the contract.[112] However, in July 1916, no doubt with concerns about the reliability of the service, the committee arranged a false alarm to be raised in the early hours of the morning, and again there was no response from Cable's office.[113] A number of factors, including wage rises, the increasing cost of fodder to feed horses, the shortage of suitable horses and reduced staff levels, led to the collapse of Cable's business. Sixty-eight of his drivers had enlisted and in June 1916 he applied for four men to be exempted at the tribunal, declaring that he had only 17 men left. However, tribunal chairman James Flint argued that Cable needed fewer men owing to the collapse in the building trade, which was another aspect of his business operations. Two of his men were exempted and the other two applications were refused.[114] This appears to have been the final straw for Cable. He closed the business, stating that he 'strove to the last to avoid the unhappy ending of what is practically my life's work in St Albans'.[115]

Shortages of materials

Coal was at the heart of the war effort, fuelling the production of munitions and other manufactured goods, providing steam power for trains and ships and generating gas to light homes and businesses and for cooking. By 1917 the situation in relation to the management, price and quality of coal supplies was critical and the government appointed a Coal Controller to oversee the running of the industry. At the time, because of the war, coal was scarce, of poor quality and expensive. To reduce the use of gas and coal the government introduced the 1916 British Summer Time Act, designed to make better use of daylight hours. At this time the council needed not only to get sufficient coal for itself during the winter but also to decide whether to stockpile coal supplies for the poorer residents. Eight firms were asked for prices, but only five were able to supply the 26 tons needed.[116]

Figure 7.5 The hard-working town clerk, Edward Percy Debenham, known as E.P.
© Chris Debenham

   Debenham, the town clerk, argued that if a reasonable supply of coal could be maintained for the city there was no need to set up yet another committee to manage it (Figure 7.5). However, the government-appointed Coal Controller insisted, and so a local Coal Control Sub-Committee was established. The Retail Coal Prices Order of 1917 gave authority for coal prices to be fixed in the city, varying according to the different types of coal. The minimum coal stock for the city was set at 750 tons, the council monitoring the figures on a monthly basis.[117] The government was worried that there would be a major coal shortage, and advertisements were run in local papers, including in St Albans, urging housewives to 'burn less fuel'.[118] By April 1918 the Board of Trade wanted further cuts in coal consumption and proposed a scheme for the distribution and supply of household coal throughout England and Wales. Coal merchant and St Albans councillor William Bennett attended a board meeting with other Hertfordshire representatives. It was decided to appoint an executive officer, responsible to the Coal Control Sub-Committee, who would enforce any orders coming from government; the board was of the opinion that the assistant city surveyor would be the best person for the job.[119] The aim was to cut domestic consumption of coal and its by-products – coke, gas and electricity. Negus, the assistant city surveyor, was appointed as the local fuel overseer of the Household Fuel and Lighting Order 1918, introduced to enforce these fuel saving measures. Negus's appointment aroused considerable criticism from the St Albans branch of the National Federation of Discharged and Demobilised Sailors and Soldiers, even though it followed government advice and reflected common practice elsewhere. The branch felt that the job should not have been given to somebody already in employment; it was only fair that one of their members should have been given this appointment as they had served their country and often been injured in the process.[120]

A notice explaining the Coal and Light Ration Order was published in the local press in June 1918. Residents had to fill in a form estimating their coal requirements for the next 12 months. The notice included helpful hints – for example, reducing the size of the grate by using firebricks – with an editorial pointing out that every pound of coal saved would 'help our soldiers and help to bring an earlier victory'.[121] At one council meeting a discussion took place about the opportunity this provided for richer households with more fireplaces to make greater savings in terms of fuel than their poorer neighbours. The editor of the *Herts Advertiser* supported this idea and also urged the wealthier residents to set an example by using the national kitchen when it opened, as this would represent a real saving in terms of the fuel needed to cook individual meals.[122] By October 1918 the Board of Trade's Coal Mines Department wanted to add the control of wood for burning. The Coal Control Sub-Committee had to consider and report, but no doubt world events obviated the need for a decision on this matter.[123]

Petrol was rationed from July 1916, with a tax imposed which doubled the price from 6d to 1s a gallon. Even at that price petrol was difficult to get hold of, so other propellants were found to power vehicles, including coal-gas, a by-product of the coking process. This was stored in gas bags, often bigger than the cars themselves, rigged up on the roof of vehicles. It was by no means an elegant solution and necessitated the running of pipes from the gas supply to the vehicle, sometimes across the pavement, a matter of concern to the council as a potential cause of obstruction. It is known that Horace Slade & Co. had just such an adapted vehicle, as in April 1918 the straw hat producers made an application for a standpipe on the footpath of Upper Marlborough Road 'for the supply of gas to their motor'.[124]

Material used to build and maintain the roads was in short supply, and controls on its sale and distribution were introduced in 1917 under the National Road Stone Control Committee, set up under DORA. Responsibility for roads in and around St Albans was split between the county and city councils. In June 1917 the National Road Stone Control Committee ordered the city council to produce a list of first- and second-class roads in St Albans. Granite was the primary material used to repair roads and from September 1917 quarries were limited to selling no more than 20 per cent of their outstanding stock for the repair of Hertfordshire roads for a period of six months, the need for road-building materials to support the war effort being very acute at that time.[125] Other unrestricted materials suitable for road repairs were also in short supply, and the council had to get approval to purchase blue paving bricks to repair the pavements in many of the old streets of the city.[126]

The council needed to make the most of the limited resources at its disposal, including buildings. Because the Corn Exchange was being used as a temporary courthouse in August 1914, while alterations were being made to the town hall, it escaped immediate requisition. Months later it was being used on Sundays as a rest room for the wives of billeted soldiers and during the week as a meeting place for the many Belgian refugees who had come to live in the city. However, its availability soon came to the notice of the military and it was requisitioned in October 1915 until the summer of 1918. The army used it as a cookhouse at one time, and the building's final wartime function was to house the national kitchen, as mentioned above.[127]

Supporting the war effort

The mayor and councillors' support for the war effort went beyond their civic and tribunal duties. They were involved in numerous voluntary efforts organised to support a range of good causes. As early as 6 August 1914 the council established a fund to encourage public donations towards the support of the families of soldiers and those made unemployed as a result of the war.[128]

Mayor Flint, responding to calls from the Lord Mayor of London for charitable donations, set up the Red Cross Shilling Fund in February 1916.[129] In addition to individual contributions and donations from churches and concerts, an average of £275 was received weekly for the shilling fund from firms and employees in the city. Regular donations were made from the fund. In November 1916, for instance, £700 went to the headquarters of the Red Cross and the Order of St John and £117 to the Hertfordshire branch of the Red Cross.[130]

With paper in such short supply, Flint followed a ratepayer's suggestion and set up a wastepaper collection fund in April 1916. Boy scouts collected the paper, which was stored in the library basement before being sorted. By September nearly six tons had been sent for processing, the profits being distributed primarily between the city's three hospitals.[131] In a drive to save paper the council stopped printing the minutes of committee meetings, but did continue to print reports.[132]

The army in the city expressed gratitude to the council on a number of occasions, especially with regard to billeting arrangements. The Commanding Officer, 59th North Midland Division, thanked the council on behalf of the soldiers for the measures taken to provide for their health and physical comfort while stationed in St Albans.[133] A letter from Lt-Col. Lane of the veterinary hospital thanked Flint for all the help received when another command took over. The wounded, too, expressed their appreciation. A tapestry of 42 regimental badges was made by soldiers in Ward F11 of the County of Middlesex War Hospital at Napsbury as a memorial of the war. It was presented to the council and displayed in the library.[134]

Conclusion

Throughout the war St Albans City Council endeavoured to run the city as efficiently as possible under difficult conditions. Barring the loss of control of the city police to the county, it succeeded in all aspects of its role. The wartime mayors, especially the long-serving Flint, sat on almost every committee, including the sub-committees formed for particular wartime purposes. Alderman Green acknowledged Flint's wartime role:

> It is a position of great honour, but it is a position of great responsibility. It means practically giving up the whole of one's time to the office and that, fortunately, Mr Alderman Flint has been able to do in the past because he has practically given up the work of his profession to devote himself to the interests of the town.[135]

There were many financial costs associated with the war effort, not least the loss of income from buildings. In the two years from March 1915 the council received less income from the buildings taken over by the army than had been generated in peacetime.[136] The council's financial resources were stretched as it took care of the families of employees who had enlisted and had to pay higher bills for labour and goods owing to the increased cost of living and shortages of materials. While shouldering the burden of administering the day-to-day needs of the city in wartime under the increasingly close direction of central government, the councillors must have been acutely aware that the autonomy they had enjoyed before the war was likely to be a serious casualty of the conflict.

Notes

1. The mayor was chairman of the magistrates' bench in St Albans.
2. See Chapters 3 and 4 for further information about billeting.
3. 'The mayor's health', *Herts Advertiser* (*HA*), 24 October 1914.
4. 'Councillor B.C. Edwards: St Albans to lose an ex-mayor', *HA*, 26 January 1918.
5. 'Municipal elections no contest probable', *HA*, 10 October 1914.
6. 'Mayor Flint the mayor delegate', *HA*, 16 October 1915. Pineapple: St Albans Pubs Database 1720–1918, SAHAAS Library.
7. 'The mayor of St Albans' *HA*, 23 September 1915.
8. *Pictorial Record: St Albans*, 1915, pp. 2–3, 8, 13–14, 16, 19–21; Hertfordshire Archives & Local Studies (HALS), SBR/1750, St Albans City Council Year Book, 1915.
9. 'Death of Dr H.E. May', *HA*, 22 March 1929. E.P. Debenham was appointed town clerk in 1909.
10. HALS, SBR/894A, City Council Minute Book (CMB), 1912–16. See Chapter 1 for details of boundary extension.
11. HALS, SBR/904, Watch Committee Minutes (WCM), 1912–22, 6 August 1918.
12. HALS, SBR/904, WCM, 15 September 1914.
13. 'Hard worked police', *HA*, 24 October 1914.
14. HALS, SBR/871, Urban Authority & General Purposes Committee (UAGPC) Minute Book, 1914–20, 3 November 1914.
15. 'Aeroplane over St Albans', *HA*, 28 November 1914.
16. 'What to do in air raids', *HA*, 26 June 1915.
17. HALS SBR/1901, Town Clerk Out Letter Book (TCOL), 1914–15, letter to Captain Thorpe, 11 September 1915.
18. HALS, SBR/871, UAGPC, 7 September 1915.
19. 'Lighting regulations: mayor's request to citizens', *HA*, 11 September 1915.
20. HALS, SBR/894A, CMB, 21 September 1915.
21. HALS, SBR/904, WCM, 14 October 1915.
22. HALS, SBR/871, UAGPC, 30 October 1916.
23. 'The mayor, church bells and Zeppelins', *HA*, 30 October 1915.
24. HALS, SBR/871, UAGPC, 4 December 1917.
25. 'Air raids', *HA*, 23 June 1917.
26. 'The mayor's warning', *HA*, 21 July 1917.

27. HALS, SBR/871, UAGPC, 17 October 1917.

28. 'The Red Cross', *HA*, 3 November 1917.

29. HALS, SBR/3687, CMB, 1916–20, 5 February 1918.

30. HALS, SBR/904, WCM, 16 November 1915.

31. 'Police enlistments', *HA*, 18 December 1915.

32. 'Breaches of the lighting order', *HA*, 16 October 1915.

33. 'Motor offences at St Albans', *HA*, 9 January 1915.

34. 'St Albans lighting ... military motor lights must be lowered', *HA*, 23 October 1915.

35. 'New lighting order', *HA*, 25 December 1915.

36. 'Constables convicted', *HA*, 20 July 1918.

37. HALS, SBR/904, WCM, 23 May 1916.

38. 'St Albans police force', *HA*, 21 April 1917. HALS, SBR/904, WCM, 28 June 1916 regarding appointment of Peck.

39. HALS, SBR/904, WCM, 31 May 1916, 20 June 1916.

40. HALS, SBR/871, UAGPC, 1 December 1914.

41. HALS, SBR/871, UAGPC, 29 December 1914.

42. HALS, SBR/871, UAGPC, 17 November 1914.

43. HALS, SBR/871, UAGPC, 29 December 1914.

44. HALS, SBR/1901, TCOL, 27 August 1915, letter to Lieut. Geoffrey S. Williams.

45. HALS, SBR/871, UAGPC, 23 February 1915.

46. HALS, SBR/1901, TCOL, 5 August 1915, letter to Captain Rodwell.

47. HALS, SBR/871, UAGPC, 6 June 1916.

48. HALS, SBR/871, UAGPC, 11 July 1916.

49. HALS, SBR/871, UAGPC, 29 October 1918.

50. HALS, SBR/871, UAGPC, 1 February 1916.

51. This is the junction of London Road, Chequer Street, High Street and Holywell Hill.

52. HALS, SBR/871, UAGPC, 28 November 1916, 3 January 1917, 30 October 1917; SBR/3687, CMB, 17 July 1917.

53. HALS, SBR/871, UAGPC, 30 November 1915. See Chapter 3.

54. HALS, SBR/3687, CMB, 17 July 1917.

55. It is believed Grange Estate was on the east side of St Peter's Street.

56. HALS, SBR/871, UAGPC, 11 September 1914.

57. HALS, SBR/871, UAGPC, 17 August 1914.

58. HALS, SBR/871, UAGPC, 17 August 1914.

59. HALS, SBR/894A, CMB, 8 February 1916.

60. HALS, SBR/871, UAGPC, 5 April 1916, 6 June 1916.

61. HALS, SBR/894A, CMB, 18 April 1916.

62. HALS, SBR/3687, CMB, 24 July 1917; SBR/871, UAGPC, 8 August 1917.

63. 'Visit to the sewage farm', *HA*, 18 May 1918.

64. 'Metropolitan managers meet', *HA*, 17 August 1918.

65. HALS, SBR/3687, CMB, 9 November 1916, 6 February 1917, 14 May 1917, 24 July 1917.

66. 'Public lavatories', *HA*, 31 October 1914.

67. HALS, SBR/894A, CMB, 17 November 1914.

68. HALS, SBR/871, UAGPC, 23 February 1915.

69. HALS, SBR/894A, CMB, 9 November 1914.

70. HALS, SBR/Interim Catalogue, Medical Officer of Health Report (MOHR), 1914.

71. The Royal Army Medical Corps took over Bricket House in September 1914. Previously it had a 15-bed field hospital in Old London Road. See Chapter 3.

72. C. Aitken, *Childwickbury* (Redbourn, 2011), pp. 66–7.

73. HALS, SBR/3687, CMB, 20 February 1917.

74. 'Hertfordshire County Council', *HA*, 22 June 1918.

75. 'Healthy St Albans', *HA*, 27 March 1915.

76. HALS, SBR/871, UAGPC, 30 October 1916.

77. 'The fly peril and how to combat it', *HA*, 5 June 1915.

78. HALS, SBR/Interim Catalogue, MOHR, 1915.

79. HALS, SBR/871, UAGPC, 5 March 1918.

80. HALS, SBR/Interim Catalogue, MOHR, 1914.

81. HALS, SBR/871, UAGPC, 5 January 1916, 7 March 1916.

82. HALS, SBR/Interim Catalogue, MOHR, 17 September 1918.

83. HALS, SBR/Interim Catalogue, MOHR. See also Chapter 4 regarding births at the Union Infirmary.

84. HALS, SBR/1901, TCOL, 30 September 1914, to Mr A. Pearce.

85. HALS, SBR/871, UAGPC, 29 September 1914.

86. HALS, SBR/871, UAGPC, 3 November 1914.

87. HALS, SBR/1901, TCOL, 16 August 1915, letter to Lieut Col. E.J. Cross MD, Officer Commanding, RAMC, Saxmundham.

88. HALS, SBR/871, UAGPC, 6 August 1914.

89. HALS, SBR/871, UAGPC, 6 June 1916.

90. HALS, SBR/3687, CMB, 20 February 1917.

91. HALS, SBR/871, UAGPC, 18 June 1918.

92. HALS, SBR/3687, CMB, 14 May 1917.

93. HALS, SBR/894A, CMB, 1 June 1915.

94. HALS, SBR/871, UAGPC, 5 April 1916; SBR/3687, CMB, 16 October 1916.

95. HALS, SBR/904, WCM, 12 December 1916.

96. HALS, SBR/904, WCM, 18 January 1917.

97. HALS, SBR/904, WCM, 1 May 1917.

98. HALS, SBR/3687, CMB, 9 November 1917.

99. 'Police pay', *HA*, 14 September 1918. HALS, WCM, 29 October, 19 November 1918.

100. Grace Costin, Oxford, <http://www.wikipedia.org/wiki/Timeline_of_Oxford> accessed 17 February 2016.

101. HALS, SBR/904, WCM, 24 July 1917.

102. 'Women police: two for St Albans advocated', *HA*, 13 April 1918. 'Women police: influential memorial', *HA*, 20 April 1918. T. Cox, 'Herts police in the Great War', Herts at War project lecture, 9 April 2015, Letchworth Garden City Heritage Foundation.

103. Correspondence, *HA*, 27 October 1917.

104. HALS, SBR/3687, CMB, 9 November 1917'; 'Specials', *HA*, 17 November 1917.

105. HALS, SBR/871, UAGPC, 22 May 1917.

106. HALS, SBR/3687, CMB, 29 July 1919.

107. HALS, SBR/2915, Agreement, John Cable Ltd and the Mayor for horsing the fire engine, 30 April 1914; SBR/2921: Agreement, John Cable Ltd and the Mayor for removal of bedding etc. to and from Sisters Hospital, 26 May 1914; SBR/2946: Agreement, John Cable Ltd and the Mayor for the collection of house refuse, 30 April 1913.

108. 'Correspondence: "John Cable Ltd"', *HA*, 1 July 1916.

109. HALS, SBR/871, UAGPC, 1 December 1914.

110. HALS, SBR/894A, CMB, 15 December 1914.

111. HALS, SBR/871, UAGPC, 26 January 1915, 27 April 1915, 7 March 1916.

112. HALS, SBR/871, UAGPC, 23 February 1915.

113. HALS, SBR/871, UAGPC, 25 July 1916.

114. 'St Albans tribunal: Messrs Cable and Co.'s Men', *HA*, 6 June 1916.

115. 'Correspondence: "John Cable Ltd"', *HA*, 1 July 1916.

116. HALS, SBR/3687, CMB, 17 July 1917; SBR/871, UAGPC, 31 July 1917.

117. HALS, SBR/871, UAGPC, 4 September 1917, 18 September 1917, 17 October 1917.

118. 'To the housewives of St Albans, burn less fuel', *HA*, 22 December 1917.

119. HALS, SBR/3687, CMB, 16 April 1918.

120. HALS, SBR/871, UAGPC, 30 July 1918.

121. Museum of St Albans, 'National War Savings Committee No. 46 hints on fuel economy'; notice published in *HA*, 15 June 1918.

122. 'St Albans City Council', *HA*, 21 September 1918. See Chapter 6 for further information about the national kitchen.

123. HALS, SBR/871, UAGPC, 16 October 1918.

124. See 'Gas-bags on wheels – fuel problems & solutions during WW1', Mary Evans Picture Library, <http://blog.maryevans.com/2014/01/gas-bags-on-wheels-a-solution-to-petrol-shortages-during-ww1.html> accessed 21 January 2014. HALS, SBR/871, UAGPC, 3 April 1918.

125. HALS, SBR/871, UAGPC, 4 September 1917.

126. HALS, SBR/871, UAGPC, 5 June 1917, 5 September 1917. SBR/3687, CMB, 17 October 1917.

127. 'Tommy's visitors', *HA* 5 December 1914; HALS, SBR/871, UAGPC, 23 March 1915; SBR/894A CMB, 20 October 1915; SBR/871, UAGPC, 16 April 1918. The British Women's Temperance Association ran the Sunday rest room. See Chapter 4 for further information about Belgian refugees.

128. HALS, SBR/871, UAGPC, 6 August 1914.

129. HALS, SBR/871, UAGPC, 1 February 1916.

130. HALS, SBR/894A, CMB, 9 November 1916, 23 July 1918. It cost just under £5,000 a week to run the Red Cross nationwide and by July 1918 this had increased to £10,000 a day.

131. HALS, SBR/894A, CMB, 18 April 1916; SBR/3687, CMB, 19 September 1916, 14 May 1917.

132. HALS, SBR/871, UAGPC, 8 March 1917.

133. HALS, SBR/3687, CMB, 28 June 1916.

134. Ibid., 22 May 1918. The tapestry was displayed in the First World War exhibition at the Museum of St Albans in 2014.

135. 'Mayor's installation', *HA*, 10 November 1917.

136. HALS, SBR/871, UAGPC, 8 August 1917.

CHAPTER 8

In the wake of the war

11 November 1918: The armistice had been signed! The news had been eagerly expected and a large crowd gathered outside the town hall, where the county council was in session. On receiving the news the chairman, the Rt Hon. T.F. Halsey, at once suspended the meeting and with the rest of the council stepped onto the balcony and proclaimed that the armistice had been signed and that hostilities had ceased.[1]

T he announcement was greeted with cheers and singing of the national anthem. Flags and bunting appeared everywhere and in the afternoon more crowds, including several hundred troops, paraded to Market Place. Biddy Hodge, then a small child, remembered being held up to see over the fence at Belmont Hill. 'The Torch Bearers (with live torches) marched down Holywell Hill and massed on the Belmont Playing Fields.'[2] In the evening another huge crowd gathered in Market Place; the city band played, the street lights were lit again and there was singing, dancing and flag-waving.

In the immediate aftermath of the armistice the city was faced simultaneously with four tasks: thanksgiving for the peace, the continuing influenza epidemic, commemoration of the dead and the absorption of returned troops, both able-bodied and disabled, into the workforce. These immediate tasks, however, had to be dealt with by a society also confronting other challenges. Suffragism, labour problems and housing were national issues before the war and, although they had largely been shelved for its duration, they had not disappeared. However, the war itself and its enormous and unexpected expense had affected them in different ways. Although they were not settled immediately, we can see the way they were beginning to be faced in St Albans in the months that followed the end of the war.

Peace at last

The signing of the Treaty of Versailles on 29 June 1919 officially ended the war. The siren on the town hall which should have announced the signing failed, and the news reached the city by way of the evening papers; it was followed by wild celebrations in the streets until after midnight. All the church bells rang, and so many fireworks were set off that the noise was deafening and even frightening. 'It was a night of nights ... and when it was augmented by a wild and hilarious display of Terpsichorean gymnastics ... the spectacle beggared description.'[3] The next day services of thanksgiving took place in all the churches. The king declared Saturday 19 July 1919 a national holiday, with beacons and bonfires lit across the country. Many residents may have gone up to London for the magnificent celebrations there, but the celebrations in St Albans were equally enthusiastic, a city-wide party catering for every element of the population.

In preparation the council decided that the market would be held on Friday instead of Saturday, shops were asked to stay open until 7pm on Friday if possible, so they could close on Saturday, and 'public buildings were decorated and residents asked to make the city as gay in appearance as possible'.[4] The mayor read out the king's message. At least 1,000 ex-servicemen from around the city were entertained at a dinner on the Friday evening, and on Saturday there were military sports in Clarence Park.[5] The Schools Sports Association organised sports in the St Albans Grammar School playing fields at Belmont Hill for 2,500 children, for whom the St Albans Cooperative Society later provided tea in their schools. Although it was damp, the festivities continued with dancing in the playing fields until 9.30pm, followed by fireworks. The *Herts Advertiser* commented wryly on the contrast with Luton's celebration, which ended with riots: 'Instead of participating in setting the local Town Hall on Fire (as at Luton) how much better it was to be seated with the St Albans ex-servicemen openly light-hearted and enjoying to the full the really first-class entertainment which had been provided.'[6]

These festive Peace Day celebrations were followed on 21 August by a more sombre event arranged by the National Federation of Discharged and Demobilised Sailors and Soldiers.[7] A formal procession of ex-servicemen, with the mayor and council in their robes, proceeded to the cenotaph constructed for the day in front of the clock tower, where many wreaths were placed (Figure 8.1).

The cenotaph was guarded by boy scouts from morning until 7pm, when they removed the floral tributes and conveyed them to Soldiers' Corner in Hatfield Road cemetery. From the cenotaph the procession continued to the Abbey Orchard, where a crowd of 8,000 to 10,000 gathered for a

Figure 8.1 Cenotaph memorial surrounded by wreaths in front of the clock tower, 21 August 1919. © Ian Tonkin

drumhead service to which several bands and choirs contributed. Both church and nonconformity were represented, the dean conducting a service and Lt-Col. Frank Wheeler, former minister of Trinity church and an army chaplain, giving an address.[8] The abbey bells were half muffled at evensong, ending 'a holy and memorable day'.[9]

And finally, on 11 November 1919, the first anniversary of Armistice Day was marked. In accordance with the king's request for two minutes silence 'at the eleventh hour of the eleventh day of the eleventh month ... the syren [sic] on the Town Hall sent forth its weird shriek', flags fell to half-mast and traffic stopped. There was no formality, just 'intense silence'.[10]

Influenza post-war

At this time of joy and relief the influenza epidemic continued to claim lives and affect the city in a number of ways. The national kitchen was closed for several weeks in November 1918, as staff were sick.[11] The sub-post office in St Peter's Street closed in December, the only person still fit being the sub-postmaster's wife. Unable to manage on her own, she received no help from the General Post Office at the Peahen Buildings, as their staff were ill too. One of the saddest cases was that of the Dorling family. The father, Frederick, a private in the Royal Army Medical Corps

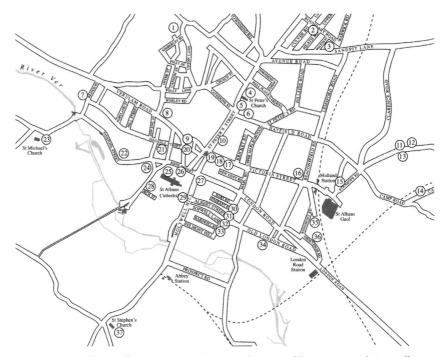

Figure 8.2 Map showing the approximate locations of First World War memorials in St Albans.
Key: Civic, military, workplace and school memorials:

1. St Andrew's Chapel, off Union Lane (*now Normandy Rd*)
2. Primitive Methodist Church, Boundary Road (*now at Hatfield Road Methodist church*)
3. St Saviour's Church, Sandpit Lane
4. St Peter's Church, St Peter's Street
5. Civic memorial, St Peter's Green
6. Hatfield Road Boys' School (*memorial lost*)
7. St Michael's memorial hall, Branch Road
8. Christ Church, Verulam Road (*memorial lost*)
9. Abbey parish memorial Verulam Road
10. London County and Westminster Bank, St Peter's Street (*Now NatWest Bank*)
11. Hatfield Road Methodist Church
12. St Paul's Church, Hatfield Road
13. Soldier's Corner, Hatfield Road cemetery
14. Salvation Army printing works, Campfield Road (*Now at Salvation Army HQ, Victoria Street*)
15. Quaker Adult School, Stanhope Road
16. Trinity Congregational Church, Beaconsfield Road
17. Baptist Tabernacle Church, Victoria Street (*now at Marshalswick Baptist Church*)
18. Salvation Army Citadel, Victoria Street
19. Town Hall memorial, Market Place
20. Dagnall Street Baptist Church, Upper Dagnall Street
21. Abbey parish memorial Lower Dagnall Street
22. Abbey parish memorial Fishpool Street
23. St Michael's Church, St Michael's Street
24. St Albans (*Grammar*) School, Romeland
25. The Cathedral and Abbey Church of Saint Alban
26. Abbey parish memorial High Street
27. General Post Office, Holywell Hill (*now at Ashley Road sorting office*)
28. Abbey parish memorial Orchard Street
29. Abbey parish memorial Holywell Hill
30. Abbey parish memorial Pageant Road
31. Abbey parish memorial Albert Street
32. Abbey parish memorial Sopwell Lane
33. Abbey parish memorial Bardwell Road
34. St John's Church, Old London Road
35. Vyse, Sons & Co., Ridgmont Road
36. Edwin Lee & Sons, Grosvenor Road
37. St Stephen's Church, Watling Street

(Volunteers), and his 18-year-old step-daughter died within a few days of one another in November 1918 and were buried together. His wife, who also had flu, could not attend the funeral, and one of her other nine children was in hospital with the illness.[12] The medical officer of health, Dr Henry E. May, reported 27 deaths from flu in the first quarter of 1919,[13] and during the rest of the year there were some milder cases, but only five more deaths.[14]

Acts of commemoration

Amidst the rejoicing there was also grief for the men who would never come home. In the Abbey parish several of the 18 temporary wooden street shrines erected in 1916/17[15] were replaced by permanent memorials and now form part of a unique collection.[16] Many others were erected after the war; in all, more than 40 in a variety of forms were put up in the city between 1919 and 1925 (Figure 8.2).

Most churches erected memorials. St Peter's church ultimately decided on a plaque, dedicated by Lord Cavan on Sunday 21 May 1921, after he had unveiled the civic memorial at St Peter's Green.[17] St Peter's has also a fine window presented by Mrs Mead in memory of her husband, who died in 1915, and their two sons, who died in action in France in 1914 and 1915.[18] When St Michael's church appealed for funds to erect a memorial triptych under the west window in December 1922 Lady Grimston proposed that any surplus be put toward a parish hall as part of the commemoration.[19] The plaque in the church was dedicated in January 1924 and the hall, still in use, was erected in 1925. St Stephen's church dedicated an oak altar rail and choir stalls.[20]

St John's church in Old London Road (a daughter church of St Peter's) erected as a memorial hall an old army hut which served as a parish centre,[21] demolished with the church in the 1950s; the elegant cross at St Saviour's can still be seen in the church grounds. A tablet listing 45 men of the parish who died is referred to in a history of Christ Church,[22] although it no longer exists. It is notable in containing the name of Edward Warner, one of St Albans' two recipients of the Victoria Cross. Most memorials were paid for by public subscription; the exception, that of Dagnall Street Baptist church, was the gift of an anonymous donor.

A planned plaque in the abbey came to nothing, but the names are included in the Diocesan Books of Remembrance displayed there. The abbey, as the centre of the diocese, pays tribute to a wider area and contains

Figure 8.3 Canon George
Henry Pownall Glossop.
© Peter Glossop

the memorial west window, designed by Ninian Comper, honouring the
deaths of 12,778 men and women from the diocese. There are three Books
of Remembrance in the Memorial Chapel containing all their names,
the pages of which are turned daily. There is also in the chapel a tablet
listing all the officers and men of the Hertfordshire Yeomanry who died
in the war. Here, too, was a painting, 'The Passing of Queen Eleanor' by
Harpenden artist Frank Salisbury, given by Alderman Arthur Faulkner
and his wife in 1918 in memory of Hertfordshire men who had died.[23] In
addition, there are several plaques and other memorials to St Albans men[24]
and a beautiful crystal cross on the nave screen, given by Canon and Mrs
Glossop in commemoration of the deaths of two of their sons (Figure 8.3).

Other memorials in the city include the window in St Andrew's chapel
at the city hospital (now offices), dedicated to staff killed in both world
wars. The Post Office plaque is now in the Ashley Road sorting office, and
several businesses also erected tablets that can still be seen today, although
most of the businesses themselves have long since ceased trading. The
only known school memorial in St Albans is the one at St Albans School.

Because memorials were usually paid for by individual subscription
men are sometimes recorded who did not live in that area or attend that

church, but were included because they had friends or relatives there who wished to remember them. Others were neglected because there was no remaining family, or the family could not afford to subscribe. Some St Albans people are commemorated only elsewhere: for example, Charlotte Day, a member of the Women's Royal Air Force (WRAF), who died from influenza on 30 November 1918, is commemorated on the WRAF memorial in the north transept of York Minster.[25]

Many men were recorded in multiple locations, such as the civic memorial, schools, workplaces, churches and others.[26] An outstanding example of such a man is Hugh Gunn Calder, who appears on at least nine.[27]

Suggestions as to the form of a permanent civic memorial ranged from a replica of the medieval Eleanor Cross (which once stood near the clock tower),[28] bungalows for disabled servicemen, and lastly, the cross which stands today on St Peter's Green. The city council decided that the bungalows were not really necessary,[29] although housing for demobilised men was regarded by many citizens as a far more pressing need than any other form of commemoration. In spite of this, possibly for financial reasons, the War Memorials Committee made their final decision on 3 April 1920 and at a meeting of subscribers to the fund in July the mayor, William Green, reported that he had received £1,320 in donations from 171 subscribers towards three projects: the purchase of Bricket House to serve as headquarters of the St Albans District Nursing Association and as a nursing home (£497), a civic memorial (£574) and a scholarship fund for children of war fatalities (£248).[30] The first of these projects to be realised was the purchase of Bricket House from the Mayor's Thanksgiving Fund and private donations, including the memorial fund. Completed within a month, it was opened in April 1920.[31]

Just a year later the second memorial project was completed. This was the civic memorial on St Peter's Green, a cross designed by Sir Edgar Wigram, a local architect, and carved by Charles Alderton of Harpenden.[32] It was unveiled on Sunday 21 May 1921. The ceremony began at 3pm with a procession 'in State' from the town hall to the memorial headed by the ex-servicemen's band and led by the mayor and the council, with all ex-servicemen invited to join in the procession[33] (Figure 8.4). The names of the dead having already been collected for this memorial, the council paid for an inscribed roll of honour to be placed in the lobby of the town hall. This work was completed in November 1920. The names on both, in alphabetical order, are as comprehensive as the council were able to ascertain.

Figure 8.4 The unveiling of the civic war memorial at St Peter's Green on 21 May 1921. © St Albans Museums (2006_5628)

The third memorial project, the scholarships fund, was established for two boys and two girls at a value of £20 per child per annum for a period of three years at St Albans Grammar School and St Albans High School for Girls. The successful applicants in 1921 were Edward Seldon, Mary Hart and Marjorie Thiele.[34] A fourth scholarship was awarded in 1924 and the fund closed in 1927.[35]

The first military casualties in St Albans were buried in the Hatfield Road cemetery. Later, with the opening of the County of Middlesex War Hospital at Napsbury, the numbers of war dead at the cemetery increased. Although this was outside the boundaries of St Albans, the government had decreed that it was not appropriate that military casualties should suffer the indignity of being buried alongside 'pauper lunatics'.[36] A 'Heroes Corner', bringing all the war dead together in one place, had been proposed by the *Herts Advertiser* in late July 1916,[37] and the council approved the idea. A plot of ground 'near the circular mound in the centre of the cemetery' was chosen and renamed 'Soldiers Corner'. The location was highly suitable; the cemetery's flat, spacious, minimally landscaped site facilitated the formalities of military funerals, with their gun carriages and ranks of soldiers. The council assumed responsibility for Soldiers' Corner in 1916. The double fees for those dying beyond the city boundary were waived and the dead regarded as 'resident' in case the higher fees might 'entail hardship'. The council erected and paid for temporary crosses on each grave.[38] In November 1919 it offered to maintain the ground for these graves 'in perpetuity' at the town's expense,[39] although ultimately these responsibilities were ceded to the Commonwealth (formerly Imperial) War Graves Commission (CWGC).

As a result of the numbers of dead to be commemorated the cemetery was entitled to a Cross of Sacrifice, which was dedicated on 24 October 1920 by the bishop of St Albans.[40] The cross, designed by Sir Reginald Blomfield, was installed on CWGC sites across the world. Surprisingly, St Albans council questioned the commission's careful selection of Portland stone for the monument, receiving a restrained reply from Blomfield's representative, who explained that, from an artistic point of view, he was 'inclined to [use] Portland on account of its clean sharp lines and clean, even grained surface. These [showed up] his design to the fullest advantage.'[41] Soldiers, sailors and airmen are buried there, two-thirds of them beside the Cross of Sacrifice. They include combatants from every part of Britain, as well as Canada, Australia and South Africa, buried together.

The city was also offered two trophies as 'memorials'. In 1915 a captured German field gun was offered by the War Office Trophies Committee,[42] while in 1919 the National War Savings Committee offered St Albans a captured German tank as a reward for its success in selling so many war bond subscriptions. The city council was initially inclined to accept both offers, but public opinion was against the idea, as expressed in letters to the *Herts Advertiser* from demobilised soldiers such as F.N. Beckitt, who felt 'Those of us who have returned or will return are "fed-up" with the sight of such things.'[43] A scathing editorial in the newspaper[44] led to a reversal of the city council's views and the offers were declined.[45]

Demobilised men return home

The armistice did not end the war: until the Treaty of Versailles was signed hostilities could have been resumed at any time. British forces were also fighting in the civil war in northern Russia and troops were still needed to maintain peace within the empire. Moreover, it was logistically impossible to ship all war-service troops home at once.

Miners and men with scarce industrial skills were prioritised; those who had volunteered early in the war (for the duration) were next, and so forth,

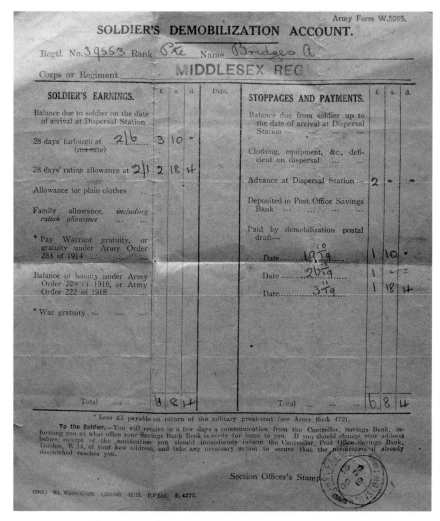

Figure 8.5 Demobilisation certificate issued to Alfred Bridges. © Phyllis Nicholls

with conscripts and the regular army last in line, especially the 18-year-olds of 1918, who would have seen little or no active service. Demobilisation of a limited number of pivotal men could be requested, though St Albans was slow to take advantage.[46] However, by the end of December 1918 the *Herts Advertiser* considered enough men had returned that the paper could ask for happy Christmas reunion stories to report. By February the increased numbers on the ration list showed that nearly 1,000 men had already returned to the city.[47] In fact, most servicemen were back in civilian life by the end of 1919,[48] each man issued with a bundle of papers: seven different

THOMAS ALFRED BICKERTON
30-6-1898 - 4-1-1994

Figure 8.6 Thomas Bickerton, soldier and prisoner of war. © Michael Bickerton

certificates, including a voucher for a suit of clothes (or an allowance of 52s 6d for clothing), a voucher for the return of his army greatcoat and a summary of his military career (Figure 8.5).

British prisoners of war (POWs) returned quickly; the German army was demoralised by the end of the war and wanted to go home themselves. Thomas Bickerton (Figure 8.6) was then in a camp at Kleinblittersdorf in Alsace-Lorraine. When the armistice was signed the prisoners there were marched in a party of 500–600 men to the French front lines – hard work in their physical condition – and about five miles from the French front their guards 'waved us towards the front and said "Alle weg" which means "Off you go", or that is what I understood it to mean'.[49]

Civilian POW Ernest O'Dell, the Thomas Cook representative in Karlsbad, Austria, was arrested in 1914. His group were permitted at the armistice to go home via Switzerland, but their captors would not sign their passports, so they travelled via Trieste, Venice, Padua, Milan, Turin, Paris and Le Havre, but still managed to reach Southampton in December 1918.[50]

The 'War Page' of the *Herts Advertiser* began to carry fewer obituaries and more accounts from returned POWs reporting the horrors they had experienced, as well as news about the parties to welcome them back.

Frederick and Amy Dearbergh, generous supporters of the troops, gave a tea for 39 returned POWs in February 1919, at which Amy declared: 'For all you have done and suffered for us, we cannot thank you enough but we do thank you warmly and always shall, over and over again.'[51]

So many men with differing needs returning in a relatively short period of time caused problems of absorption. Of the c.1,000 men who had returned to St Albans by 21 February 1919, 486 were unemployed.[52] At the beginning of the war several companies in St Albans had guaranteed to keep jobs open for returning servicemen, but the economic situation at the end of the war altered everything and demobilised men received varying treatment.

Demobilised teachers were eagerly welcomed back by the schools. The headmaster of the Abbey School, William G. Alderton, returned at the beginning of February 1919, thus releasing his *locum tenens*, William Cowley, to return to his job as assistant master at Hatfield Road Boys' School.[53] Mr Bunn returned from his work for the Admiralty to resume his post at the St Albans Technical Institute; for a year from 1 July 1919 he also advised the Local Training Committee of the Ministry of Labour on training disabled soldiers.[54]

The case of the butcher Edward Hawkins Smith, who was allowed by the St Albans Local Food Control Committee to sell to unregistered ration-holders for two months in order to re-establish his business, is described in Chapter 6. Less formal support was shown to Henry Salvidge, who opened a coffee stall in Market Place in early 1920 (Figure 8.7). The council and the police turned a blind eye to the fact that, on days other than market days, he was strictly speaking blocking the highway, but they refused to allow him to expand his business with unsanctioned shutters, footboards and advertisement posters or to let him stay open later or leave his stall in position overnight. In October 1921 he was forced to quit, as it was felt that his stall was getting in the way of the increasing traffic.[55]

Still less sympathetically treated was Alfred Bridges, who had been a 'hat and cap presser' before the war. Having tried from the beginning to volunteer and being rejected because of his short stature and short sight, he was nevertheless conscripted in March 1916. Unable to get his old job back at E. Day & Co., he went to the employment exchange in October 1919 and was told by one of the members 'Your father is my gardener, he must keep you on the wages he gets from me.'[56]

Among the documents given each man on demobilisation was an 'Out of Work Donation Policy'. Basically an *ex gratia* payment, this was intended

Figure 8.7 Ex-soldier's coffee stall in Market Place, c.1921. © Francis Frith Collection

to be available for a strictly limited period. However, the government had underestimated the time it would take ex-servicemen to find work and they were forced to grant extensions. Various solutions to the unemployment problem were attempted. The building of new houses and the extension of the sewage scheme offered employment opportunities for many men, but councillors reported several instances in which jobs had been turned down because the wages were too low.[57] When the sewage farm project at Fleetville was finally put out to tender at the end of June the council still hoped to employ demobilised soldiers for the job.[58] Another opportunity arose in May 1921, when the sub-committee responsible for Clarence Park proposed building terraces around the football pitch.[59]

As early as September 1914, the government recognised the need for training schemes to be set up to help disabled ex-servicemen learn skills that would enable them to find employment. This task became the responsibility of the Ministry of Pensions after 1916. The implementation of these schemes was delegated to the Soldiers' and Sailors' Families' Association (SSFA). When Ernest Gape retired from the onerous work of the SSFA in June 1918, Kathleen Tyrwhitt Drake took over the task.[60] For her services she was awarded an MBE in April 1920. After the war the SSFA also arranged training for able-bodied ex-servicemen and discharged munitions workers. Although these schemes were quite successful, they often required training away from home and married men were reluctant to go on them until the allowance for families was increased.[61] Additionally, in February 1919 there were about 180 young people aged 15–16 unemployed. The lecture room at the county museum was let for a month as an unemployment and training centre for girls, but this was discontinued as the girls did soon find jobs.[62]

The King's National Roll was a scheme created in 1919 to encourage the employment of disabled men. The roll listed employers of over ten men who undertook to employ a minimum of 5 per cent of disabled men in accordance with the terms of the National Scheme for the Employment of the Disabled, and employers who took part were encouraged to use an official stamp indicating their participation. Between its launch on 15 September 1919 and 31 December 1919 some 9,524 employers nationally were recorded. Of the 89 employers in Hertfordshire 15 were in St Albans, and their names were recorded on the King's National Roll.[63]

Servicemen themselves realised the need for other forms of support and during the war two major organisations had been formed for this purpose. The Comrades of the Great War was a national non-political society founded in 1917 to support ex-servicemen and women.[64] In addition to commemorating those who had died and fostering comradeship and patriotism in the young, their objects were to help discharged soldiers and sailors, encourage the training and employment of the disabled and assist the families of those who had died. A St Albans branch was founded in June 1918 and at the opening meeting it was reported that there were already 100 members. The high degree of support which the Comrades felt it necessary to provide may be deduced from the fact that, when H. Reade had to resign as secretary in January 1919 owing to ill-health, his replacement, A.E. Sharpe, was 'at home to members every evening from 6–9'.[65]

The other major support group in St Albans was the National Federation of Discharged and Demobilised Sailors and Soldiers, which had its first monthly meeting at the Abbey Institute in September 1918.[66] While the Comrades intended to provide social and economic support, the Federation had in addition a political agenda. The following March they were calling for the council to supply housing for those with none or who were living in slums.[67]

At the beginning of January 1919 the St Albans branches of the Comrades and the Federation jointly promoted the formation of 'a first-rate club on non-political lines' for ex-servicemen. Trustees of the Abbey Institute offered rooms, with running costs to be paid by the club.[68] The

Ex-Servicemen's Club officially opened on 27 February 1919, but on 10 February it had already hosted a supper for returned POWs, followed by a social gathering welcoming any ex-serviceman 'and a lady friend'.[69] The Comrades and the Federation, with the National Association of Discharged Sailors and Soldiers and the Officers Association, merged in 1921 to become the British Legion.[70] The first 'Poppy Day' was held on 11 November 1921.

On a more social level, the new mayor, Arthur Faulkner, began as soon as elected in 1918 to arrange a performance of Handel's *Messiah* to be held the following March at the drill hall. The event was attended by the city council in full regalia and honoured demobilised men, POWs and the 'parents and wives of sailors, soldiers and airmen who are or have been with the Colours in the present war'.[71]

Lingering problems

Some effects of the military occupation of the city lingered for the next year or more. There were troops in the city until at least mid-1919. The rifle ranges were in use until the end of July[72] and some 300 soldiers remained, their duties included guarding German POWs in St Albans gaol.[73] The POWs continued to provide agricultural and other labour, as ex-servicemen were mostly unwilling to work for the available wages.[74] In June 1919 the Hertfordshire Agricultural Executive Committee warned that POWs might be withdrawn soon and farmers should consider other arrangements for the harvest,[75] but we do not know how soon that was carried out; German POWs in Britain were gradually repatriated throughout 1919.[76] The army were still occupying Clarence Park in July 1919, which was a cause of great annoyance to the St Albans City Football Club, who were unable to play there. When the troops finally departed the park required considerable restoration before the grounds were fit for the football and cricket teams to use in 1919–20. Other locations in use by the military at the end of the war, such as the veterinary hospital on St Stephen's Hill, the war supply depot, the Abbey Institute and some church halls, all required repair before their pre-war purposes could be resumed. Bricket House Red Cross Hospital closed on 31 January 1919, although massage and electrical treatment for the disabled continued there.[77] The County of Middlesex War Hospital at Napsbury closed on 1 August 1919 and the building returned to its original use as a mental hospital.[78]

Food problems did not end with the armistice either. One particular area of concern was milk supplies. In December 1918 the St Albans Local

Food Control Committee introduced a rationing scheme, which limited the sale of milk to half a pint a day per person. A priority card for infants and invalids was available on production of a medical certificate testifying to a need for extra milk.[79] Concern about children's health was reflected in the distribution by the Mayor's Relief Fund of milk worth several hundred pounds by September 1919.[80] Although ration books expired in May 1919 rationing was only gradually phased out, finally ending in November 1920. The food control committee continued to meet until the end of June 1920.

By early 1919 life was already gradually returning to pre-war routines; sports, aside from football and cricket, were possible again and other clubs and societies quickly resumed their previous activities. Fundraising concentrated on local causes, such as the local hospitals; some events were even presented without an objective. Before the war's end, however, the pre-war problems of labour, women's suffrage, housing and education were re-emerging in St Albans, as throughout the country.

The Labour movement

Although there was something of a truce between employers and workers, there were still tensions everywhere throughout the war and, with the returning troops, the situation worsened. The shortage of jobs in addition to the increased cost of living during the war, the expectations of higher wages such as had been earned in war-work and increased taxes due to the enormous costs of the war all exacerbated the situation and labour problems erupted more strongly than ever.

There had been a branch of the National Amalgamated Society of Operative Painters and Decorators in St Albans since around the turn of the century, membership of which increased enormously in line with the growth of the building trade after the war. In July 1919 the St Albans branch went on strike to be paid skilled labour rates, but the dispute was settled satisfactorily within a few days.[81] In December 1919 the girls at the Abbey silk mills walked out on the advice of the National Federation of Women Workers; this case also, although we do not know the details, was settled satisfactorily.[82] These disputes were minor, but they show the mood of the time.

The national rail strike in September 1919, however, was more serious, and the coal miners' strike in October 1920 even more so. The latter caused public lighting to be cut by 50 per cent and restricted the use of coal, gas and electricity for businesses.[83] It lasted only a fortnight, but caused problems to many businesses – not only, for instance, the straw hat makers in St Albans but also the bleachers and dyers who supplied them, as well as the merchants who bought their hats.

Even companies such as E. Day & Co., which had done well during the war, suffered in these conditions. They revived their straw hat trade when an initial post-war boom occurred, with returning soldiers creating a large demand for 'saucy' boaters – and a fine summer reinforcing this – but changing fashions were diminishing the bonnet and boater trade. Day's helmet department continued to receive army contracts after the war, but in November 1920 the industry suffered another blow with the imposition of minimum wages in the hat, cap and millinery trades. By 1923 Day's was in serious financial trouble and was forced into liquidation, despite supplying government contracts until the day they closed.[84]

The struggle of demobilised men and munitions workers to find work was aggravated by the fact that many women workers were loath to give up the freedom of earning their own wages. Employers were also happy to retain women workers, who earned a lower wage than men. In August 1919 the Restoration of Pre-War Practices Act was passed which demanded that within two months of its passage employers must restore any trade practice (in particular, the employment of women in jobs previously done by men) to its pre-war state and to maintain such for at least one year. The fines for non-compliance were a very hefty £25 per day. In August 1920 the Military Cork Headdress Trade Union attempted to make a case against Day's for infringing this law, but the case was dismissed. The union tried again in December, assembling a host of helmet makers to attest that helmets had never been made by women before the war, but Day's successfully defended themselves, basically because their process was entirely new. The judge decided that the only offence was that no men had been employed in this work since the war, and that this must be corrected. There was no fine.[85] Day's was successful, but in general the law was effective. It is significant, however, that in December 1919, only four months after that act was passed, the Sex Disqualification (Removal) Act of 1919 made it illegal to exclude women from jobs because of their sex. Women had entered the workforce.

Although there had been little union activity in St Albans during the war the Trades and Labour Council (TLC) had become increasingly active. The St Albans Cooperative Society, representing 2,000 households, had affiliated with the TLC in 1917 and in October 1918 the St Albans Labour Party was re-formed.[86] There were vocal supporters of organised labour on the tribunal and on the food control committee, but there was growing feeling that the city council was not giving labour serious consideration. As the war continued food shortages, complaints about the inequality of distribution and the need for fair rationing caused growing resentment among the working classes and, by 1918, became the subject of many heated discussions at TLC meetings and increased support for the Labour party.

The strength of the developing political movement is apparent in the following examples. Frederick Clift was a linotype operator and probably a member of the St Albans Typographical Society who sat on the food control committee as a private individual. When he was asked informally in 1917 to represent the TLC on the committee he threatened to resign, perceiving this as not respecting the TLC's position.[87] Benjamin Wouldham was a TLC representative on the St Albans City Military Service Tribunal. He demonstrated a similar ideological conviction when he resigned in June 1918, feeling unable as a trade unionist to act under the Military Service (No. 2) Act, which he perceived as weakening the power of the unions.[88] In this instance the TLC decided that a labour representative was necessary and nominated George Dimond.[89]

The role of women

Before the war campaigns for women's political representation were becoming increasingly fierce, but they had been set aside during the war. By the end of the war the situation had completely changed. Women had played such important roles on the home front that the Representation of the People Act was passed by a majority of 385 to 55 in the House of Commons in February 1918 with no further militant pressure. It gave the vote to women over 30, providing that they or their husbands either owned or rented property valued at £5 per annum or more. It also enfranchised all men over 21 with no such proviso. Nationally, the size of the electorate tripled. According to Frederick Preece, responsible for the electoral roll in St Albans, the number of voters in the Mid-Hertfordshire constituency rose from 5,500 to 13,000.[90]

It is often suggested that the government gave women the right to vote in recognition of their wartime work in munitions but that is, of course, a gross simplification. Women were intensely involved in the constant fundraising taking place during the war. The amounts of money raised in St Albans, as everywhere, during the war were significant. In addition to over £500,000 raised through war savings campaigns, and a further £300,000 as a result of the post-war Victory campaign described in Chapter 4, funds were raised for comforts for POWs, for the wounded in St Albans and abroad, for the Red Cross and for innumerable other wartime causes. At the same time local causes such as the St Albans hospitals and church missions continued to receive support. Much of this money was raised by concerts, teas, fêtes and flag days, all arranged, promoted, contributed to and staffed by women.

The committees of the various clubs and organisations which struggled on through the war depended largely on women. More importantly, women played increasingly prominent roles on the food control committee, the Board of Guardians, the St Albans Rural Military Service Tribunal and other civic committees. In the later years of the war, with enfranchisement looming larger, women were also taking on more political roles. Lady Grimston (Figure 8.8) and Lady Thomson were active in setting up the St Albans branch of the National Union of Women Workers (NUWW)[91] and in petitioning for the appointment of women police officers in St Albans.[92] They were powerful supporters of the cause, but there was some resentment of their titles among labour supporters. In February 1918 the NUWW suggested that Lady Thomson be co-opted as city councillor, and she was proposed by Alderman William Green. The proposal was voted down, with the wish expressed that women should rather come in by 'the Big Door' (election),[93] but this was partly due to opposition from the TLC, at whose meeting the week before a member had expressed sarcastic remarks about 'Lady de Tompkins'.[94]

Other women had appeared on the political scene during the war. Edith Garrett illustrates the increase in women's power resulting from their

Figure 8.8 Lady Grimston, a member of the Voluntary Aid Detachment, who worked at Bricket House military hospital in St Albans during the war. © Lord Verulam

wartime activities. She and her husband Albert, a textile expert, moved to St Albans in 1912. In 1916 they both enthusiastically took up the cause of promoting war savings schemes (more fully described in Chapter 4). She and her husband were joint honorary secretaries of the local fundraising committee, a position she held until at least 1932. Her contribution to the city's successful sales of war bonds and certificates was so significant that in April 1920 she was awarded an MBE in recognition of her work.

Perhaps the most significant indication in St Albans of the developing role of women was the election to the city council in November 1919 of Margaret Wix, who held the seat until 1949. She became the first female mayor of the city in 1924 and an alderman in 1936. In 1925 Frances Glossop became both county and city magistrate and the Countess of Verulam (formerly Violet, Lady Grimston) a city magistrate. Other women joined them gradually. There were women elected to the county council from 1919,[95] but the first St Albans female representative was Edith Garrett in 1929. She remained in office until 1940, when she retired and left the city.

Political changes
No council elections had been held since the start of the war. However, in the same week that the armistice was declared St Albans installed a new mayor for the first time since November 1915. The outgoing mayor, James Flint, was a hard act to follow, but Alderman Arthur Faulkner described in his speech upon election his plans to take action on the issue of housing, to raise funds for the St Albans and District Nursing Association, to prepare for the national drive the following December to sell war bonds and to host a performance of the *Messiah* in March, honouring the families of servicemen.[96]

National changes also swiftly followed. Lloyd George called a general election for 14 December 1918.[97] The coalition won a landslide victory and Lloyd George remained prime minister, but there were significant changes within the coalition. This had no effect on St Albans, where the sitting member since 1906, Sir Hildred Carlile, was elected unopposed. However, he resigned through ill-health in 1919 and a fiercely fought by-election was held in December 1919. Sir Edward Francis Fremantle (the county medical officer, a Coalition Unionist) won the election with 9,621 votes, but John William Brown for Labour was very close behind at 8,908. This growing strength of the Labour party had been shown in the city council elections the previous month, when two Labour representatives, William H. Bond and Stephen J. Simmons, were elected in the East Ward.

The housing crisis

Housing and education were matters of great concern to both women and the Labour movement. Housing had already become a major issue before the war: far too many houses in the city were 'unfit for purpose'. As with labour unrest and suffrage, this problem had been shelved during the war, partly driven in this case by the shortage of men and materials; no planning applications were made between September 1915 and September 1919 in St Albans.[98] As early as 1916, however, concerns were expressed nationally about the need for improved housing when the men returned and in 1917 a need was reported to the Local Government Board for 50 more houses in St Albans for working-class families and an estimated 200 by the end of the war.[99]

The situation described in the 1924 Housing Survey[100] initiated by the bishop of St Albans to study the quality of working-class housing in the older parts of the city must have long pre-dated the war. The survey, carried out by the St Albans Housing Enquiry Committee, covered 27 streets (718 houses), about 20 per cent of working-class houses in St Albans. Although many houses were found to be in good condition, the sanitation and general state of repair of many appalled the visitors. There were 107 houses in which more than one married couple shared a bedroom.

By the summer of 1918 the housing problem was being hotly debated by a number of organisations representing several churches, labour, women and ex-servicemen. The council began making plans for house building in January 1919[101] and on 14 February 1919 the government pledged help to councils so that rates would increase by no more than 1d in the pound, which was a great encouragement to local authorities. The city council set up an advisory committee for the proposed housing scheme which included two representatives each of the NUWW, the Friendly Societies Council, the TLC and the Discharged Sailors and Soldiers Association. When this committee of interested parties was established it was specifically required that women be 'included if possible'.[102]

Two sites were considered. One was Townsend (where Waverley Road meets Townsend Road), where 100 houses could be built. The other was at Sportsman's Hall (at the corner of Prospect Road and Cottonmill Lane), for 50 houses. Both sites were purchased, but the Ministry of Health did not approve the Sportsman's Hall site.

Tenders for houses on the Townsend site were submitted by mid-July 1920 and that of James Bushell of Worley Road was accepted. There were to be four types of houses, 25 houses were to be built every four months, and the entire scheme to be finished by 15 February 1922. Criteria for applications gave priority to local ex-servicemen in lower-grade accommodation, for which there were 200 applications, and the council's firm stand on this was shown in their rejection of an application in April 1922 from a Mr Jackson of Oxford Street, London.[103] The economic problems of the 1920s hindered further vitally necessary improvements in housing and sewage, and it was not until 1925 that any real progress was made.

Changes in education

Yet another act of major social importance, the Education Act (1918), was passed before the end of the war. The significant provisions of the act were to raise the school-leaving age from 12 to 14; to prohibit the employment of children under 12 and limit it between 12 and 14; to transfer most of the financial burden of education to central government; and to place an emphasis on improving the health of the nation's children. Compliance affected both county and city councils, as the rest of the country, in several ways. One result of the act's encouragement of further education for children over 11 years of age in St Albans was the opening on 4 October 1920 of the St Albans Central School and Pupil Teacher Centre for girls in the old School of Art & Craft in Victoria Street.[104] Fully subscribed on opening, with 73 pupils and ten pupil teachers, the school proposed expansion the following year.[105] A similar school for boys was also planned.[106] The act also led to the trial of an unemployment centre for girls, as mentioned earlier.

Conclusion

By 1920 St Albans would have appeared in many ways a different city to that which it had been in 1914. There were more unaccompanied women in public places; probably more men in the streets owing to lack of work, the many disabled very obvious. There were fewer horses, but more cars and motorcycles. Some businesses, large and small, even well-established ones, had disappeared, and there were many memorials. This was the public face of the much deeper changes in the city. Women were not only in public places but also in public positions. The loss of active men and the memorials reflected both the lasting grief and the escalating labour problems. Higher costs and continuing shortages in the shops were expressions of the enormous economic burden of the war. But it was still the same city. The people who had guided the city through the war were the same people who faced and met these new challenges.

Notes

1. 'Armistice Day', *Herts Advertiser* (*HA*), 16 November 1918.
2. St Albans School archive, letter from Biddy Hodge, 6 September 2001. The school (formerly St Albans Grammar School) had asked for reminiscences of the war and Biddy remembered seeing a member of staff, Bill Barrett, at the celebrations.
3. 'Peace Night', *HA*, 5 July 1919.
4. 'Peace Day arrangements', *HA*, 12 July 1919.
5. See Chapter 3 for a description of these sports.
6. 'Joy Day. City en fete', *HA*, 26 July 1919.
7. 'Honouring the dead', *HA*, 23 August 1919.
8. The church is now called Trinity United Reformed Church.
9. 'The Drumhead service', *HA*, 23 August 1919. Drumhead services are usually held in the field with military drums providing a temporary altar. The tradition dates back many centuries and continues to the present day, for example, the VJ Day 70th anniversary ceremony held in London on 15 August 2015 <https://www.gov.uk/government/news/vj-day-70-royal-marines-rehearse-drumhead-service-ahead-of-national-commemorations> accessed 4 April 2016.
10. 'Armistice Day', *HA*, 15 November 1919.
11. See Chapter 6 for further information about the national kitchen.
12. 'Father and daughter buried', *HA*, 9 November 1918.
13. Hertfordshire Archives and Local Studies (HALS), SBR/3384, City Council Correspondence File, 1918, unnumbered collection of correspondence.
14. HALS, SBR/Interim Catalogue, Medical Officer of Health Reports (MOHR), 1905–25, annual report 1919.
15. The shrines are discussed in Chapter 4. For a fuller study of the street shrine movement, see J. Mein and G. Hughes, 'The war shrine movement in Hertfordshire, 1916–18', *Herts Past & Present* (forthcoming).
16. J.G.E. Cox and A. Dean, *The street memorials of St Albans Abbey parish* (Ware, 2015).
17. 'Chivalrous churchmen: memorial tablet at St Peter's', *HA*, 28 May 1921; St Peter's parish magazine, June 1921.
18. Ibid., September 1915.
19. 'War memorial at St Michael's', *HA*, 2 December 1922.
20. W.N. Wright, *The story of St Stephen's church, St Albans* (n.p., 1941), p. 10.
21. 'St John's New Mission Hall', *HA*, 1 October 1921. The site is now a small housing estate, Miller's Rise.
22. J.W. Hubbard, *Christ Church, an early account: 1850s–1943*, <http://www.ccstalbans.org.uk/index.php/our-history.php> accessed 1 February 2016. Following the deconsecration of the church no trace can be found of the tablet.
23. 'The passing of Queen Eleanor', *HA*, 21 September 1918. Sadly, the painting was stolen in 1973.
24. These memorials are marked on a trail leaflet which can be found at the abbey.
25. L. Watson, *From watches to matches: the story of my family* (Warboys, 2010), p. 75.
26. This information has been collated for the St Albans memorials and published in

the SAHAAS War Memorials Matrix (St Albans, 2013). This is available on the Society's website, <http://www.stalbanshistory.org> accessed 8 January 2016.

27. Civic Memorial, St Peter's Green; Civic roll of honour, town hall; St Paul's church; Trinity church; Spicer Street church; Thomas Cook Group, plc (formerly Thomas Cook & Son) memorial window in their HQ at Peterborough – there are no names listed, but his name appears in the Order of Service from the dedication; Commonwealth (formerly Imperial) War Graves Commission (CWGC) memorial in Gaza, Palestine; his birthplace, Ackergill, Caithness, home of his parents; Edinburgh Castle. Information provided by Jean Taylor, Calder's granddaughter.

28. Erected in the 1290s, crosses marked the places where Queen Eleanor's coffin rested en route to London for burial.

29. 'St Albans City Council', *HA*, 14 February 1920.

30. HALS, SBR/884, Miscellaneous Committees Minute Book (MCMB), 1919–21, 9 July 1920.

31. 'Opening of Bricket House', *HA*, 1 May 1920.

32. HALS, SBR/884, MCMB, 17 September 1920.

33. 'The Glorious Dead', *HA*, 28 May 1921.

34. HALS, SBR/885, MCMB, 1921–4, 5 September 1921.

35. HALS, SBR/3563, Miscellaneous papers on the War Scholarship Fund, 1921–7.

36. P. Barham, *Forgotten lunatics of the Great War* (London, 2007), p. 57.

37. 'Editorial: "Our Heroes' Corner"', *HA*, 29 July 1916.

38. 'St Albans City Council: the soldiers' graves', *HA*, 17 November 1917.

39. HALS, SBR/884, MCMB, 28 November 1919, in reference to a letter from the CWGC representative, Captain Newham.

40. 'Fleetville's heroes: the cemetery war cross', *HA*, 30 October 1920.

41. HALS, SBR/884, MCMB, 2 December 1919.

42. HALS, SBR/871, Urban Authority & General Purposes Committee Minute Book (UAGPC), 1914–20, Highways etc. sub-committee, 23 November 1915.

43. 'Correspondence: "no tank please"', *HA*, 24 May 1919.

44. 'Editorial', *HA*, 20 December 1919.

45. 'St Albans City Council', *HA*, 14 February 1920.

46. 'Correspondence: "demobilisation"', *HA*, 14 December 1918.

47. 'St Albans City Council', *HA*, 1 March 1919.

48. <http://www.1914–1918.net/demobilisation.htm>, accessed 30 January 2016.

49. T.A. Bickerton, *The wartime experiences of an ordinary 'Tommy'* (typescript, 1964), p. 1.

50. 'Returning POWs', *HA*, 21 December 1918.

51. 'Repatriated prisoners', *HA*, 8 February 1919.

52. 'St Albans City Council', *HA*, 1 March 1919.

53. 'Demobilised teachers', *HA*, 8 February 1919.

54. HALS, HCC 21/11, Hertfordshire County Council (HCC) Education Committee Minute Book, 1917–20, 23 June 1919.

55. HALS, SBR/884, MCMB, 31 January 1920, 15 March 1920; SBR/885, MCMB, 26 September 1921, 22 October 1921, 20 January 1923.

56. P.D. Nicholls, *The diary of Private A.A. Bridges* (Cirencester, 2014), p. 167.

57. 'St Albans City Council', *HA*, 1 March 1919.

58. 'St Albans City Council', *HA*, 28 June 1919.

59. D. Taverner and P.A. Taylor, *The city at war: a tribute to the city's most glorious saints* (n.p., c.2014).

60. Kathleen Tyrwhitt Drake, eldest daughter of Revd W.T. and Mrs Harriett Tyrwhitt Drake, volunteered to serve in the SSFA at the very start of the war. Initially devoting herself to the women's side of the work, when Gape retired she became district chairman of the St Albans division of the War Pensions Committee. See 'Death of Miss K. Tyrwhitt Drake', *HA*, 13 October 1944.

61. 'War Pensions Committee', *HA*, 30 March 1918; 'Herts war pensions', *HA*, 1 June 1918.

62. Museum of St Albans, Hertfordshire County Museum Minute Book, 13 September 1919; HALS, HCC HEd5/19/1 St Albans City Local Education Authority Sub-Committee Minute Book, 1913–21, 26 February 1919.

63. Dangerfield Printing Co.; E. Day (St Albans) Ltd; Marcus Day & Co.; Grimston Tyres, Ltd; Sir Howard Grubb & Sons; Kingsbury Works, Ltd; Edwin Lee & Sons, Ltd; Thomas Mercer; Thomas Oakley & Co., Ltd; H.A. Richardson; St Albans Cooperative Society; St Albans Council; A.W. Sharp; W.J. Shore; Horace Slade & Co. (HMSO, *The King's National Roll* [the national scheme for the employment, on a percentage basis, of disabled ex-service men] [London, 1920]). If the minister of labour thought it reasonable there might be a reduction in this percentage. Many of these firms became limited companies toward the end or just after the war and are listed as they were registered in 1920.

64. <http://www.legion-memorabilia.org.uk/badges/comrades.htm>, accessed 30 January 2016.

65. 'Comrades of the Great War', *HA*, 18 January 1919.

66. 'Notice', *HA*, 31 August 1918; The Cathedral and Abbey Church of Saint Alban Muniment Room, Abbey Institute Minute Book, January 1919.

67. HALS, SBR/871, UAGPC, 11 March 1919; 'Ex-servicemen's demands', *HA*, 15 March 1919. See the section on Housing below.

68. The Cathedral and Abbey Church of Saint Alban Muniment Room, Abbey Institute Minute Book, January 1919.

69. 'Correspondence: "club for ex servicemen"', *HA*, 1 February 1919.

70. <http://support.britishlegion.org.uk/app/answers/detail/a_id/1243/~/history-of-the-royal-british-legion>, accessed 30 January 2016.

71. 'Correspondence: "the mayor's Messiah performance"', *HA*, 25 January 1919.

72. See *HA* weekly notices on the front page.

73. 'St Albans Football Club AGM', *HA*, 19 July 1919.

74. 'City Council', *HA*, 1 March 1919.

75. 'Herts Agricultural Executive Committee', *HA*, 21 June 1919.

76. P. Panayi, *Prisoners of War and Internees (Great Britain)*, <http://www.encyclopedia.1914–1918-online.net/article/prisoners_of_war_and_internees_great_britain>, accessed 21 January 2016.

77.   'Bricket House; record of valuable war work', *HA*, 8 February 1919.

78.   <http://1914–1918.net/hospitals_uk.htm>, accessed 21 January 2016.

79.   HALS, SBR/863, St Albans Local Food Control Committee Minute Book, 1917–20, 10 December 1918.

80.   Ibid., 29 September 1919. For more about the Mayor's Relief Fund, see Chapter 7.

81.   'Painters' strike at St Albans', *HA*, 19 July 1919.

82.   'Correspondence: "the silk mill dispute"', *HA*, 13 December 1919. The *HA* refers to this Federation, although the National Union of Women Workers was stronger in St Albans and is perhaps more likely to have acted in this.

83.   'The straw hat trade in St Albans and Luton', *Hatters' Gazette*, 15 November 1920, p. 516.

84.   Day's helmet department was bought up by its manager, Thomas Noblett, and three friends, who established a new firm, Helmets Ltd, which was still trading in 2015.

85.   'Legal: "helmet making by females"', *Hatters' Gazette*, 15 September 1920; 'Legal: "females and helmet making"', 15 December 1920.

86.   'Labour, important meeting at St Albans', *HA*, 5 October 1918. There had been a St Albans Labour party before the war, but it apparently became inactive after 1914: see 'St Albans Labour party's protest', *HA*, 12 October 1914.

87.   'Trades Council and food control', *HA*, 8 December 1917.

88.   'St Albans Trades and Labour Council', *HA*, 7 June 1918.

89.   'St Albans Trades and Labour Council', *HA*, 1 August 1918.

90.   'From 5,500 to 13,000', *HA*, 4 May 1918.

91.   In January 1918 the NUWW became the National Council of Women. 'Editorial, local food control', *HA*, 23 February 1918; 'National Council of Women', *HA*, 19 July 1919.

92.   'War philanthropy', *HA*, 6 July 1918.

93.   'St Albans City Council', *HA*, 23 February 1918.

94.   'The voice of Labour', *HA*, 16 February 1918.

95.   A Miss Bradford for Watford had that honour.

96.   'The mayoralty: Alderman A. Faulkner's election', *HA*, 16 November 1918.

97.   The votes were not counted until 28 December to allow for absentee votes from soldiers overseas to arrive.

98.   Based on data extracted from HALS SBR/871, UAGPC, results of planning applications.

99.   HALS, SBR/874, Urban Authority Committee Highways Sub-committee Minute Book, 1914–18, Return for the LGB, 2 October 1917; SBR/871, UAGPC, 2 October 1917.

100. HALS, SBR/3146, Report of a Housing Survey, 1924, St Albans Housing Enquiry Committee.

101. HALS, SBR/871, UAGPC, Further Report of the Highways and Plans and Nuisances sub-committee, 2 January 1919.

102. 'St Albans City Council', *HA*, 17 May 1919.

103. HALS, SBR/885, MCMB, 26 April 1922.

104. The school moved to Fleetville in 1931 and was renamed St Albans Girls' Grammar School in 1938.

105. HALS, HCC 21D/8, HCC Education Finance and General Purposes Sub-Committee, 1915–21, 13 December 1920.

106. Ibid.

Select bibliography

Official publications

Acts of Parliament
Local Government Board's Provisional Order Confirmation (No. 12) Act, 3 & 4 Geo. V, c. cxxxci

British Parliamentary Papers
Board of Agriculture and Fisheries, Wages and conditions of employment in agriculture vol. I. General Report; 1919 (Cd 24) IX.1
Board of Trade, Department of Labour Statistics, Report on Changes in Rates of Wages and Hours of Labour in the United Kingdom in 1913, with Comparative Statistics (1914–16, Cd 7635)
Board of Trade, Department of Labour Statistics, Standard Time Rates of Wages in the United Kingdom at 1 October 1913 (1914, Cd 7194)
Statutory rules and orders, 1918, no. 55. Defence of the Realm Ministry of Food, 1917–18 (000)XXVI

HMSO
The King's National Roll (the national scheme for the employment, on a percentage basis, of disabled ex-service men) (London, 1920)
Ministry of Munitions, *The history of the Ministry of Munitions*, the National Factories, VIII, Pt 2 (London, 1922)
War Office, *Musketry Regulations Pt.2 – Rifle Ranges and Musketry Appliances* (London, 1910)
War Office, *Manual of military law* (London, 1914)
War Office, *Group and class systems. Notes on administration*, February 1916 (London, 1916)

Primary sources

The Cathedral and Abbey Church of Saint Alban Muniment Room
Abbey Institute Minute Book, 1915–34
Hall, H.R. Wilton, *A Chronicle of the Cathedral Church 1914–1920* (n.d.)

Hertfordshire Archives and Local Studies
Agriculture
AEC/1 Hertfordshire War Agricultural Committee Minute Book, 1916–19

AEC/3–4 Executive Committee of the Hertfordshire War Agricultural Committee Minute
  Books, 1917–18
AEC/8 Hertfordshire Women's War Agricultural Council Executive Committee Minute
  Book, 1916–20
AEC/20 Hertfordshire War Agricultural Committee correspondence, Mid-Herts Division,
  1916–20
AEC/22 Hertfordshire War Agricultural Committee, Cultivation of Lands Order (1917),
  Register of Notices (Mid-Herts Division), 1916–20

Diocese and churches

DP91/25/1 Christ Church Parish Account Book, 1897–1921
DP93/29/5–6 St Peter's parish magazines, 1910–24
DP93C/29/2 St Paul's parish magazines, 1910–19
DP96A/11/2 St Saviour's parish magazines, 1913–23

Gorhambury estate archives

DE/V E167–73 Correspondence and papers, 1914–16
DE/V E180–86 Correspondence and papers, 1919–21
DE/V F1437 1–2 Correspondence and papers concerning service of employees of Lord
  Grimston's businesses during the war, 1914–19
DE/V F1553 Papers relating to Lord Grimston's position in the First World War, 1916–19
DE/V F1687/3–4 Letters to Lady Verulam from her husband, 1914–20
DE/V Q58 Correspondence, papers and leaflets including St Albans and District British
  Red Cross accounts, 1917

Hertfordshire County Council

HCC 21/9 Hertfordshire County Council Education Committee Minute Book, 1914–15
HCC 21/11 Education Committee Minute Books, 1914–20
HCC 21D/8 Finance & General Purposes Sub-Committee Minute Books, 1915–21
HCC HEd5/19/1 St Albans City Local Education Authority Sub-Committee Minute Books,
  1913–21

Hertfordshire Territorial Forces Association

TAFA/1–2 Association Minute Books, 1908–27

Public utilities

PUE 3/3 North Metropolitan Co. Board Minute Book, 1910–17
PUG 13/1/5–6 St Albans Gas Co. Directors' and Shareholders' Minute Book, 1907–21

St Albans Board of Guardians and Union Workhouse

BG/STA/17–19 Minute Books, 1913–20
HSS/8/6/1 St Albans Union rough Minute Book, 1911–30

St Albans City archive

SBR/863 St Albans Local Food Control Committee Minute Book, 1917–20
SBR/865 St Albans City Tribunal Minute Book, 1915–18
SBR/871–2 Urban Authority & General Purposes Committee Minute Book, 1914–23
SBR/874 Urban Authority Committee Highways Sub-Committee Minute Book, 1914–18
SBR/882–5 Miscellaneous Committees Minute Books, 1912–24
SBR/894A City Council Minute Book No. 10, 1912–16
SBR/904 Watch Committee Minute Book, 1912–22

SBR/1666 Market Toll Account Book, 1912–22

SBR/1749–56 City of St Albans Year Books, 1914–18

SBR/1813–4 St Albans City Tribunal (Military Service Act cases) Registers, 1916–18

SBR/1815 St Albans City Tribunal (Lord Derby Scheme cases) Register, 1916–18

SBR/1900–06 Town Clerk Out Letters Books, 1913–21

SBR/1943 Council Out Letter Book (mostly to government departments), 1912–20

SBR/2867 Agreement between Mayor etc. and National Telephone Co. re way leave, 1910

SBR/2915 Agreement, John Cable Ltd and the Mayor for horsing the fire engine, 30 April 1914

SBR/2921 Agreement, John Cable Ltd and the Mayor for removal of bedding etc. to and from Sisters Hospital, 26 May 1914

SBR/2946 Agreement, John Cable Ltd and the Mayor for the collection of house refuse, 30 April 1913

SBR/2960 Lord Derby's Recruiting Scheme Papers, 1915

SBR/3146 Report of a Housing Survey, 1924, St Albans Housing Enquiry Committee

SBR/3384 City Council Correspondence File etc., 1916–18

SBR/3563 Miscellaneous Papers on the War Scholarship Fund, 1921–27

SBR/3566 Miscellaneous Minutes of the Housing Committee, 1917–20

SBR/3572 St Albans and Mid Herts Hospital and Dispensary: Management Committee Annual Statements, 1914–19

SBR/3580 St Albans Housing Enquiry, 1924

SBR/3687 City Council Minute Book, 1916–20

SBR/3736 Miscellaneous Housing Committee Minute Book, 1925–29

SBR/Interim Catalogue Medical Officer of Health Reports, 1905–25

St Albans City Petty Sessions

PS21/2/22 Petty Sessions Register, 1915–19

PS21/4/1 Register of Clubs, 1903–56

PS21/10/7 Alehouse Licensing Minute Book, 1916

Schools

HEd2/27/1 Garden Fields School Log Book, 1896–1931

HEd2/28/1 Priory Park School Log Book, 1901–31

Urban District Councils

UDC/4/68/1 Berkhamsted Tribunal Papers, 1915

Miscellaneous

Acc 3727 St Albans & District Chamber of Commerce Executive Committee Minute Book, 1908–17

Acc 3883 Benskin's Watford Brewery Ltd papers, 1648–1970

Acc 3959 B. Anderson, *Nearly a century: the history of Hill End Mental Hospital, St Albans, 1899–1995* (1998)

Acc 5148 St Albans Typographical Society Minute Book, 1899–1949

D/ECk F55 Harriet Suzanna Tyrwhitt Drake's diary, 1914

Imperial War Museums

17/3 (141) 0 Aeroplane Raids 1918 – Reports compiled by the Intelligence Section, GHQ Home Defence, May 1918

Documents.4899 private papers of H.C. Cossins
E.J.1106 Birklands School magazine, 1915–18
Museum of St Albans
Leaflet, *City of St Albans Defence Of The Realm (Consolidation) Regulations 1914*
Hertfordshire County Museum Minute Book, 1919

The National Archives
CAB 23/8/480 War Cabinet minutes, 1918
FO 383/508 'Letter from Swiss legation', 1 July 1919
HO 144/304/B4882 Nationality and naturalisation papers for Friedrich Sander, 1889
MH 10/195–197 Local Government Board Circulars. Military Service Regulations, 1915–19
MH 47/141/1 *Comparison of Previous List of Certified Exemptions with list of 4th April, 1916, showing the material alterations apart from age limits*
MH 47/142/1 *Group and Class Systems, Notes on Administration*, 1916–18
MH 47/142/2 *Schedule of Protected Occupations*, 7 July 1917
MH 47/142/3 *List of Certified Occupations*, 26 September 1918
MUN 4/5307 Liquidation of contracts, 1919–20
MUN 4/5311 Liquidation of contracts, 1918–19
MUN 5/72/324/1 Minutes of Dilution Section, Department of Labour, confidential memo of the DA section of the Labour Department
WO 33/729 *Emergency Scheme B – Reinforcement of Central Force North of the Thames by Troops from Aldershot/Salisbury Plain Training Centre*, 1915
WO 33/782 *Composition of the Headquarters of Home Forces*, October 1916
WO 33/812 Distribution of Home Defence Troops (corrected to 1 March 1917)
WO 33/837 *Distribution of Home Defence Troops and Reserve Units at Summer Stations, 1917*
WO 33/843 *Composition of Headquarters Home Forces*, October 1917
WO 363/W1638 Soldiers' papers, Harry J. Wilson

Private collections
Hall, H.R. Wilton, *Notes and memoranda relating to St Saviour's church*, Book 5, 1914–16 (in hands of incumbent of St Saviour's Church)
Stocker, W., *Letters of Private William Stocker*, 1/5th (London) Field Ambulance (in private hands)

Royal Air Force Museum
X001–3532 Personal diary, *A short life and a gay one: diary of Frank Best 1893–1917*
X006–7001 Orderly Book of No. 74 Squadron (RFC), 1917–18

St Albans & Hertfordshire Architectural & Archaeological Society (SAHAAS) Library
Bickerton, T.A., *The wartime experiences of an ordinary 'Tommy'* (n.p., 1964)
SAHAAS Council Minute Book, 1915–19
SAHAAS General Meetings Minute Book, 1914–20

St Albans School archive
Letter from Biddy Hodge, 6 September 2001
Letter from headmaster to the chairman of governors, 25 July 1914
St Albans Grammar School Minute Book, 1910–16

Miscellaneous
British Red Cross Archives, Hospital Record Card 493, Bricket House Red Cross Hospital
St Albans High School for Girls archive, School Report 1919 and School Record Book
Verulam Golf Club Ltd, General Committee Minute Book, 1912–18

Published primary sources

Books
Broom, D., *My St Albans memories: an oral history of life and times in St Albans* (St Albans, 2001).
Chapin, H., *Soldier and dramatist: being the letters of Harold Chapin*, 2nd edn (London, 1917).
City of St Alban [*sic*], *City Extension 1913, Proceedings*.
Hall, H.R. Wilton (compiled Lapthorn, D.), *Bernard's Heath and the Great War: extracts from the diary of H.R. Wilton Hall* (St Albans, 2009).
Mellersh, H.E.L., *Schoolboy into war* (London, 1978).
War record of 21st London Regiment (1st Surrey Rifles) 1914–1919 (London, 1927).

Newspapers, magazines and directories
Baptists Handbook
Bedfordshire Advertiser and Luton Times
Daily Herald
Hatters' Gazette
Hertfordshire News and County Advertiser (St Albans)
Herts Advertiser
Kelly's Directory of St Albans, Harpenden and Hatfield (various)
Kelly's Trade Directory for Hertfordshire (London, 1922)
Letchworth Citizen
London Gazette
Luton News & Bedfordshire Chronicle
Milling Journal
Pictorial Record: St Albans (New Series, London, 1915)
The Times

Secondary sources

Books and articles
Acland, K., 'A town voluntary aid detachment', *Journal of the RAMC*, 51/2 (1928), pp. 121–4.
Aitken, C., *Childwickbury* (Redbourn, 2011).

Anon, *Memorial trail*, Cathedral and Abbey Church of St Alban leaflet.

Anon, *St Albans roll of honour* (St Albans, n.d.).

Armstrong, A., *Farmworkers: a social and economic history, 1770–1980* (London, 1988).

Ashmore, E.B., *Air defence* (London, 1929).

Barham, P., *Forgotten lunatics of the Great War* (New Haven and London, c.2004).

Barnett, L.M., *British food policy during the First World War* (London, 1985).

Beckett, I.F.W., *Home Front, 1914–1918. How Britain survived the Great War* (Richmond, 2006).

Billings, T., *84 bus to St Albans: an illustrated local history* (St Albans, 2003).

Bloom, U., *Youth at the gate* (London, 1959).

Bourne, J., *Britain and the Great War, 1914–18* (London, 1989).

Bowyer, C., *Albert Ball VC* (Manchester, 2002).

Brittain, F., *Milestones of 100 years of Hertfordshire scouting* (n.p., 2008).

Brittain, F., *Milestones of 105 years of Hertfordshire scouting* (Borehamwood, 2013).

Broadberry, S. and Harrison, M. (eds), *The economics of World War 1* (Cambridge, 2005).

Broadberry, S. and Howlett, P., 'The United Kingdom in World War I, business as usual?' in S. Broadberry and M. Harrison (eds), *The economics of World War I* (Cambridge, 2005), pp. 215–17.

Budd, K. and Church, D., *St Albans Bowling Club, the first hundred years: 1903–2003* (St Albans, 2003).

Burton, K.G., *A penknife to a mountain: the early years of the National Savings Committee* (London, 1999).

Carrington, B., *Care in crisis – the story of the Hertfordshire British Red Cross 1907–1994* (Whittlebury, 1995).

Chorlton, M., *Forgotten aerodromes of World War 1* (Manchester, 2014).

Corbett, J., *Celebration: the story of a parish: SS Alban and Stephen, 1840–1990* (St Albans, 1990).

Cox, J.G.E. and Dean, A., *The street memorials of St Albans Abbey parish*, 2nd edn (1978; Ware, 2015).

Crellin, C., *Where God had a people: Quakers in St Albans over three hundred years* (St Albans, 1999).

Dewey, P., *British agriculture in the First World War* (London, 2014).

Dyer, J. et al., *The story of Luton* (Luton, 1964).

'E. Day (St Albans) Ltd', *St Albans as a Visitors' Resort ... The official handbook, etc.* (Cheltenham, 1919).

Ellsworth-Jones, W., *We will not fight: the untold story of the First World War's conscientious objectors* (London, 2008).

Eyles, A., with Stone, K., *Cinemas of Hertfordshire* (Hatfield, 2002 [1st edn. 1985]).

Fookes, M., *Made in St Albans* (St Albans, 1997).

Fox, A., *A history of the National Union of Boot and Shoe Operatives, 1874–1957* (Oxford, 1958).

Freeman, M., '"Splendid display, pompous spectacle": historical pageants in twentieth-century Britain', *Social History*, 38 (2013), pp. 423–55.

Freeman, M., *St Albans: a history* (Lancaster, 2008).

Friswell, N.C., *Northmet: a history of the North Metropolitan Electric Power Supply Company* (Horsham, 2000).

Fry, P., *Samuel Ryder: the man behind the Ryder Cup* (Weymouth, 2000).

Gardner, E.J., *Marlborough Road, 1898–1998* (St Albans, 1998).

Goslin, G., *St Albans to Bedford, including the Hemel Hempstead branch* (Midhurst, 2003).

Gourvish, T.R. and Wilson, R.G., *The British brewing industry, 1830–1980* (Cambridge, 1994).

Gregory, A., *The last great war: British society and the First World War* (Cambridge, 2008).

Grieves, K., *The politics of manpower, 1914–1918* (Manchester, 1988).

Hallifax, S., '"Over by Christmas": British popular opinion and the short war in 1914', *First World War Studies*, 1 (2010), pp. 103–21.

Harris, J. (ed.), *Civil society in British history* (Oxford, 2003).

Heywood, J.S., *Children in care: the development of the service for the deprived child* (London, 1959).

Horn, P., *Rural life in England in the First World War* (London, 1984).

James, E.A., *British regiments, 1914–1918* (London, 1978).

Jennings, P., *The local: a history of the English pub* (Stroud, 2007).

Kernahan, J.C., *The experiences of a recruiting officer* (London, 1915).

King, A., *Memorials of the Great War in Britain: the symbolism and politics of remembrance* (London, 1998).

McDermott, J., *British military service tribunals, 1916–1918: 'a very much abused body of men'* (Manchester, 2011).

MacGill, P., *The amateur army* (London, 1915).

McWhirr, A., *St Albans city fire brigade* (Leicester, 2007).

Mercer, T., *Mercer chronometers, history, maintenance and repair* (Ashbourne, 2003).

Mein, J. and Hughes, G., 'The war shrine movement in Hertfordshire, 1916–18', *Herts Past & Present*, (forthcoming).

Meyer, J., *Men of war: masculinity and the First World War in Britain* (Basingstoke, 2009).

Mitchinson, K.W., *Defending Albion: Britain's home army, 1908–1919* (Basingstoke, 2005).

Moody, B., *The light of other days: a short history of the St Albans & Hertfordshire Architectural & Archaeological Society, 1845 to 1995* (St Albans, 1995).

Morley, W.H., *More such days, 1910–1952, being a continuation of the story of the church and parish of St Saviour, St Albans* (n.p., 1952).

Neighbour, M., *St Albans' own East End, volume I: outsiders* (Hoddesdon, 2012).

Nicholls, P.D., *The diary of Private A.A. Bridges* (Cirencester, 2014).

Offer, A., *The First World War: an agrarian interpretation* (Oxford, 1989).

Parker, D., *Hertfordshire children in war and peace, 1914–1939* (Hatfield, 2007).

Pearce, C., *Comrades in conscience: the story of an English community's opposition to the Great War* (London, 2001).

Peatling, B. and Smith, B. (eds), *Always a scout: a glimpse into St Albans scouting since 1908* (Gateshead, 1984).

Petty, F., *The Pudding Lady's recipe book with practical hints* (London, 1917).

Prothero, R.E., Lord Ernle, *English farming past and present* (London, 1961, 1st edn London, 1912).

Sainsbury, J.D., *Herts V.R.* (Welwyn, 2005).

Searle, G.R., *A new England? Peace and war, 1886–1914* (Oxford, 2004).

Simkins, P., *Kitchener's army: the raising of the new armies, 1914–1916* (Barnsley, 2007).

Simmonds, A.G.V., *Britain and World War One* (London, 2012).

Simons, R.G., *Cricket in Hertfordshire* (Hertford, 1996).

Sisson, G.M., 'Mirror images', *Vistas in Astronomy*, 35 (1992), pp. 345–97.

Strachan, H., *The First World War*, vol. 1 (Oxford, 2001).

Swinson, A., *Frederick Sander, the Orchid King* (London, 1970).

Taverner, D. and Taylor, P.A., *The city at war: a tribute to the city's most glorious saints* (n.p., c.2014).

Toms, E., *The story of St Albans* (St Albans, 1962).

Turner, D., *With cheerful zeal: a history of the Dagnall Street baptist church* (London, 1999).

Waller, P.J., 'Altercation over civil society: the bitter cry of the Edwardian middle classes', in J. Harris (ed.), *Civil society in British history* (Oxford, 2003), pp. 115–34.

Waller, P.J., *Town, city and nation: England, 1850–1914* (Oxford, 1983).

Watson, L., *From watches to matches: the story of my family* (Warboys, 2010).

Watson, N., *Born not for ourselves: the story of St Albans School* (St Albans, 2014).

Watson, N., *St Albans High School for Girls – an illustrated history* (London, 2002).

Whitaker, A., *Brewers in Hertfordshire: a historical gazetteer* (Hatfield, 2006).

Wilson, R.G., 'The changing taste for beer in Victorian Britain', in R.G. Wilson and T.R. Gourvish (eds), *The dynamics of international brewing since 1800* (London, 1998), pp. 93–104.

Wilson, R.G. and Gourvish, T.R. (eds), *The dynamics of international brewing since 1800* (London, 1998).

Wolfe, H., *Labour supply and regulation* (London, 1923).

Wright, W.N., *The story of St Stephen's church, St Albans* (n.p., 1941).

Radio
BBC Radio 4, *1913: The Year Before* (2013).

Unpublished secondary sources

Cox, T., 'Herts police in the Great War', Herts at War project lecture, 9 April 2015, Letchworth Garden City Heritage Foundation.

Hallifax, S., 'Citizens at war: the experience of the Great War in Essex, 1914–1918', DPhil thesis (University of Oxford, 2010).

Mein, J., *The rise and fall of the pub in Victorian St Albans* (St Albans, 2011) (available in SAHAAS library).

Moody, B., 'The museum of St Albans, a history', copy of lecture given to SAHAAS in 1999 (available in SAHAAS library).

Websites

Bank of England: www.bankofengland.co.uk

British government: www.gov.uk/government/news/vj-day-70-royal-marines-rehearse-drumhead-service-ahead-of-national-commemorations

British Red Cross: www.redcross.org

Christ Church, St Albans: www.ccstalbans.org.uk

Comrades of the Great War, British Legion Memorabilia Collectors Club: www.legion-memorabilia.org.uk/badges/comrades.htm

Financial Times: www.ft.com

Find My Past: www.findmypast.co.uk

Forgotten Books: www.forgottenbooks.com

Graces Guide: www.gracesguide.co.uk/Albert Ball

Hansard, House of Commons: hansard.millbanksystems.com

Imperial War Museums: www.iwm.org.uk

International Encyclopedia of the Great War: encyclopedia.1914–1918-online.net/home/

London Irish Rifles Association: www.londonirishrifles.com

London Transport Museum: www.ltmcollection.org

Mary Evans Picture Library: blog.maryevans.com/2014/01/gas-bags-on-wheels-a-solution-to-petrol-shortages-during-ww1.html

Our Hertford and Ware: www.ourhertfordandware.org.uk

Oxford Dictionary of National Biography: www.oxforddnb.com

Royal Bank of Scotland: www.rbsremembers.com

Royal British Legion: support.britishlegion.org.uk/app/answers/detail/a_id/1243/~/history-of-the-royal-british-legion

St Albans & Hertfordshire Architectural & Archaeological Society: www.stalbanshistory.org

Tank Banks: www.wikipedia.org

The History Press: www.thehistorypress.co.uk

The Long Long Trail: www.1914–1918.net

The National Archives: www.nationalarchives.gov.uk

The Samuel Ryder Story: www.samuelryderstory.co.uk

Third Sector: www.thirdsector.co.uk

Index